Notes on the
Gospel of John

Notes on the Gospel of John

PAUL MARSHALL ALLEN

SteinerBooks

© 2013 by Paul Marshall Allen

Published by SteinerBooks
610 Main Street, Great Barrington, MA 01230 USA

www.steinerbooks.org

All rights reserved. No part of this book may be reproduced, stored in a retrieval system, or transmitted, in any form or by any means, electronic, mechanical, photocopying, recording, or otherwise, without the prior written permission of the publisher, except for brief quotations in critical reviews and articles.

ISBN: 978-1-62148-009-9

Contents

Preface   vii

Pronunciation Key for Greek in This Book   ix

Rudolf Steiner, Lecture on the Gospel of John   xi

Second Lecture   xi

Notes from Conversations with Dr. Rudolf Freiling   xii

John 1	1	John 12	152
John 2	19	John 13	169
John 3	30	John 14	180
John 4	45	John 15	192
John 5	60	John 16	202
John 6	76	John 17	216
John 7	102	John 18	226
John 8	112	John 19	234
John 9	126	John 20	250
John 10	130	John 21	264
John 11	134		

Notes on the "I AM" Statements   42

Notes on the Apocalypse of John   241

Notes on the Epistles   241

Notes on the Composition of Mark's Gospel   272

Notes on the General Character of the Apocalypse   278

Preface

The Christian Community in New York City was officially founded on December 11, 1948, with Reverend Verner Hegg as its first resident priest. As a requirement of its incorporation in the United States there needed to be a minimum of three American-born members as signatories, not so easy to find, as many members in this country were from European lands, having immigrated before or during World War II. The three who offered to sign were Elizabeth Wright Hubbard, M.D., Anne Stockton Goodwin, and Paul Marshall Allen.

Paul had already heard a great deal about The Christian Community from Michael Chekhov as early as 1939, when he began teaching at the Chekhov Studio Theater in Ridgefield, Connecticut. He was also familiar with the literary works of the early founders, among others Friederich Rittelmeyer, Emil Bock, and Alfred Heidenreich. However, with the advent of the "Movement for Religious Renewal" in New York City, he immediately began to take an active role in the unfolding life of this religious community on West 74th Street and gradually nurtured a growing inner question as to whether he might at some later time consider attending the priest's training seminar located in Stuttgart, Germany.

Late in 1949, Dr. Rudolf Frieling, together with his wife, Margareta, was sent over from Germany to support and help build up the work of The Christian Community in North America, an assignment which actually lasted many years. Paul and Frieling soon became close friends, with their mutual love for and knowledge of German, English, and American literature; of Latin, Hebrew, and biblical texts; and extensive background in Rudolf Steiner's spiritual science. They decided that they would meet weekly to undertake an intense, in-depth study of St. John's Gospel. This study began on December 13, 1949, and was completed April 10, 1951.

Paul wrote down 266 pages of notes by hand in his neat and clear script, including extensive Greek phrases, and thus they sat in a ring-binder on our bookshelf for over sixty years. He and I have often referred to them in preparing for Bible Evenings during our many years in Camphill and, on occasion, have also shared them with Christian Community priests in various countries. However, it is now a great joy that SteinerBooks has decided to print them, thus making this unique treasure available to a much wider circle of interested friends.

I well recall throughout the intervening years Paul mentioning how warmly he remembered this special time together with Rudolf Frieling. When we visited Stuttgart for the first time in the winter of 1956, the Frielings had already returned to Germany so that Rudolf could take up the leadership of The Christian Community Movenment. During this time we had the joy and privilege of several wonderful visits with them. That was to be the last time we saw them both.

It is a pleasure to offer these notes on Paul's behalf to everyone interested in using them side-by-side with the John Gospel as a way of stimulating their own thoughts and meditations.

Joan deRis Allen

Pronunciation Key for Greek in This Book

Each Greek word in this text is preceded by a simple attempt at a phonetic pronunciation of the term. These phonetics are not intended to be exact or complete, but were developed by the editor for this particular text, only to give a suggestion of possible pronunciation. The serious student of New Testament Greek will discover that various scholars' phonetics, and so also their pronunciation, will differ from one another. The pronunciation used here reflects that given in a course of New Testament Greek attended by the editor while in Germany. Below are the indications used in this text:

	Pronounced:
a/A	as a long "a"
ä/Ä	as in "father"
ai	as a long "I," as in "aye"
au	ow as in how
i/I	as a short "i"
e/E	When indicating an "I" or "i" in the Greek word pronounced as a long "e"
e/E	When indicating an "ϵ" or "E" in the Greek word, pronounced as a short "e" with a hint of a long "a" also indicating "η" before a consonant only the vowel is held slightly longer
oi	as in boy
o/O	as a long "o"
oo	as in "who"

Rudolf Steiner
Lecture on the Gospel of John
Berlin, February 19, 1906

The formula John used for meditation, whereby his soul was led to spiritual perception, stands at the beginning of the Gospel. In there five sentences lie, which set free a spell in John's soul and brought forth great visions. The first five sentences must be taken as a formula for meditation. Then one follows John on his way and attempts to experience what he experienced. The surest way to do it is to let the formula work on your soul, and you will verify what is said in the first chapters. Thus it is intended, and thus it should be used.

The John Gospel thus becomes one of the greatest texts ever written, for it leads into the depths of the inner life of the soul. It was written so everyone who reads it can follow the same path. And this one can do. It is not a biography of Christ but a biography of the developing human soul. What Steiner describes . . . takes place in the heart of every human being. The text is a living model. Hence it has this awakening, living power which not only makes possible this, but enables them to awaken to a higher reality. John's gospel is not a profession of faith but a text which really gives strength and a self-supporting, independent higher life. The John Gospel is not addressed mainly to the human intellect, but to human beings' soul forces, and real soul experience springs from it.

Second Lecture
February 26, 1906

Every sentence of John's Gospel directs us to the higher world. When we make it alive, then we come to know Christian initiation.

John's Gospel is a description of the Christian path of initiation. One who takes it as an account of events only and an external passage does not understand it. It can be comprehended only if one has lived it through inwardly.

Christianity retains its real meaning when it is followed as an inner path. John's Gospel is a document which can be lived sentence by sentence. Every doubt disappears if one knows that what is written is to be lived through and through. Every line can be lived inwardly in the depth of the soul.

"In the beginning was, *not* the *Light* but the *Word*. The Gospel of John is not a document that may be placed side by side with the others; it expands the others from the temporal to the eternal.

(From the lecture given March 24, 1908, in Berlin.)

John meditated the contents of this gospel for seventy years before writing it.

Notes from Conversations with Dr. Rudolf Freiling: December 13, 1949–April 10, 1951

John's Gospel: Introduction divided into three parts:

The Prologue: Verses 1–5, 6–13, and 14–18:

Heavens

Christ

Earth

John 1:1–51

John 1:1–18: Prologue

John 1:1–5

1. In the beginning was the Word, and the Word was with God, and the Word was God.
2. The same was in the beginning with God.
3. All things were made by him, and without him was not anything made that was made.
4. In him was life, and the life was the light of men.
5. And the light shineth in darkness, and the darkness comprehended it not.

    I. THE PRIMEVAL STORY. THE TRINITY, CREATION, FALL OF MAN (THE HUMAN BEING)

Verses 1–2

Vs. 1. The Word (Logos) Christ
With God—Christ with God
Was God—Christ was God.

Vs. 2. The Trinity—Three in One.

Vs. 3. Creation by the Logos

Vs. 4. Paradise: Tree of Life, Tree of Knowledge (Light)

Vs. 5. Fall of the Human Being. (Schelling's philosophy that darkness is selfishness)

    II. THE SPHERE OF HUMAN HISTORY

The human being is becoming—he or she is not yet perfect. Genesis "becoming"

John 1:6–9
Four Verses about John the Baptist

6. There was a man sent from God, whose name was John.
7. The same came for a witness, to bear witness of the Light, that all men through him might believe.
8. He was not that Light, but was sent to bear witness to that Light.
9. That was the true Light, which lighteth every man that cometh into the world.

John 1:10–13
Four Verses about Lazarus–John

10. He was in the world, and the world was made by him, and the world knew him not.
11. He came unto his own, and his own received him not.
12. But as many as received him, to them he gave the power to become the sons of God, even to them that believe on his name,
13. which were born, not of blood, nor of the will of the flesh, nor of the will of man, but of God.

Vs. 13. "Monoganus" (μονογενοῦς) from one God to one Christ in contrast to human generation, from "two," from male and female parents.

Through the Logos is the "becoming." The Logos is spoken of three times—verse 1.

This threefold repetition of the Logos connects the first and last part. The Logos and the flesh. The Logos goes to the physical sphere. Verse 14.

John 1:14

14. **And the word was made flesh and dwelt among us, and we beheld his glory, the glory as of the only begotten of the Father, full of grace and truth.**

Vs. 14. "Eskanosen"— ἐσκήνωσεν —Tent"—"Flesh"—"dwelt" verse 14, refers to the Old Testament, the Tent where Moses saw Jacob manifested. It refers to the Hebrew "Shekinah" and is spoken of in the Apocalypse and connected to the New Jerusalem.

"Glory"—radiating light from the innermost center of God.

"Father"—mentioned for the first time. So there are two steps: "Eternity," "History and Becoming." In other words, one could know the "Father" *after* the incarnation of Christ. Through Christ we see the "Father Ground of the World." "Through thy Word is the Godhead made known among men."

"Grace"—giving of life—Tree of Life.

"Truth"—that which survives the forgetfulness of Lethe—the Tree of Knowledge.

"Flesh"—the working of Christ in space—in room.

In the *Act of Consecration of Man,* we approach God as "Father" through four steps:

> "Christ"—Gospel
> "Divine Ground of the World"—Offering
> "Father God"—Transubstantiation
> "Father"—Communion
> "His Father"
> "Our Father"
> "Father"

Thus the simple Christian fundamental teaching that God is Our Father is a deep mystery, not to be approached lightly or directly, but only by degrees.

Initiation

In the Middle Ages	The Act of Consecration
1. Doctrine	1. Gospel
2. Purification (Catharsis)	2. Offering (sacrifice)
3. Illumination	3. Transubstantiation
4. Mystical Union	4. Communion

The Act of Consecration as a Descent of Christ:

1. The Spirit of the Christ—The Gospel

2. Spirit and Soul—(Inwardness)—Offering

3. Spirit and Soul and Life (etheric)—Transubstantiation, the creation of the Christ in the Bread and Wine (earth substances). The etheric body of the human being is touched by Christ working in the etheric body of the world.

4. Spirit and Soul and Life and Physical—Communion

The Act of Consecration as an Elevating of Ourselves to Meet Christ:

1. Gospel—Our daily consciousness

2. Offering—Picture consciousness, *Imagination*. Pictures for us: Cup, Bread, Mingling of Water and Wine, Incense. Smoke, etc.

3. Transubstantiation—Consciousness of *Inspiration*

4. Communion—*Intuition,* the divine reaching of the Spiritual World.

John 1:15–18

15. John bare witness of him, and cried saying, This was he of whom I spoke, he that cometh after me is preferred before me, for he was before me.

16. And of his fullness have we all received, and grace for grace.

17. For the law was given by Moses, but grace and truth came by Jesus Christ.
18. No man hath seen God at any time; the only begotten Son, which is in the bosom of the Father, he hath declared him.

Vs. 15. "after", "before"—The working of Christ in time. The entrance of Christ into the sphere of time. "Protos"—πρῶτος—presupposes no. 3. It is used as a superlative, excluding sense.

Vs. 16. "Glory" "fullness"—"Plaromätos"—πληρώματος

Pleroma—Hamburg cycle on the John Gospel: (Lecture 4)—*All* of the Elohim in Christ. Full consciousness of the Sun Logos.—the direct light of the sevenfold Elohim instead of the reflected light of the one—Jahve.

After the incarnation:

1) He dwelt in us—We made a place for him
2) We beheld his glory—We saw him (more active)
3) We all have taken out of His fullness (most active)

These correspond to:

1) Christmas
2) Easter
3) Whitsuntide

"Grace" (schäritos)—χάριτος—The soul's capacity for doing right out of the inner self. *Grace* and an *inner recognition of Truth* came through Christ (see 17 below.). Christ never uses "Grace" in *any* of the Gospels except in the Publican's Prayer and the words in Greek are: "God, have *pity* on me."

"We"—Ego—The greater "I" over the "I"s = We. Not "we" of blood-ties, but a "We" which is beyond blood ties—a "super-We." In the High Priestly Prayer of Chapter 17 of John, this "We" appears again.

Vs. 17. "Grace and Truth"—go into the sphere of the "becoming." "Jesus Christ" used for the first time.

Vs. 18. "God"—The Father God—inconceivable. "Super personal"—beyond all reach, dwelling in eternal spacelessness, timeless silence.

But through the Logos (Christ), he becomes conceivable.

"Bosom of the Father"—Christ hears the Inspiration in the Heart of God.

As Christ hears the heart of the Father God and makes him audible, so Lazarus-John, "He whom Jesus loved" hears the heart of Christ and makes him audible through the Gospel of John.

Thus the mystery of the Heart is set forth. You always have this threefold order:

1. The Father
2. The Son
3. Humanity (Mankind)

"He hath declared him"—remarkable verb here: a guiding out, a bringing out of the hidden. Like the presentation of the sacred images from the dark rooms of the temples of ancient Egypt and holding up these sacred images and pictures of the gods before the people on special holy days; even to putting them into boats on the Nile. This is echoed in the Corpus Christi processions which even include boats (floats) today in Roman Catholic countries.

So, Christ brings out the hidden picture of the Father God from the eternal silence. Christ becomes the leader in this beholding of the Father God, this perceiving of the universal Father. Thus, we can understand that, "He who sees me, sees the Father."

This Verse 18 ends the Prologue to John's Gospel, and with this Prologue in Heaven and Earth, we are about to see the curtain rise on the unfolding Drama.

(On the importance for the universe of a reading of the Gospel of John, see *The Effects of Esoteric Development*, Anthroposophic Press, 1997.)

(December 27, 1949)

John 1:19-40

19. And this is the record of John, when the Jews sent priests and Levites from Jerusalem to ask him, Who art thou?
20. And he confessed and denied not; but confessed, I am not the Christ,
21. And they asked him, What then? Art thou Elias? and he saith, I am not. Art thou that prophet? And he answered No.
22. Then they said unto him, Who art thou? That we may give an answer to them that sent us. What sayest thou of thyself?
23. He said, I am the voice of one crying in the wilderness, Make straight the way of the Lord, as said the prophet Esaias.
24. And they which were sent were of the Pharisees.
25. And they asked him, and said unto him, Why baptizest thou then, if thou be not that Christ, not Elias, neither that prophet?
26. John answered them saying, I baptize with water, but there standeth one among you, whom ye know not.
27. He it is, who coming after me is preferred before me, whose shoe latchet I am not worthy to unloose.
28. These things were done in Bethabara beyond Jordan, where John was baptizing.
29. The next day John seeth Jesus coming unto him, and saith, Behold the Lamb of God, which taketh away the sin of the World.
30. This is he of whom I said, After me cometh a man which is preferred before me: for he was before me.
31. And I knew him not: but that he should be made manifest to Israel, therefore am I come baptizing with water.

32. And John bare record, saying, I saw the Spirit descending from heaven like a dove, and it abode upon him.

33. And I knew him not: but he that sent me to baptize with water, the same said unto me, Upon whom thou shalt see the Spirit descending, and remaining on him, the same is he which baptizeth with the Holy Ghost.

34. And I saw, and bare record that this is the Son of God.

35. Again the next day after, John stood and two of his disciples;

36. And looking upon Jesus as he walked, he saith, Behold the Lamb of God!

37. And the two disciples heard him speak and they followed Jesus.

38. Then Jesus turned, and saw them following, and saith unto them, What seek ye? They said unto him, Rabbi (which is to say, being interpreted, Master), where dwellest thou?

39. He saith unto them, Come and see. They came and saw where he dwelt, and abode with him that day: for it was about the tenth hour.

40. One of the two which heard John speak, and followed him, was Andrew, Simon Peter's brother.

Vs. 19. Levites—in Greek, "Levetäs"—Λευίτας: First of two groups to come to John—they were of the Sadducees (Pharisees come, v. 24). The Sadducees were genuine materialists. They did not believe in life after death, in the Messiah, or any spiritual questions at all. Typical of materialistic people of today. Preoccupied entirely with the physical body. They were exclusively political in tendency and action. They ask an exclusively materialistic question, "Who art thou?" See Acts 23:1-9.

It is important to remember that the Jews were destined to provide the physical body for the incarnation of Christ. They had therefore an instinctively exclusive attitude regarding the physical, material as being *all*. Therefore, when Christ came and they did not recognize him, they continued straight onward in the physical interest and came to Ahriman, the intense materialism. This is typified in the Sadducees. On the other hand, the Pharisees typify the tendency to the opposite, they looked for the Messiah, but thought he would, in a twinkling, change everything external, set up an outward physical government, and change the whole outer order of things. Therefore they had no use for Christ. The Pharisees were a truly fanatical religious order, sticking to old traditions in a really narrow Jesuitical sense, but with a real materialism attached.

The Old Testament does not give any really direct evidence of the survival after death, of the soul, in a personal way. There are a few fleeting references: Abraham and Isaac who were "gathered to their fathers, the Witch of Endor, and Daniel Chapter 12. But this very interesting 12th Chapter of Daniel presents a picture which is strongly Persian in character, the influence of the Babylonian Exile, and is not Jewish in character. Here Michael is mentioned. In the Psalms is a mention of immortality in a personal sense, but not in a clear way. The Witch of Endor says she sees "Gods"—in Hebrew, "Elohim"—and this is a very uneasy passage for theologians, who claim it is a pagan survival, but really, of course, it is an actual occult séance experience which she has.

It was the Greeks who developed the idea of the soul surviving the bodily death—for example, Socrates speaks of how free he will be after death when his pneuma is freed from his body, etc.

However, it is only with the resurrection of Christ that the resurrection-body became a possibility, and the possibility to be free, still retaining one's own *individuality* become manifest. This is a unique thing with the Christ, and this is why, whenever Paul mentioned the resurrection to the Jews, they rose up in wrath. The whole concept of the Jews was the preservation of the physical body, and for the thought of a resurrection-body they had no gift. Therefore the Pharisees were disappointed when the *physical* was not spoken of as outlasting death.

Vs. 20. "I am not"—This "I am not" is balanced by Peter's words, "I am not," at the opposite end of the Gospel of John (Notably, 18:17, etc). This is a frame, and within this frame is placed the whole great group of the "I AM" statements of Christ. Only once does anyone other than Christ say "I am" in this Gospel, and that is the man born blind, in Chapter 9—notably, Verse 9: "I am he."

One thing to remember about John's Gospel is that it begins after the Baptism in the Jordan, and ends *before* the Ascension. Nor does it contain any account of the Last Supper. BUT the aroma, the perfume of these events is pervading the entire Gospel to a tremendous degree. Throughout the Gospel we feel and see the *effects* of these events. The High Priestly Prayer at the end of the Gospel is an effect of the Ascension. The "I Am" statements, especially "I Am the bread," and "I Am the true vine," are pictures in the deepest sense, effects, intuitions of the Last Supper. And this first part of the Gospel takes us to the moment when the Baptism is accomplished, but the effect remains as a reality, a deep reality. Dr. Steiner points out that the pictures of Imagination have to be blotted out in order to prepare room for Intuition, to provide a place for Intuition in our consciousness. Thus in John's Gospel we can see that the Imagination pictures of the Last Supper, Baptism and Ascension have been blotted out of John's consciousness to give a place for a presentation of the Intuitive effects of these great events. This is one of the miraculous secrets underlying the character of this Gospel.

Vs. 21. This mention of Elias is interesting because it brings out a contradiction. We know John was Elias, and other Gospels say so, and always when there is a contradiction in the Gospels, a great secret, a mystery is pointed to. In Greek, here John says simply, "Am Not"—not "I." In their questions about his being a prophet, we can remember this refers to the fact that the Jews were always looking for prophets physically appearing who were to be the forerunners of Christ. Thus, their question was a natural one.

Vs. 23. "the voice of one crying in the wilderness"—aramo- ἐρήμῳ. Refer here to Dr. Steiner's lectures, notably on the Gospel of John, where he speaks of "eremit," etc.

Vs. 24. The Pharisees. See above.

Vs. 25. In a typical narrow way, they question him first about who he is and then about his work. They question him as to his right, his legitimacy, in using the sacrament of baptism. Does he have the right to baptize? A typical narrow-minded question.

Vs. 26. The first mention of the physical presence of Christ, whom they do not know, do not recognize. Note that Christ does not speak. He is only "one" who is present among them, a mysterious person.

Thus in the first act of this drama, following the Prologue, there is a conversation between several persons about a single Person. Then this Person, as it were, walks across the stage. He simply appears, but that is all. He does not speak, he only passes among them. This is a gesture, not a speech. But they do not recognize him, so he appears as though disguised. He is more spoken of than seen.

Vs. 28. Note that the Baptism has already taken place. (Bethany means "House of Need" = the earth!)

"Bęthäbärä"—Βηθαβαρᾶ—, beyond Jordan. The best Greek texts give the correct name for this town as "Bethäneä"—Βηθανια— beyond Jordan (Bethany in English). "Beth" means "house." "thea" means "poverty." Therefore, "Bethanea" (Bethany) means "House of Poverty." Likewise, "Bethlehem" means "House of Bread." This "Bethanea," "House of Poverty," may be linked with the first Beatitude, "the poor in spirit." But the more important link is with another Bethany in Chapter 11: Bethany, the home of Lazarus. In verses 40, 41, and 42 in Chapter 10, John the Baptist is mentioned as we have said. In Chapter 10 (v. 40–42), the name "John" rings out three times, and in the very next verse (11:1), the name "Lazarus" sounds! Thus, the initiation of Lazarus-John is clearly indicated. But more than this, the two places are connected: (10:40) "the place where John at first baptized" (Bethany beyond Jordan) and (11:1) "Bethany, the town of Lazarus, Mary and Martha." So the deep connection is unmistakably pointed to. It is interesting that the Bethany that was the home of Lazarus, is today called

"El Lazarus" by the Arabs of Palestine, thus connecting it with Lazarus.

Vs. 29. "The next day"—This is the second act of the drama, the second day. This has a deep meaning, because four days are clearly pointed to in this chapter: (v. 29) "the next day" (v. 35),"the next day after" (the third day), and (v. 43) the day following (the fourth day). Then there are three more days which follow, making a total of 4 + 3 = 7—a full week, and on the seventh day (the last of the three days) is the Wedding of Cana! This has its counterpoint in another week at the other end of John's Gospel, where another week is carefully articulated, day by day, in like manner—Passion Week! Again evidence of the deep wisdom of the composition of John's Gospel.

"John sees Jesus coming to him"—One always sees the Christ coming thus toward one. Note that Christ does not speak as yet. He still is a silent figure, "coming" across the stage of the drama. He still is in the realm of gesture, not of speech. The Christ is shown among men—this is a "showing" of the Christ. And John, in presence of this "coming," this "showing," of the Christ, expresses himself in the Apocalyptic pictures of the Lamb and the Dove. Christ's coming to us is "shown" to us in the form of pictures, in Imaginations, which arose in the soul of John in the moment of the Baptism which has already taken place, and which he now describes as in the past. We know from Dr. Steiner that the sacrament can (but does not always of necessity) bring forth such a loosening of the etheric body, so that pictures in etheric form can be seen, thus the Dove.

"... which taketh away the sins of the world"—This is a poor translation. The Greek is more in the nature of one who "lifts," who "carries," the heaviness of the sins of the world. Here Christ is indicated as having the power of lifting, of overcoming the heaviness of sin by taking, from the bottom up, the objective sin of the world. Human beings are powerless to do this, but Christ overcomes the heaviness. He lifts it up. He does not change karma, but adds to karma the power to bear it, to carry it. Christ could not change karma, otherwise the Deed of Golgotha would have no effect for us, as it does through karma.

John 1:1–51

It is John who "shows" the Christ as he saw him through the Baptism, that the Christ might be manifest as the Lamb. This is clearly indicated in verses 29–31.

Vs. 32. "And I, John, bare record."—this is the very style of the Apocalypse, for, as we have said, an apocalyptic-picture came from the Baptism. This is a link to the Apocalypse. This is the mystical experience of John at the time of the Baptism, now recounted.

Vs. 33. "He that sent me"—Refers to God. "And remaining on him" (manon)—μένον—This word "remaining," and "abode" (v. 32) and "dwell," "tarry" (Chapter 21:22, 23) and "abide" ("My words abide in you") and "mansions"—("In my house are many mansions") are the same word in Greek! It means that which remains, the opposite of transitory. It unites all these passages as John intended that they should be united, but the translators apparently thought it was not good always to translate one word the same way. Yet, in using all of these synonyms, they destroyed the harmony of the Gospel to a degree! The saying about "many mansions" for example, points us to a spiritual sphere where we may always feel at home. (In this particular section of the Greek text, all of the Greek words for "seeing" are used in turn!)

Vs. 34. "And I saw and bare record that this is the Son of God"—The other Gospels speak of a voice from heaven saying, "This is my Beloved Son," but John does not speak of this. He simply speaks out of the reflection from within his soul, out of the spiritual experience which he had and bears witness "that this is the Son of God!" It is a direct intuition.

Vs. 35. This introduces the third day of this week, as we have said. Two of John's disciples are present.

Vs. 36. John "looks"—he perceives Christ in action, "coming"—"walking." Thus he expresses himself to his disciples.

Vs. 37. This "heard" is not trivial. They really understood John. John pointed them to the Christ. He gave them up to Christ. This was a great sacrifice, a noble act, for the relation between teacher and student was very deep and far-reaching in those days, far different from today. So John sacrificed them and this was not easy to do, and despite the economy of words in this verse, we must feel that John's perception of the Christ Being was a very real thing, otherwise he could not have given up these two so apparently easily. Immediately they follow Jesus. There is a great depth and beauty in the simplicity of these words, as a sacrifice of heroic proportions is involved.

Vs. 38. Two secrets are contained in the verbs, "turned" and "saw." The disciples asked nothing, put no questions, but simply followed. It was Christ who first saw them after he turned. (Note: he says "What," whereas one would have expected him to say, "Who"—but he already knew the answer.) Now, in this third day, *Christ speaks for the first time in John's Gospel.* "What seek Ye? The answer to this question refers again to the verb of which we spoke before (Verse 33, above), "Where dwellest thou?" They might have asked "Where is the spiritual sphere where you are at home?"

Vs. 39. "Come and see." Dr. Steiner indicates that there must be a "coming" first—we must act before spiritual knowledge can be given to us or can be had. Thus they had to act first. "They came and saw where he dwelt and abode with him that day." Again the verb "came," and only then did they attain the spiritual "sight," so they "saw." The words "dwelt" and "abode" are one verb in Greek, of which we have spoken (v. 33 above).

"For it was about the tenth hour." This means it was about 4:00 pm, an important time of the day, because the sun has run its course. The outer activities of life are nearing completion, and it is possible to enter more deeply into the coming of the night. It is a time when pictures of spiritual reality can arise before the soul, when apocalyptic pictures can present themselves to one who "abides" with Christ.

Vs. 40. "Andrew, Simon Peter's brother"—Here we have the identification of the first of the two who had been John's disciples and who had the deep experience of John's recognition of the Christ and sacrifice to Him. This is Andrew, and in the Russian Church he is spoken of as "The First-Called," because of this experience we have spoken of. "Seeing" is specifically related to the Greeks. (see Ch. 14: 8-9) Philip is especially representative of the Greeks.

John 1:41–51

41. He first findeth his own brother Simon, and saith unto him, We have found the Messiah, which is, being interpreted, the Christ.

42. And he brought him to Jesus. And when Jesus beheld him, he said, Thou art Simon the son of Jonas: thou shalt be called Cephas, which is by interpretation, A stone.

43. The day following Jesus would go forth into Galilee, and findeth Phillip, and saith unto him, Follow me.

44. Now Phillip was of Bethsaida, the city of Andrew and Peter.

45. Philip findeth Nathanael, and saith unto him, We have found him, of whom Moses in the law, and the prophets, did write: Jesus of Nazareth, the son of Joseph.

46. And Nathanael said unto him, Can there any good thing come out of Nazareth? Philip saith unto him, Come and see.

47. Jesus saw Nathanael coming to him, and saith of him, Behold an Israelite indeed, in whom there is no guile!

48. Nathanael saith unto him, Whence knowest thou me? Jesus answered and said unto him, Before that Phillip called thee, whence thou wast under the fig tree, I saw thee.

49. Nathanael answered and saith unto him, Rabbi, thou art the Son of God, thou art King of Israel.

50. Jesus then answered and said unto him, Because I said unto thee, I saw thee under a fig tree, believest thou? Thou shalt see greater things than these.

51. And he saith unto him, Verily, verily, I say unto you, hereafter ye shall see heaven open and the angels of God ascending and descending upon the Son of Man.

Vs. 42. "Simon, Son of Jonas"—this name is used again at the end of the Gospel of John: "Simon, Son of Jonas, lovest thou me"—another connection of the beginning and end of the Gospel, first and last chapters. "Cephas"—correct translation: "a rock."

Vs. 43. Christ finds five disciples—not twelve. Andrew, the other, Simon, Phillip, Nathanael. In St. John's Gospel, the figures 7, 3, 5, and 12 have special significance. For example, $5 + 7 = 12$, etc. "Findeth"—This is a special word. It indicates that one has been seeking Christ before he finds him. There is a destiny in it: they were looking for Christ.

"Follow me"—Like with "come," one has to put one's self into movement. First become active—"come," and then one "sees."

Vs. 46. "Come and see": see the note for vs. 40 above.

Vs. 47. "seeth Nathanael coming"—He observes his destiny, Christ sees his destiny, observes him "coming"—he has Intuition regarding him.

Nathanael means "God-given." John means "Grace of God."

"Behold an Israelite"—this refers to the fifth degree of Initiation, the one who bears the Holy Ghost. He is the bearer of the spirit of the community, a community spirit.

"no guile"—correct translation: "no spot"

"no shade" of Ahriman (see below—Jews)

In the Old Testament there is also a Trinity:

1. Abraham: Ab = Father; Ram high lofty (later added "Ha"—of the people). This is a picture of the Father God.
2. Isaac: the Son who is prepared to be sacrificed and prefigures Christ.
3. Jacob: Israel, he who has twelve sons, twelve tribes, prefigures the twelve disciples—Jacob in Hebrew is James. This is the figure which prefigures the twelve disciples who were to bear the Holy Ghost in themselves after Pentecost.

John always refers to two conditions of thought in a special way:

"Israelites" Those who, in a pure sense, bore in themselves the possibility to receive the Christ.

"Jews"—A negative sense—those who had hardened themselves in the old laws and cult so they could not receive the Christ but would fall into Ahriman's hands.

Vs. 48. "Whence knowest thou me?" How did you know that I had reached the Israelite stage of development?

"Under the fig tree"—Like Buddha under the Bodhi tree. (RS lectures)

Vs. 49. "the King of Israel"—the true Israelite spirit speaks through Nathanael, the community spirit, looking for its king. "the Son of God"—Nathanael recognizes Christ, who, in verse 51, sees the "Son of Man"—the possibility of *the human being*—in him!

This passage is balanced in Chapter 12:13.

"They (the people) took branches of palm and went forth to meet him, and cried Hosannah: blessed is the King of Israel"—Here, what was recognized by an individual in Nathanael, was taken up in an exalted spirit by the people. They saw him as he really was—in a moment of great uplift.

But this was forgotten when the moment was passed, and the next time he was named "King of the Jews"—significant difference. But between these two moments Christ cursed the fig tree (not mentioned in John's Gospel, but in the other Gospels). He cursed, rejected, the old clairvoyance (Nathanael, Buddha) and initiated the new clairvoyance which can only come through Christ. Those who follow the old clairvoyance from this time onward, fall into the hands of Ahriman—the true "King of the Jews."

Vs. 51. "angels of God . . . upon the Son of Man." This is a new kind of existence for Christ—points to his incarnation in the flesh. (There are twelve passages in John's Gospel where the "Son of Man" is spoken of. This is the first.) In his "Letters to the Members,"

Dr. Steiner points out that the divine world, passing through humanity, through human experiences, gets something more.

In this verse, Christ points to the dream experience of Jacob (James)—the ladder—and shows that what was then only a dream experience, now begins in actuality, in reality. The dream is about to be fulfilled. Human beings will see the Spiritual Hierarchies anew, but in movement. This movement is important, because the Angels sometimes look earthward and bring heaven to earth, then they look heavenward and take the deeds of the earth into the heavens.

Jacob's dream: He had to depart from the fixed life of the Jews and depart Eastward, to Laban, i.e., to Babylonia, and there his deepening personal consciousness was darkened down to receive the dream—experience of the ladder. He had to go to the East and come in contact with Eastern cults, in order for this to be made manifest. Leaving the fixed home gave spiritual possibility.

John 2:1-25

John 2:1-17

1. And the third day there was a marriage in Cana of Galilee, and the mother of Jesus was there,

2. and both Jesus was called, and his disciples, to the marriage.

3. And when they wanted wine, the mother of Jesus saith unto him, They have no wine.

4. Jesus saith unto her, Woman what have I to do with thee? Mine hour is not yet come.

5. His mother saith unto the servants, Whatsoever he saith unto you, do it.

6. And there were set there six waterpots of stone, after the manner of purifying of the Jews, containing two or three firkins apiece.

7. Jesus saith unto them, Fill the waterpots with water. And they filled them to the brim.

8. And he saith unto them, Draw out now, and bear unto the governor of the feast. And they bare it.

9. When the ruler of the feast had tasted the water that was made wine, and knew not whence it was (but the servants which drew the water knew), the governor of the feast called the bridegroom,

10. And saith unto him, Every man at the beginning doth set forth good wine, and when men have well drunk, then that which is worse, but thou has kept the good wine until now.

11. This beginning of miracles did Jesus in Cana of Galilee, and manifested forth his glory; and the disciples believed on him.

12. After this he went down to Capernaum, he, and his mother, and his brethren, and his disciples, and they ontinued there not many days.

13. And the Jews Passover was at hand, and Jesus went up to Jerusalem,

14. and found in the temple those that sold oxen and sheep and doves, and the changers of money sitting:

15. And when he had made a scourge of small cords, he drove them all out of the temple, and the sheep and the oxen, and poured out the changers' money, and over threw the tables;

16. And said unto them that sold doves, Take these things hence; make not my father's house an house of merchandise.

17. And his disciples remembered that it was written, The zeal of thine house hath eaten me up.

Vs. 11. "This beginning"—The Greek word "ärschan"—αρχὴν—the same word opens the Gospel of John!—It means, among other things, "In Principle."

In the lectures on the Hierarchies, Dr. Steiner speaks of the "Archai": they are the Spirits of Personality—the "Originators"—the "Originating Spirits"—they originate, and the human being is the result.

So we have the word "beginning" referring to "the original," "the principle," the "key," the "pattern"—of all the miracles to follow.

Changing Water into Wine: this is the "key" miracle, the "pattern" of all that is to follow.

Water: impersonal element

Wine: personal element. It leads the soul more into the body, even negative, and one feels oneself to be "more of a human" when drunk, but in a negative sense, of course!

The grape is a kind of cosmos enclosed in its skin. Each grape is an individual entity, individual ego, self-enclosed, and the skin surrounds all of it. The wine derived therefrom can lead one deeper into oneself, into one's own ego! Through changing the water into wine, the Christ agrees to the divine nature of the Ego!

"Miracle": In Greek "semai-o"—σημείώ—this is the general word for "miracle" used by John. It is incorrectly translated, should be "token" or "sign." And there are seven "tokens" or "signs" in John's Gospel.

But this word "semaio" refers to the "knowledge aspect" of the signs.

Thus, the turning of water into Wine represents the "key token," "the original sign," "the in-principle token, or sign" of all "signs" to follow.

The Act of Consecration of Man

It is an act, a deed, in conformity with the entire Act of the Christ, the entire life of Christ upon earth.

The Four Parts:

1. The Gospel—Refers to the preaching and teaching life of Christ

2. The Offering—Refers to the Deed, the sacrifice upon Golgotha, catharsis, purging, sacrifice.

3. The Transubstantiation—Refers to the Resurrection of the Christ

4. The Communion—Refers to the experience of Pentecost, when the Christ poured the Holy Spirit out upon all the disciples, when the Christ became possible for all to attain for themselves.

"How can we know the Christ is present in the Act of Consecration?" Not because by a call or ritual or magic or incantation, we summon Him. It is like a rendezvous we have: "If you come there each day at twelve o'clock, I will be there." He is there because the

Act of Consecration is a keeping of the rendezvous with Him, and He is there, because we come to the rendezvous He has set! We act "out of the revelation of Christ, in reverence for Christ, in mindfulness of Christ's deed."

The Act of Consecration of Man is a kind of picture of what the human being can become through Christ. The human being is still in process of becoming!

The early Christians wished to commemorate the Deed, the entire life, of Christ upon the earth, and this they did through the Mass.

The word "Mass" actually has no meaning at all! It comes from the words the priest speaks at the end of the Mass: "Ite missa est"—a kind of dismissal—they can go home now! And they took this joyfully, and looked forward to these words and named the whole Act thus.

Roman Catholicism: Had the ritual, the Mass, but not individual freedom—no individuality.

Protestantism: did away with the dogma and brought individual freedom.

The Christian Community: Restores the Mass, but keeps the individual freedom—has no dogma at all.

"Dominus vobiscum" "The Lord be with you" is changed to "Christ in You"—The Christ not with you as an external being, but *in you* as a personal experience. There is a great difference.

When Adam and Eve dwelt in Paradise they were clothed in light, in the aura of God. Afterward, through the Fall, they became naked—they lost "the garment of Light" in which they were clothed. Thus they felt "ashamed"—but this "shame" was not ordinary mortification. It was a deep soul experience for them, of a kind we cannot imagine; it is certainly deeper than shame.

The Protestant Church did away with the vestments and left only the black cassock, symbolic of the material, the physical body, the utter materialism, the picture of the human being considered only physically—a body about to die, to dissolve. Perhaps they were more truthful than they knew. For the present age sees everything "naked," without the spiritual body at all: we see the human, buildings, and everything only as matter, and the spiritual forces and bodies remain only a mystery. They are "veiled" to our sight. We need to realize that it is only through Christ that these hidden mysteries can be found again. For example, for the life body- the etheric—the body of life forces—we have no knowledge at all. No wonder Adam and Eve felt "naked."

There are four words used by John which are translated generally as "miracle":

1. "Thauma"—θαῦμα—a feeling in the soul of astonishment, wondering. The feeling aspect.

2. "Semai-on"—συμείων—a knowledge aspect. This is the word used by John, generally, "the sign," "the rune," "the token"—something which brings understanding. There are seven of these in John's Gospel. (From this word we get the English "semaphore.") This is the thinking aspect.

3. "Teräs"—τέρας—a "shock," a "striking thing," something which comes in "out of the routine" producing a shock in the soul. Has to do with the effect on the will, on the actions. It is like the tail of a comet, producing a shock in the beholder.

4. "Dunämes"—δύναμις: Used especially in Luke's Gospel with regard to describing or naming the healings by Christ. It has to do with the effect upon others of that which is extraordinary, striking, powerful. Refers to the will aspect, similar to "Teras."

The speaking of Christ: In John's Gospel, Christ generally speaks either three or seven times. This is an important part of the composition of the Gospel as a whole. Example: In John 2 at the Cana Wedding, the Christ speaks three times: Verses 4, 7, and 8. In other places he speaks three or seven times.

Divisions into Chapters and Verses

The division into chapters was done first. This was in the thirteenth century in the time of Thomas Aquinas, and at that time it was a very new thing. The division into verses was not made until the seventeenth century. The separation of the words, space between the words, shows increasing ability to space and separate thoughts, a symptom of more ability in abstract thinking.

John, Chapter 2: The Marriage at Cana. This is explained in detail in Dr. Steiner's lectures on this Gospel—(Hamburg Series).

Vs. 4. "Woman"—here Jesus addressed the female principle. Not a term of contempt—see Dr. Steiner's lectures. Balanced by Verse 26 in Chapter 19: "Woman, behold thy son."

"Mine Hour is not yet come": This is a formula of John's Gospel. Later, in Chapter 17: "Father, the hour is come." These are two polar opposites that explain each other. This first sign at the wedding is done when His hour had not come. When His hour had come, He penetrated the substance of bread and wine at the Last Supper and through His blood shed upon Golgotha.

Vs. 6. With regard to the water, Rudolf Steiner points out that this was freshly drawn water from the well.

Vs. 8–9. "The governor of the feast," "the ruler of the feast"—this is the same word in Greek—"Ärschitreklenos"—αρχιτρικλίνος— The tables were arranged so that three persons lay side-by-side on three sides of the table, and the fourth side was left open for serving. These couches were called "Treclenae"—τρίκλινει— our word "recline" is contained therein. The "master" or "majordomo" or "chamberlain" of the feast was called "Archi-triclinos." This word or person is named three times in this chapter, verses 8 and 9—again a secret of three.

Vs. 9. "bridegroom"—This name is "noomphe-on"—νυμφίον—in Greek. It also occurs three times in the Gospel of John. Of course this word has a double meaning as John uses it, where it can be taken externally, and in another case, it refers to Christ himself.

Vs. 10. "the good wine"—in Greek "good" is "kälon"—καλὸν. This is the same word "Kälos"—καλός—in "The good shepherd." It is not only "good" but had the undertone of "the beautiful" as well, though one cannot translate it this way directly, because it would be too sentimental and would not be understood correctly.

This whole verse can be thought of as the state of the human ego (the wine) without Christ. The wine (blood) is related to the ego, is the bearer of the ego. For example, a young man of seventeen or eighteen years experiences in great joy the unfolding of his ego. It is a joyful thing for him. This is the "good wine" which is served first. Then if the Christ impulse does not come to him, he comes, at perhaps age forty, to the "worse wine"—his ego begins to be a burden to him, and perhaps he commits suicide. So this verse is a picture of the way one may go without Christ.

Dostoyevski: It is interesting that of the seven "signs" in this Gospel of John, Dostoyevski uses two—the first and the last (the seventh) for the spiritual background of his two greatest novels. He relates the Wedding of Cana to the death experience of Father Zossima in "Brothers Karamazov,"—a very strange connection, but there is a deep meaning in it. And the other, the raising of Lazarus, he puts in his "Crime and Punsishment" in relation to Raskolnikov.

Water—Wine—Reincarnation

From Rudolf Steiner's lecture—Dusseldorf, February 9, 1906: "The Christian Mystery"

"So that human beings would come to regard their present incarnation as their only one, it was necessary to separate the brain from knowledge of higher principles in the human being—*Atman, Bhuddi,* and *Manas*—and any knowledge of reincarnation. Wine was given to humanity for this purpose. Earlier only water had been used in all temple rituals, then wine was introduced. Indeed, a divine being, Bacchus (or Dionysus) was the representative of wine. John, the most deeply initiated of Christ's disciples, revealed in his Gospel the significance of wine for inner development (John 2:1-11). Water was transformed into wine during the Marriage at

Cana in Galilee. Humanity was so transformed through the use of wine that people were no longer able to understand reincarnation. At that time, the use of water in offerings was transformed into wine; now we are about to change wine back into water. Anyone who wants to ascend to the highest realms of existence must refrain from drinking even a single drop of alcohol."

Vs. 11. This was explained before, "Manifested" this is "declared" —see v. 18 in Chapter 1.

"Glory," "doxa"—the aura around the sun. A significant picture. The "streaming-out" quality of the Father God manifested by the Son—Christ. This is spoken of in the Persian text of Zarathustra, as one of the qualities which would be a part of the anticipated Messiah. It is a shining, streaming quality.

"His disciples believed on Him." This is not the correct translation. It should be "began to believe." It is the past perfect form of the verb. Thus here is a "beginning" of belief—of faith. This is the beginning of faith in John's Gospel.

Vs. 12. "The Jew's Passover": There are three references to the Passover in the Gospel of John, and they are in important places:

1. Following the first sign—the Cana Wedding
2. Following the fourth Sign—the Feeding of the 5,000
3. Following the seventh sign—the Raising of Lazarus.

Vs. 14. "The Temple"—this must not be confused with Solomon's Temple. That temple was destroyed in 586 B.C. when the Jews were taken into Babylonian Exile. Then, at the time of the Maccabees, at the return from Babylon, in 520 B.C., they rebuilt it, but on a much more modest scale, much smaller, because as returning exiles they were much poorer. Then in the time of Herod, the Temple of Jesus' time was built up. It took about forty-six years to build and was very sumptuous and shining with gold covered domes and pinnacles in the sunlight. Herod was not a Jew, but an Idoumian, and because of this, he always felt uneasy at heart with the Jews and tried to "make up" to them by building this gorgeous Temple. It was one of the wonders of the world at that time. And in Christ's time it was still under construction in part, and building stones and rubble lay about, and the people took some of these stones to throw at Christ at a later time. When Titus attacked Jerusalem, he did not want to destroy the Temple of Herod—he knew of its beauty by reputation—and wanted it taken intact, but it caught fire during the attack and was burned to the ground.

One part of the Temple remained as a fragment, a ruin, from Solomon's original Temple; "Solomon's porch"—and both Christ and the disciples enjoyed this because of its association with Solomon, and various scenes of the Gospel took place there.

The temple was in a depraved state. It had become a place of money and commerce and merchandise.

Verses 15 and 16. The Christ did not act out of human anger. That is a trivialization of the text. Note that He was not violent with all of them: He said to those that sold doves, Take these things hence. He was much gentler with the doves!

Vs. 17. "The zeal"—is a quotation from the Psalms. It refers to the enthusiasm of Christ for the cleanliness of the Temple—"eaten me up," "consumed me."

John 2:18–25

18. Then answered the Jews and saith unto him, What sign shewest thou unto us, seeing that thou doest these things?

19. Jesus answered and said unto them, Destroy this temple, and in three days I will raise it up.

20. Then said the Jews, Forty and six years was this temple in building, and wilt thou rear it up in three days?

21. But he spake of the temple of his body.

22. When therefore he was risen from the dead, his disciples remembered that he had said this unto them; and they believed the scripture, and the word which Jesus had said.

23. Now when he was in Jerusalem at the Passover, in the feast day, many believed in his name, when they saw the miracles which he did.

24. But Jesus did not commit himself unto them, because he knew all men.

25. And needed not that any should testify of man, for he knew what was in man.

Vs. 19. The prophecy of the Resurrection.

V. 20. See above regarding the Temple.

V. 21. Here is a double use of "Temple" as "body." He found a Temple in a state of decay, an unworthy state, depraved. He attacked the decay of religions. When His hour was come, he would restore religion through His Resurrection. Note that it is "The Jews" that John refers to here.

V. 22. "Remembered" – In Greek this is a kind of "mirroring" of the deeds of Christ. Dr. Steiner speaks in the lectures on the *Fifth Gospel*, that after Pentecost, the disciples distinctly remembered many of the sayings and deeds of Christ which they had forgotten. Then they were able to reflect upon them. John did not write this Gospel until in his old age, and after he had meditated on the deeds of Christ for many, many years. This is why he did not give many full details as did the other Evangelists about the Gospels, because he had so thoroughly worked upon his recollections, and reflections of Christ through years of meditation. So often we find him giving only a very short description where others go into many details. There are two exceptions: "The man born blind" and "The Raising of Lazarus." Here the details are very vivid, dramatic and complete because these two "signs" had so strongly impressed themselves upon John. They had a very deep meaning for him.

Vss. 23–25. "miracles"—"Semai-on" (see page 23 above, these notes. They believed (had faith), through the knowledge aspect of the "signs." The Greek "began to believe."

These three verses are a key to the next scene—that of Nicodemus, and should not be separated from it by a new chapter heading. This is an illustration of the way the chapter readings are a barrier to the flow of the text and the compositional relationships of the Gospel.

Vs. 25. "Knew all men," (1) all inclusive, a prophecy of what is to come. Greek text does not have the word "men"—"man" three times. "Testify of man," "knew what was in man," 'there was a man." Here again it is a threefold use of the word "man"—Christ "knew what was in man"—a preface to "there was a man"—whose name was Nicodemus. Thus we are led into the next event, the meeting with Nicodemus, whom Christ could penetrate with his vision, since "he knew all" and could answer Nicodemus' questions.

John 3:1–36
The Nicodemus Chapter

In reference to this see the lectures of Dr. Steiner on John's Gospel.

1. There was a man of the Pharisees, named Nicodemus, a ruler of the Jews.
2. The same came to Jesus by night, and said unto him, Rabbi, we know that thou art a teacher come from God, for no man can do these miracles that thou doest, except God be with him.
3. Jesus answered and said unto him, Verily, verily, I say unto thee, except a man be born again, he cannot see the kingdom of God.
4. Nicodemus saith unto him, How can a man be born when he is old? Can he enter the second time into his mother's womb, and be born?
5. Jesus answered, Verily, verily, I say unto thee, except a man be born of water and of the spirit, he cannot enter into the kingdom of God.
6. That which is born of the flesh is flesh, and that which is born of the spirit is spirit.
7. Marvel not that I said unto thee, Ye must be born again.
8. The wind bloweth where it listeth, and thou hearest the sound thereof, but canst not tell where it cometh, and whither it goeth: so is every one that is born of the spirit.
9. Nicodemus answered and said unto him, How can these things be?
10. Jesus answered and said unto him, Art thou a master of Israel, and knowest not these things?

John 3:1–36

11. Verily verily, I say unto thee, we speak that we do know, and testify what we have seen: and ye received not our witness.

12. If I have told you earthly things, and you believe not, how shall ye believe, if I tell you of heavenly things?

13. And no man hath ascended up to heaven, but he that came down from heaven, even the Son of Man which is in heaven.

14. And as Moses lifted up the serpent in the wilderness, even so must the Son of Man be lifted up:

15. That whosoever believeth in him should not perish, but have eternal life.

16. For God so loved the world, that he gave his only begotten Son, that whosoever believeth in him should not perish, but have everlasting life.

17. For God sent not his Son into the world to condemn the world, but that the world through him might be saved.

18. He that believeth on him is not condemned: but he that believeth not is condemned already, because he hath not believed in the name of the only begotten Son of God.

19. And this is the condemnation, that light is come into the world, and men loved darkness rather than light, because their deeds were evil.

20. For everyone that doeth evil hateth the light, neither cometh to the light, lest his deeds should be reproved.

21. But he that doeth truth cometh to the light, that his deeds may be made manifest, that they are wrought in God.

22. After these things came Jesus and his disciples into the land of Judea, and there he tarried with them, and baptized.

23. And John was also baptizing in Aenon near to Salim, because there was much water there, and they came, and were baptized.

24. For John was not yet cast into prison.

25. Then there arose a question between some of John's disciples and the Jews about purifying.

26. And they came unto John, and said unto him, Rabbi, he that was with thee beyond Jordan, to whom thou barest witness, behold the same baptizeth, and all men come to him.

27. John answered and said, A man can receive nothing, except it be given him from heaven.

28. Ye yourselves bear me witness, that I said, I am not the Christ, but that I am sent before him.

29. He that hath the bride is the bridegroom, but the friend of the bridegroom, which standeth and heareth him, rejoiceth greatly because of the bridegroom's voice; this my joy is therefore fulfilled.

30. He must increase, but I must decrease.

31. He that hath cometh from above is above all; he that is of the earth is earthly, and speaketh of the earth, he that cometh from heaven is above all.

32. And what he hath seen and heard, that he tesifieth, and no man receives his testimony.

33. He that hath received his testimony hath set to his seal that God is true.

34. For he whom God hath sent speaketh the words of God, for God giveth not the spirit by measure unto him.

35. The Father loveth the Son, and hath given all things into his hand.

36. He that believeth on the Son hath everlasting life, and he that believeth not the Son shall not see life, but the wrath of God abideth on him.

Vs. 2. "Came by night"—Here the time only is given. There is no indication of the place—no space details at all, only the time. Night is important. Note the Pharisaical pride of Nicodemus. He says "We know"—speaking out of group pride. He looks down on Jesus.

Note the number of times each of these two speak in this famous dialogue: Nicodemus three times, verses 2, 4, and 9. Note how Nicodemus speaks:

Vs. 2. A prideful statement, full.

Vs. 4. Condensation, shrinking: only two questions—the mood of his soul has changed.

Vs. 2. He shrinks yet more—only one short question! He decreases thus! In the last moments (vs 10-11) Christ almost annihilates him, reducing him utterly.

Vs. 3. Jesus also speaks three times, but increasing in volume. The first (vs 3) is a short statement. The second (vs 5-8) is longer, and the third (vs 10-21) is longest of all. So while Nicodemus decreases in size and speech, Christ increases. "A man be born again": In Greek, "from above," "cannot see": in contrast to "cannot enter" (vs. 5), which comes later. A preliminary: one must see before one enters.

Vs. 4. This is the second speech of Nicodemus. Less arrogant. Now questions instead of assertions—less sure. Nicodemus himself is old. He is a representative of the Jerusalem Jews. These questions he asks are not foolish, they have a deeper meaning. How can a human being reach the creative power which will keep one young, overcoming the forces of stiffness, age, death, the intellect (Jews)—Ahriman, but still keep upright in consciousness—how to remain human? This is behind the question.

Vs. 5. "Water"—In the background of all these events is the baptism in the Jordan, though as we have said, John does not specifically describe it. It is the background of these events:

1. The Cana wedding—water and wine
2. The Nicodemus scene—water and spirit
3. The Samaritan Woman—water of life
4. The pool of Bethesda—

"Spirit," "pnoimä"—πνεῦμα—in Greek. This is the "breath" of the spirit world. It can be thought of as "air of spirit."

"Enter": Contrast to "see" (vs. 3)—"See" is to have knowledge, while "enter" is a "going in" through the will activity.

"Baptism": By water and remembrance of the human being's origin in the Godhead, and the Fall (to the past). By Spirit, the Holy Ghost (to the future) when the human spirit, through the undefiled, undimmed Holy Spirit, can be reunited to the Godhead.

Vs. 6. "Flesh": this is the same word as is used in "And the Word became "Flesh."

Vs. 7. "Born again"—Greek, "born again from above."

Vs. 8. "The wind"—the Greek word is "pnoimä"—πνεῦμα.

"Hearest," etc.—Soul, feeling quality.

In olden times the wind was evidence of a spiritual presence. Wotan is an example of this. In the Bible, David and the rustling of the wind in the leaves of the olive tree—the voice of God speaking in the wind.

"Cometh, goeth": breathing, the movement, the rhythm, the soul qualities of the "pnoimä,"—πνεῦμα: "spirit." For the human being there is always something hidden, a mystery. This reference to the wind is an example of this. Another is the fact that human beings look ahead of themselves. They cannot see behind; that is a mystery. Therefore, whenever the Bible speaks of "looking backward," "turning," "turned and saw," etc., this refers to a mystery, an esoteric turning, especially in reference to Christ. It is a turning in response to a mystery.

Vs. 9. "How can these things be?": The smallest speech of all for Nicodemus. This question indicates a real mystery from the material standpoint. How can one reach the "Eternal Feminine" and find rejuvenation, the creative forces in age and intellectuality? This points to a most modern question.

Vs. 10. Now begins the third part of Christ's share in the dialogue. Here Jesus "shrinks" Nicodemus more and more, even with a gentle contempt; He has to do this, to shrink him even to the point of putting him through the eye of the needle, of driving him through the floor! Ever reducing him. It is then that Nicodemus can form a cup for the revelation of the Christ. This revelation is given in the verses through Verse 21.

But we must be very grateful for people like Nicodemus, who called forth these revelations from Christ. We must never look down upon them, because without them, the revelation might never have been given! Christ was not a "walking encyclopedia" who simply gave out these things indiscriminately. He had first to be asked, the cup had to be formed by these individuals, then the answers came out, not as premeditations, but as specific answers, revelations, in reply to the need of the moment.

Vs. 11. "We"—It is now Christ who says "We," as a kind of reply to Nicodemus' original "We" in his first statement (vs. 2). Here Christ assumes the superior position, and Nicodemus, who, as in Verse 2, was filled with importance, as an old man, a ruler of the Pharisees, is now shrunken, now reduced.

"witness," a kind of humility. It is as though he said, "You would be a teacher, and are not even a disciple [a witness]."

Vs. 12. "Ye believe not": There is no fire in his attitude, no warmth in it.

Vs. 13. "Which is in heaven": He who has his eternal Being, existence, in Heaven, which is always there, even if he is dwelling temporarily upon the earth. Like the verse, "Before Abraham was, I AM," it is not a case of time, for example, "is," "was," "will be," because Christ is eternal, existing outside of time. This brings us to Moses (next verse).

Vs. 14. "Moses"—Christ is approaching the great central, key teaching, the cornerstone of Christian revelation (vs. 16), and in order to do this, he turns to a picture which Nicodemus, as a Jewish scholar, would know well: the raising of the serpent in the wilderness by Moses. It is an imagination (image) over which Nicodemus would have mediated many times.

"Lifted up": This is the Greek word "hupsosen"—ὕψωσεν—a famous formula used by John to foretell the Crucifixion. It is used exactly three times in the Gospel of John, Chapters 3, 8, and 12.

Vs. 15. Here Christ comes nearer the key revelation, but does not reveal it yet! It is only an approach.

Vs. 16. This is the great climax of the teaching. Here is the picture of Golgotha revealed fully for Nicodemus to see. Here is a heavenly Mystery, not an earthly one. This is the summit of the whole of Christianity. The English translation is just about accurate.

The Nicodemus and Samaritan Woman Dialogues:

1. Nicodemus represents the Jerusalem Jews—a scholar of advanced age. He represents a modern human being in whom the ego forces are fully developed intellectually. He is related to the sun—to the day—but he comes to Christ by night—very significant—he seeks the night which is really the sphere of the woman—(the moon) because he is seeking the Eternal Feminine—birth—the creative life forces which are lost to him in age. Note the few external details here: only night is mentioned (similar to Faust).

2. The Samaritan Woman dialogue is very different. Here the external details are many, down to the finest degree. The hour is noon when the sun stands highest in the heavens. The woman—in ancient times women were not so developed as now—seeks her ego forces—and Christ perceives this at once because he speaks immediately about her husbands—her disordered search for her ego forces! And thus she saw he was a prophet.

Thus these two great dialogues concern a man and a woman and Christ between them.

One of the interesting things about this Gospel is that scholars have tried to prove that it was not the work of John in his old age. But some few years ago in Germany, a psychologist wrote a book in which he said the stories are exactly in the fragmentary style and absolute psychology of an old man. He said that an old man starts a story, loses the thread, rambles, etc., and that this Gospel does exactly that; thus it is the work of an old man! But he was wrong because he did not perceive the marvelous composition, and did not realize that, whereas John in the Nicodemus story, for example, is very brief in details and apparently wanders, in the very next story, the Samaritan Woman, he is very exact in the details, to the finest degree! He did not grasp the real meaning behind the difference in these two narratives as John relates them. Thus he missed one of the great mysteries of the Gospel of John.

Vs. 16. This verse is a threefold unity:

1. For God ... the world
2. That he ... begotten Son
3. That whosoever ... everlasting life.
4. This is the foretaste, prophecy, of Golgotha.

"Loved," "agäpasen"—ἠγάπησεν : "ägäpa,"—ἀγάπη, "ägäpas"—ἀγάπης, the usual Greek word of St. John's Gospel, translated as "Love." It is special, not like "fela-o," φιλέω, as a friend, one we like (see pages 39 and 139 of these notes).

"Should not perish"—this is a kind of menace, a pointing to the abyss into which one can fall if one does not have Christ.—A warning.

"Everlasting Life"—Greek "ai-one-on"—αἰώνιον—"everlasting," that which goes through the aeons, which is eternal.

Vs. 17. "not to condemn": "This is addressed to Nicodemus especially, because he is a Pharisee. This group was a kind of organization. They looked for the Messiah to condemn, to judge the world. They thought that the Messiah would come and immediately the world would be judged and condemned; the end of the world would come. They looked for this with a kind of grim self-satisfaction.

"might be saved": a special formula of St. John.

"sotha"—σωθη.

"saviour" "sotar"—σωτήρ.

Vs. 18. To the Pharisees and Nicodemus as such. "The name," etc. This refers to the prologue, especially verse 18. The name is something special, denoting the essence, the real nature. The name of the Christ is "I AM."

Vs. 19. A further explanation of "condemnation." The third verse where this is mentioned.

"Light and Darkness" refers to the Prologue.

"Loved Darkness": The opposite of "God so Loved"

in verse 16 above.

"Love of Heaven" (Godlike)
"Love of Evil" (Evil, Devil-like) } must have both

Vs. 20. "Doeth evil, hateth light," — this hate is the opposite of "love."

Doing evil results in hatred.

Doing good results in love.

"This "doing evil" is against the spiritual world.

This verse is the negative of Verse 16.

Vs. 21. "Doing truth" as against "knowing truth"—"Doing" is the will activity. "Knowing" is thought activity. "Doing truth" is doing what will last for the world, what will not disappear in decay. Note the difference, not doing good *in* the world, but *for* the world. It is a "lifting up" and refers to Verse 14 above.

This ends the present reference to Nicodemus. But he reappears twice more (three times in all)—

1) In the "night"—the spiritual world. (Chapter 3)
2) With the Pharisees, where he breaks the "we" of which he spoke in Chapter 3:2, and where he becomes an independent being, separated from the "we" of the Pharisees (Chapter 7). External light.
3) After the Resurrection, with Joseph of Arimathea, in Chapter 19, where he becomes a Christian.

So we find that Nicodemus meets Christ three times:

1) In the spiritual world, the sphere of the Holy Spirit.
2) In the ego, as an independent being, the sphere of Christ, the Son.
3) In the Resurrection, in God the Father.

This is a Trinity!

"Love,": "ägäpa"—ἀγάπη: see pages 37 and 139 of these notes.

John, in the Epistles, does not love the world. God loves the world. (Ch. 3:16).

The following Sevenfold use of Love: see page 41 of these notes.

1. God loves Christ (1), the disciples (2), and the world (3).
2. Christ loves God (4) and the disciples (5).
3. Disciples love Christ (6) and each other (7).

Vs. 22. "Judea"—John has more ego consciousness, hence he gives more concrete details regarding the activity of Jesus than do the other Evangelists. They tell only of Jesus going to Judea once, whereas Christ said they loved to go there often!

Vs. 25. "Purifying": Greek, "Cäthärismu"—καθαρισμοῦ—About salvation, baptism, initiation, discipleship.

Vs. 26. "All men come to him"—A kind of reproach, a criticism, a cynical remark, as though to say, "they all followed you (John Baptist) and now he has taken them all away; they all run after him (Christ)."

John answers this in Verse 32: "No man receiveth his testimony."

Vs. 27. John answers the reproach in part.

"Except it be given him from heaven"—This is a formula from St. John. It is repeated three times in the Gospel: The negative of this "given" is found in the speech of Pilate:

Three times these formulae are used by John:

1) "from above"
2) "from heaven"
3) "from God."

Vs. 29. "bridegroom," "bride"—The mood of the Wedding at Cana in Galilee, the reflection of the event.

"Friend"—This is referred to three times:

1) "friend of the bridegroom" (Chapter 3:29)
2) "our friend Lazarus" (Chapter 11:11)
3) "I have called you friends" (Chapter 15:15)

The negative: "Caesar's friend Pilate" (Chapter 19)

"the bridegroom's voice"—This is referred to three times:

1) "bridegroom's voice" (Chapter 3:29)
2) "shepherd's voice" (Chapter 10:3)
3) "my voice" with Pilate (Chapter 18:37)

"Joy is fulfilled"—Points to the reference in the High Priestly Prayer: "that they might have my joy fulfilled in themselves." (Chapter 17, verse 13)

Vs. 30: "Increase"—"Decrease": Points to the Nicodemus scene, where the Christ increases in words and meaning and Nicodemus decreases in words and meaning.

Vs. 31. "From above"—The Christ. "of earth"—man.

Christ brings the better half of the human being from the heavens.

Vs. 32. "seen and heard"—this is a mirroring of the Nicodemus scene, Chapter 3, Vs 11, "seen," know, told, etc.

"No man"—See reference to John v. 26 (page 40 of these notes. "all men" versus "no man."

Vs. 33. "Set to his seal"—An active thing, an adding of something to what is already known. Refers to Chapter 6:27, also to the Seals of the Apocalypse.

Vs. 34. "by measure"—One aspect is give by Dr. Steiner. The ancient wisdom was given "by measure" (Greek, "matroo"—μέτρου—as in the Greek epics, the Vedas, etc., in poetic form. It was given from the etheric, not through the understanding of the ego. Christ speaks through the Ego in John's Gospel.

Vs. 35. "The Father loveth the Son." Refer to "Love" (page 37 of these notes). This is the first reference to this. "The Father loves the disciples"; see Chapter 14 of John's Gospel.

Vs. 36. This verse is a mirroring, a reflection, of Verse 16: "For God so loved," etc.

But this is, in a sense, an opposite at the same time, for here the wrath, the Judgment is spoken of. The wrath is the mirror of the love.

Again, there appears in this verse the threefold form, three clearly articulated parts.

Notes on the "I AM" Statements

These are always divided into three parts, which reflect the Trinity:

1) The Father principle: The basis, the beginning, the "I AM" statement itself.

2) The Son principle: the consequences, the impulse in the individual, the personal action, the condition, the word "it."

3) The Holy Spirit: The "plaromä"—πλήρωμα—the fullness of the statement, the glory of it, the streaming-out quality, the fulfillment of it in spirit, the extension to humanity.

The Physical Body: Our body becomes visible through the matter that fills it. There is an invisible web of forming and shaping forces. The body of Christ is an invisible web of forming and shaping forces upon the framework of the body.

The Blood: Is an invisible force. Not the matter or earthly substance. The blood receives the finest, most delicate motions of your soul through your thoughts, feelings and emotions. It is a real spiritual power in the world which spiritualized the blood of Jesus of Nazareth.

Elevation: Invisible, spiritual powers coming from above. We lift up substances from the earth to meet this. When these substances of the earth meet Christ, there is a possibility of coming together. It is a kind of predestined connection between the supersensible world and the earthly elements. It is like a bright cloud coming down from heaven. This is like a "grounding" of the supersensible substance (as in "grounding" of electrical current in the earth).

"with"—touches the earthly sphere in this moment of Transubstantiation.

"in"—penetrates, disappears into the earthly substance. The light radiates from them.

"be"—"it is" Christ's body and blood—the elevation—it has a radiating glory then.

There is much more reality in it than we perhaps think. There is an organic relationship between Elevation and Transubstantiation: lifted and lighted, light and light in weight. The Elevation is a lifting the substance up and out of the earthly sphere of the heaviness and darkness to the light.

Raphael's last picture, in part unfinished, stood by his bed when he died. It shows the Transfiguration on Mt. Tabor. The Christ is in a state of elevation above the earth, hovering above the earth. Not spoken of thus in the Gospels. It is an elevation of the physical body of Christ. He is penetrated by the supersensible light, taken out of the darkness and heaviness of the earth and given to the sphere of light. Thus Raphael expressed the elevation.

"Our Father"—the Lord's Prayer prayed after the Transubstantiation and before the Communion. "Heaven" and "Earth" have met again. "Daily Bread" points toward the Communion. "The Lord's Prayer" here gives the strength it does because it has the spiritual Transubstantiation Act as a background and points to the Communion.

If we meet a *reality,* we are never the same again. It has an effect, either positive or negative, upon us. We cannot be the same as we were before. We are either richer or poorer than before. It either adds to or steals from us, and this is the meaning of Christ's statement, "like a thief in the night."

"Who is worthy to take communion?" We must take it with devotion knowing that, really, we are unworthy, being ill and conscious of it, realizing the distance between us and Christ, but he comes to us, in spite of our being sinners—then he can help us. Then being "unworthy" is really being "worthy."

Why two substances—bread and wine? In the thirteenth century, the Church abolished the giving of the Cup, only the Host was given, but in the Act of Consecration of Man both are given.

Body: It is a structure of forming, shape-giving forces.

Blood: Bearer of the ego, the "I am," is a power of streaming life-forces.

Two Ways of Comprehending the Spiritual World:

Apollonian: The day, the sunlight, the clear form of things, temples, statues, body. Consonants.

Dionysian: The night, the enthusiasm, the streaming inner power of life, like an inner river. Vowels, Blood.

These represent the right form and shape of our eternal body.

Death attacks the Body—Bread

Devil attacks the Blood—Wine. Devil brings the wrong kind of life.

The Ego: the greatest gift to the human being which at the same time has the power of becoming the greatest danger. The I AM is the human being's greatest dignity. The animal cannot say "I Am."

Free Will: We are free from God for being free for Him! This is the true meaning of the Gospel of John.

John 4:1–54

1. When therefore the Lord knew how the Pharisees had heard that Jesus made and baptized more disciples than John,
2. (though Jesus himself baptized not, but his disciples)
3. He left Judaea, and departed again into Galilee.
4. And he must needs go through Samaria
5. Then he cometh to a city of Samaria, which is called Sychar, near to the parcel of ground that Jacob gave to his son Joseph.
6. Now Jacob's well was there, Jesus therefore, being wearied with his journey, sat thus on the well, and it was about the sixth hour.
7. There cometh a woman of Samaria to draw water. Jesus saith unto her, Give me to drink.
8. (For his disciples were gone away unto the city to buy meat.)
9. Then saith the woman of Samaria unto him, How is it that thou, being a Jew, askest drink of me, which am a woman of Samaria? For the Jews have no dealings with the Samaritans.
10. Jesus answered and said unto her, If thou knewest the gift of God, and who it is that saith to thee, Give me to drink, thou wouldst have asked of him, and he would have given thee living water.
11. The woman saith unto him, Sir, thou hast nothing to draw with, and the well is deep; from whence hast then thou that living water?
12. Art thou greater than our father Jacob, which gave us the well, and drank thereof himself, and his children, and his cattle?

13. Jesus answered and said unto her, "Whosoever drinketh of this water shall thirst again,

14. But whosoever drinketh of the water that I shall give him shall never thirst; but the water that I give him shall be in him a well of water springing up into everlasting life.

15. The woman sayeth unto him, Sir, give me this water, that I thirst not, neither come hither to draw.

16. Jesus saith unto her, Go, call thy husband, and come hither.

17. The woman answered and said, I have no husband. Jesus said unto her, Thou hast well said, I have no husband,

18. For thou hast had five husbands, and he whom thou hast is not thy husband, in that saidst thou truly.

19. The woman sayeth unto him, Sir, I perceive that thou art a prophet.

20. Our fathers worshipped in this mountain, and ye say, that in Jerusalem is the place where men ought to worship.

21. Jesus saith unto her, Woman, believe me, the hour cometh, when ye shall neither in this mountain, nor yet at Jerusalem, worship the Father.

22. Ye worship ye know not what: we know what we worship, for salvation is of the Jews.

23. But the hour cometh, and now is, when the true worshippers shall worship the Father in spirit and in truth, for the Father seeketh such to worship him.

24. God is a Spirit, and they that worship him must worship him in spirit and in truth.

25. The woman saith unto him, I know that Messias cometh, which is called Christ, when he is come, he will tell us all things.

26. Jesus saith unto her, I that speak unto thee am he.

John 4:1–54

27. And upon this came his disciples, and marveled that he talked with the woman, yet no man said, What seekest thou? or Why talkest thou with her?

28. The woman then left her waterpot and went her way unto the city, and saith to the men,

29. Come, see a man, which told me all things that ever I did: is not this the Christ?

30. Then they went out of the city and came unto him.

31. In the meanwhile his disciples prayed him, saying, Master, eat.

32. But he said unto them, I have meat to eat that ye know not of.

33. Therefore said the disciples one to another, Hath any man brought him ought to eat?

34. Jesus sayeth unto them, My meat is to do the will of him who sent me, and to finish his work.

35. Say not ye, there are four months, and then cometh harvest? Behold, I say unto you, lift up your eyes and look on the fields; for they are white already to harvest.

36. And he that reapeth receiveth wages, and gathereth fruit unto life eternal, that both he that soweth and he that reapeth may rejoice together.

37. And herein is that saying true, One soweth, and another reapeth.

38. I sent you to reap that whereon you bestowed no labor; other men labored, and ye are entered into their labors.

39. And many of the Samaritans of that city believed on him for the saying of the woman, which testified, He told me all that ever I did.

40. So when the Samaritans were come unto him, they besought him that he would tarry with them, and he abode there two days.

41. And many more believed because of his own word;

42. And said unto the woman, Now we believe, not because of thy saying, for we have heard him ourselves and know that this is indeed the Christ, the Savior of the World.

43. Now after two days he departed thence, and went into Galilee.

44. For Jesus himself testified that a prophet hath no honor in his own country.

45. Then when he was come into Galilee, the Galileans received him, having seen all the things that he did at Jerusalem at the feast, for they also went unto the feast.

46. So Jesus came again into Cana of Galilee, where he made the water wine. And there was a certain nobleman, whose son was sick at Capernaum.

47. When he heard that Jesus was come out of Judea into Galilee, he went unto him, and besought him that he would come down, and heal his son, for he was at the point of death.

48. Then said Jesus unto him, Except ye see signs and wonders, ye will not believe.

49. The nobleman saith unto him, Sir, come down ere my child die.

50. Jesus saith unto him, Go thy way, thy son liveth. And the man believed the word that Jesus had spoken unto him, and he went his way.

51. And as he was now going down, his servants met him, and told him saying, Thy son liveth.

52. Then he enquired of them the hour when he began to amend. And they said unto him, Yesterday at the seventh hour the fever left him.

53. So the father knew that it was the same hour, in which Jesus said unto him, Thy son liveth, and himself believed, and his whole house.

54. This is again the second miracle that Jesus did, when he was come out of Judea into Galilee.

Vs. 1–3. There is much confusion here over the word "Lord." Jesus left Judea and went into Galilee to leave Judea free for the work of John the Baptist. Judea: represents the head, the hardening forces, the brain, the dying existence of the physical.

Galilee: represents the etheric, the life forces, the atmosphere in which Christ could work.

Samaria: That part of Palestine ruled by the Israelite Kings of the North. It is among these people that the Elohistic divinity arose. At the South was Judea, home of the Jews. The ten Tribes of Israel lived in the North. In 586 the Babylonians under Nebuchadnezzar destroyed Jerusalem. The Judeans were worshippers of Jahve. The exile in Babylon lasted fifty years, and on their return, the Judeans were fanatical, narrow, hard Jews. When they returned, the Jews began to rebuild Jerusalem, and the Samaritans wished to help them build the wall, as they considered themselves Jews also. But the Jews refused their help, and sent them home, an insult they never forgave. They considered Samaria a "little Babylon," and its people to be not genuine Jews. There had been three Judean Kings: Saul, David, and Solomon. The ten tribes of the North who later finally wandered away little-by-little, were ruled by other Kings.

"Codex Samaritana": The Samaritans considered themselves Jews—which they were, but only half—for they still today retain traces of the their partly-Babylonian ancestry. They still have their own synagogues and type of worship. There are about four hundred families in this group today (as of 1950). They accept the Five

Books of Moses and the Book of Joshua only. This is the famous "Codex Samaritana," and they also profess to have a copy of the Law in the handwriting of Abisha, the great-grandson of Aaron.

The Maccabees: They (the Jews) attacked the Samaritans, and relations became very bitter. Suffered severely under Hyrcanus, and the Temple on Mount Gerezim was destroyed.

The Two Mountains of Samaria: Deuteronomy 27:11–13.

a) Mount Gerezim: Today a green fertile mountain, originally the Mount Olypmpus of the Samaritans. There they thought Noah's Ark had rested. From that mountain, Moses ordered blessings to be called out. In Christ's time there were eighty wells on the mountain, A fertile mountain of "life."

b) Mount Ebal: A contrast, a bald unproductive mountain. There Moses ordered curses to be called out. A barren "Mountain of death."

When the Jews in Christ's time traveled north from Jerusalem to Galilee, they purposely made a great detour, partly out of fear of the hostility between the Samaritans and themselves and because of their desire to avoid a heathen country. They went via "trans-Jordan" and the Greek area of Decapolis, preferring even heathen Greeks to the hated Samaritans.

The Samaritans differed from the Jews in that they lived more in their feelings, the heart, whereas the Jews lived more in the head, the intellect, the brain. The Samaritans lived more in the astral, the feeling sphere, and of course this could be of great danger, because a demon could so easily slip into these people.

Character of the Gospels

Matthew: The Father principle, God as Father. The physical sphere described in the details. The "masculine," the parable of "the shepherd and the lost sheep."

Mark: The Son principle, Christ as son. The etheric sphere of life forces.

Luke: The Woman principle, the mother, the feeling astral sphere. The emotions. Mary. Parables with Women figures, The feminine principle everywhere present in Luke. "The parable of the Woman who lost a penny" is the Luke balance (feminine) of the "Shepherd who lost a sheep" in Matthew (Masculine). "Remember Lot's Wife"—this verse in Luke—picture of hardening soul forces, the opposite of Mary. Christ speeches to the women of Jerusalem—special in Luke. The Mary and Martha scenes. In the Chapter 8, certain special women are introduced. The scene of the Woman who speaks to Christ out of the Crowd. The Mary-Elizabeth scenes.

Mary is the listening soul. "Hearing," Listening," "Speaking"—the Word, special terms for Luke's Gospel. The sperm, the germ of the Logos is heard by the hearing soul which receives it. There is a crossing over to the soul sphere from the eternal, the everlasting.

The beauty of the soul is always in Luke.

The Samaritans play a role in Luke because they have such strong feelings. There are two special Samaritan scenes in Luke:

"The Good Samaritan"—Chapter 10

"The Thankful Leper"—Chapter 17.

John: The Gospel of the Ego. Continues the Samaritan line introduced by Luke. The Christ is called a Samaritan.

Acts of the Apostles, written by Luke.

In Chapter 8, Simon Magus was a Samaritan who had been taken by demons, a dark figure. Simon Magus and Simon Peter are opposites—both "Simons." Simon Magus, connected with dark forces, shows what Simon Peter could have been without the influence of Christ.

Jacob's Well at Sychar

When Jacob came with his family and adherents to Sychar, he was a kind of "outsider," a sort of displaced person, and he was not permitted to use the wells of the residents. Instead he had to dig his own well, which remains to this day. Then he had to leave Sychar, because his sons got into trouble and murdered some of the Samaritans. He went to Egypt eventually, and there he died and was mummified by the Egyptian embalmers. His mummy was taken to Mount Hebron and buried there in a famous cave along with that of Abraham, Isaac, Sarah and others. This was done by Joseph. Then Joseph returned to Egypt and eventually died there, and his body also was embalmed by Egyptian embalmers. Then, four hundred years later, when Moses led the Children of Israel into Palestine, they carried the coffin of Joseph with them for forty years in the wilderness. Finally, Joseph's mummy was buried in the parcel of land which had belonged to Jacob near Mt. Ebal. Joseph could not be buried in the cave at Mt. Hebron, because the line of descent toward the Christ had meanwhile crossed over to Judah.

On the one side: Mt. Ebal, the Grave, the Curses, Death

On the other side: Mt. Gerezim, The Living Water, Well, Life.

Vs. 6. "Jesus was wearied"—John's Gospel is all embracing, inclusive of the greatest and the least details. He goes to the bottom of the human picture of the Incarnated Christ, includes many physical details, gives the most intimate details. And he gives the greatest, i.e., the Logos, etc.

All the physical details in the story are absolutely clear and alive. It is 12 Noon—Midday—the sun is at the zenith.

Vs. 7. Jesus speaks seven times in this story. This is the first.

Vs. 8. "the city"— incorrect, Greek, "Polen"—πόλιν—"town," "village," i.e., Sychar.

"meat"—incorrect: Greek: "Trofäs"—τροφὰς—"food."

Vs. 9. The woman stresses the old Jewish-Samaritan struggle. She also realizes He is a Rabbi, and the old rabbis had nothing to do with women, only contempt for them. The Talmud has many bad, dreadful references to women. The rabbis would not permit their students even to speak to women.

Vs. 10. Stands in the common everyday sphere with the first request—(verse 7)—now here, verse 10, the second speech of Christ, he raises it to a higher level. "To know"—not with your eyes! But with your knowledge—the etheric sphere.

"Living Water"—Greek, "Hudor Tson"—ὕδωρ ζῶν—this takes us to the life-force, the etheric sphere.

Vs. 12. The pride of the Samaritans in Jacob and his work is alive in this woman—after 2000 years of time had passed! Jacob lived 2000 years before the Christ. The tradition is alive; it is as though Jacob had died yesterday!

Greater"—Greek "Maitson"—μείζων—a feeling of invisible forces, a magician, a magic in it.

Vs. 13. "Whosoever drinketh of this water shall thirst again." This first statement is the third speech of the seven speeches in the series in this Gospel. Professor Betch pointed out that this "thirst" is physical, the physical sphere, and is the thirst of the soul to incarnate physically, a Buddhist concept. Buddha taught that the thirst for earth existence, incarnation, is something which is to be avoided, overcome, since earth existence is maya, illusion. But the Christian teaching is that earth existence is not an illusion, and that the human being has a task on earth.

Vs. 14. This verse contains parts two and three of this third speech of Christ. The whole verse is divided thus:

1) "Whosoever drinketh of this water shall thirst again,"
2) "But whosover drinketh of the water that I shall give him shall never thirst;"
3) "But the water that I shall give him shall be in him a well of water springing up into everlasting life."

The first part is the physical, the second is the astral, feeling sphere; the third is the etheric, the life sphere.

"Shall be"—This in Greek is "shall become"—we are to become a well, pouring out for others. This is the Greek "genasetai"

—γενήσεται—which, as in the Prologue, is translated "be, "when it should be "become."

"Springing up"—This is really "jumping up"—a correct translation of the Greek "hällomenoo"—ἁλλομένου.

"Shall never thirst"—The word "thirst" appears three times in John:

1) Samaritan Woman—4:13-15
2) I am the Bread—6:35
3) Every man a fountain—7:37-38

On the cross the counter-statement: "I am athirst." Only John gives this detail.

"Everlasting life"—Life which goes "through the aeons."

In regard to this verse: this is a prophecy, it is not fulfilled here with the Samaritan woman, because "his hour is not yet come"—Christ has first to go through Golgotha before he can give this "Living water"—before he can give it, Christ has to take into his being the condition of thirst.

These references to "thirst" are balanced by three references to the Apocalypse:

1) Revelation 7:16
2) Revelation 21:6
3) Revelation 22:17

—Thus John gives three references to Thirst.

—Then Christ athirst on the cross between them.
Then the Apocalypse gives three references to Thirst.

Vs. 16. Jesus speaks for the fourth time in this chapter.

He points to her lack, the lack of a correct approach to the male principle and union with it. "Husband"—The Babylonian, mediumistic element in the Samaritans (the "Whore of Babylon" is the Archetype of this) led this woman to sexual connections of a depraved kind in her search for the male sphere. She seeks the ego sphere.

Vs. 17. "I have no husband"—She acknowledges that she has no right connection with the male principle, that she is in search of the ego. Jesus points out that this is a fact. This begins the fifth speech of Jesus in this part.

Vs. 18. "Husband"—the Johannine word, "Bridegroom," for Christ, stands hidden behind this word in this verse.

Vs. 19. "Prophet"—The woman has confidence in Christ. It is an acknowledgment of the Christ Being, as in Luke's Gospel, by a woman, by the female principle.

Vs. 20. "worshipped in this mountain"—A pointing to Mount Gerezim, the Mountain of Life. This is a reference to the old pre-Christian worship of nature in the out-of-doors—a "summer worship"—a cosmic worship but with a heathen background. A Catholic worship, in a sense.

Vs. 20. (continued): "at Jerusalem"—
    A pointing to the Jewish, Judaic worship.
    Inwardness—a loss of the summer, nature, cosmic
        relationship.
    Indoors. It is similar to Protestantism.

    —This verse is in the nature of a *question*.

Vs. 21. "hour cometh"—To the future, "Mine hour is come."
    This is the sixth speech of Christ in this scene.
    "Neither" "Nor": Strong contrast
    The Christ points to a new relationship—a new cosmic
        relationship but with *new inwardness*.

    First Step: "This Mountain": Cosmic worship.

Second Step: "Jerusalem": Goes through the House of Inwardness, a "bottleneck." The Ego-point begins from the Jews—through their narrowness, then leads back to a regaining of the cosmic.

Vs. 22. "Salvation is of the Jews"—The way to true worship leads *through* the *narrowness* of the Jews to a new *cosmic* worship.

> Thus, those who say Christianity is a Jewish concept, is an adaptation or extension of it, simply do not know the facts which are indicated here. Christianity is that which goes *through* Jewish narrowness and *out of it* to expand into an entirely new concept on cosmic lines.

Vs. 23. "cometh and now is": this appears confusing but is not. It merely points to the fact that the *germ of the future* of which the Christ is speaking is present in the *now, the present, but as a possibility only.*

"Spirit"—Greek—"pnoimäte"—πνεύματι—see these notes page 34 above.

"the Father seeketh": The Father *seeks* worshippers, in the etheric sense. God *seeks* the human being! God *needs* the human being! An impressive thought!

Vs. 24. "Spirit and truth"

Spirit (pnoimä)—πνεῦμα—cosmic worship

Truth (älathai-ä)—ἀλήθεία—inward worship

—The Father seeks worship on both bases!

Vs. 25. "Messe-äs"—Μεσσίας—The *warm faith* of the Samaritans regarding the coming Messiah, is pointed to here by the *Woman*.

Vs. 26. This is the seventh speech of the Christ, and it is really an "I AM" statement: In Greek, begins with formula "Ago aime"—Ἐγώ ειμι—"I AM I am" It should be translated: "I am the I AM, speaking to you."

This is the first "I AM" statement in John. It is given in full sunlight at noon—the ego principle.

Note: The I AM statements are always given as "Ago aime"— Ἐγώ ειμι. In each case they should be translated as, "I am the I AM." "I AM" is Christ's name. He is identifying himself as the "I

AM." For example in the seven great I AM statements of the John Gospel: "I am the I AM Who is the Bread of Life"; "I am the I AM Who is the Light of the World," and so on, throughout the I AM statements.

Vs. 27–30. This little interlude is an extension of what the Samaritan woman did after the conversation with the Christ. It is important to note the details so clearly mentioned—the waterpot, etc.

Vs. 31–38. The disciples appear again. Behind these verses is the Mystical Food contained in the "I Am the bread of life." This is the background of the scene.

Vs. 34. Here is the mystical word "Teliasom": "Talamä"—θέλημα—related to "Talos"—τέλος—(see above) and "Tala-o"—τελέω—translated "finish"—meaning "fulfill," "complete," "finish." This is used especially in John's Gospel, and is used three times.

On the cross, Christ uses another word: "Tatalestai"—τετέλεσται—"It is fulfilled."

From this we can see the place of the human being—that the human being is needed to complete the world—to "finish" the work of the Father. Human beings are of consequence, their thoughts are necessary to the completion of creation. This is one of the fundamental ideas of Dr. Steiner in his early philosophical writings.

Vs. 35. "The fields"—Refers to the famous wheat fields near Sychar.

Vs. 37. This "another" refers to pre-Christian great men and women—initiates—who had done so much to prepare for the coming of Christ. Remember, the Samaritans were influenced by a non-Jewish world.

Vs. 38. The indication that we must thank these others, these pre-Christians.

Vs. 40. "Tarry", "Abide"—One word.

Vs. 42. "The Savior of the World" Greek, "Sotar tu cosmu" "Sotar too kosmoo"—σωτὴρ του κόσμου—This phrase is the climax of the scene with the Samarian Woman and the Samaritans as a whole.

However the word "cosmos" is not like our sense of its meaning. In the New Testament, cosmos means the earthly world, the world independent of the Creator—separated from the divine. It is the same word as used in the John 3:16 "The World." It refers to the fallen world, which has to be saved, delivered.

In the New Testament, the word "cosmic," as we understand it, "the heavens" is "ooränos"—οὐρανόσ—"cosmic" in our sense.

Vs. 43. "Galilee"—The miracles are divided in John's Gospel thus:

In Galilee:

> The Cana Wedding
> The Nobleman's Son
> The Feeding of the 5,000
> The Walking on the Sea.

These four: Nature, general

In Judea:

> The Healing of the Impotent Man
> The Healing of the Man born Blind.
> The Raising of Lazarus.

These three: Individual, personal

Judea: that which is connected with the Fall of the human being—decay.

The Judean signs are more individual in character.

The Galilean signs are more relating to nature in character.

Vs. 46. "Cana of Gaililee where he made the water wine"—This is important, not a reference for the careless or forgetful reader. No such references in John are without importance. This reference is to remind us that this is a continuation of the work begun at Cana.

So this second sign is the continuation of the first one. There is a direct connection.

"Son"—the key is "son"—the keyword. The ego principle here comes through the problem of incarnation.

Vs. 52. "Fever"- The son is ill of a fever, a condition related to the blood. The Luciferic element was too much in the warmth of the blood—too much to bear.

"Father and son"—The son is dying. The old forces coming from the past are weakening, dying, forces which would carry the son into the future. So the son can't live into the future. Thus Christ gives him the forces of life. Christ penetrated the boy with his ego.

"Son"—In Greek, first, "hoo-e-os"—υἱὸσ—(son); second, "pais"—παῖς—(boy); third—"hoo-e-os"—υἱὸς—(son).

Vs. 50. "Thy son liveth"—this is the key word here. Repeated three times (Vss. 50, 51, and 53).

Vs. 54. "Second"—This is more than a casual word. It is an indication that we are to count the number of miracles in Johns' Gospel (seven in all).

John 5:1-47

1. After this there was a feast of the Jews; and Jesus went up to Jerusalem.
2. Now there is at Jerusalem by the sheep market a pool, which is called in the Hebrew tongue Bethesda, having five porches.
3. In these lay a great multitude of impotent folk, of blind, halt, withered, waiting for the movement of the water.
4. For an angel went down at a certain season into the pool, and troubled the water: whosoever first after the troubling of the water stepped in was made whole of whatever disease he had.
5. And a certain man was there, who had an infirmity thirty and eight years.
6. When Jesus saw him lie, and knew that he had been now a long time in that case, he saith unto him, Wilt thou be made whole?
7. The impotent man answered him, Sir, I have no man, when the water is troubled, to put me into the pool: but when I am coming, another steppeth down before me.
8. Jesus saith unto him, Rise, take up thy bed, and walk.
9. And immediately the man was made whole, and took up his bed, and walked, and on the same day was the Sabbath.
10. The Jews therefore said unto him that was cured, It is the Sabbath day, it is not lawful for thee to carry thy bed.
11. He answered them, He that made me whole, the same said unto me Take up thy bed and walk.
12. Then asked they him, What man is that which said unto thee, Take up thy bed and walk?

13. And he that was healed wist not who it was, for Jesus had conveyed himself away, a multitude being in that place.

14. Afterward Jesus findeth him in the temple, and said unto him, Behold, thou are made whole; sin no more, lest a worse thing come unto thee.

15. The man departed and told the Jews that it was Jesus, which had made him whole.

16. And therefore did the Jews persecute Jesus, and sought to slay him, because he had done these things on the Sabbath day.

17. But Jesus answered them, My Father worketh hitherto, and I work.

18. Therefore the Jews sought the more to kill him, because he not only had broken the Sabbath, but said also that God was his Father, making himself equal with God.

19. Then answered Jesus and said unto them, Verily, verily, I say unto you, the Son can do nothing of himself, but what he seeth the Father do: for what things soever he doeth, these also doeth the Son likewise.

20. For the Father loveth the Son, and sheweth him all things that himself doeth, and he will shew him greater works than these, that ye may marvel.

21. For as the Father raiseth up the dead, and quickeneth them; even so the Son quickeneth whom he will.

22. For the Father judgeth no man, but hath committed all judgment unto the Son,

23. That all men should honor the Son, even as they honor the Father. He that honoreth not the Son honoreth not the Father which hath sent him.

24. Verily, verily, I say unto you, he that heareth my word, and believeth on him that sent me, hath everlasting life, and

shall not come into condemnation; but is passed from death unto life.

25. Verily, verily, I say unto you, the hour is coming, and now is, when the dead shall hear the voice of the Son of God, and they that hear shall live.

26. For as the Father hath life in himself; so hath he given unto the Son to have life in himself;

27. And hath given him authority to execute judgment also, because he is the Son of Man.

28. Marvel not at this, for the hour is coming in the which all that are in the graves shall hear his voice,

29. And shall come forth; they that have done good, unto resurrection of life; and they that have done evil, unto the resurrection of damnation.

30. I can of mine own self do nothing: as I hear, I judge, and my judgment is just; because I seek not mine own will, but the will of the Father which hath sent me.

31. If I bear witness of myself, my witness is not true.

32. There is another that beareth witness of me; and I know that the witness which he witnesseth of me is true.

33. Ye sent unto John, and he bare witness unto the truth.

34. But I received not testimony from man: but these things I say, that ye might be saved.

35. He was a burning and a shining light, and ye were willing for a season to rejoice in his light.

36. But I have greater witness than that of John: for the works which the Father hath given me to finish, the same works that I do, bear witness of me, that the Father hath sent me.

37. And the Father himself, which hath sent me, hath borne witness of me. Ye have neither heard his voice at any time, nor seen his shape.

38. And ye have not his word abiding in you, for whom he hath sent, him ye believe not.

39. Search the Scriptures, for in them ye think ye have eternal life: and they are they which testify of me.

40. And ye will not come to me, that ye might have life.

41. I receive not honor from men.

42. But I know you, that ye have not the love of God in you.

43. I am come in my Father's name, and ye receive me not; if another shall come in his own name, him ye will receive.

44. How can ye believe, which receive honor one of another, and seek not the honor that cometh from God only?

45. Do not think that I will accuse you to the Father: there is one that accuseth you, even Moses, in whom ye trust.

46. For had ye believed Moses, ye would have believed me: for he wrote of me.

47. But if ye believe not his writings, how shall ye believe my words?

Vs. 1. Behind this miracle of the Impotent Man is the Baptism in the Jordan. However, if we compare these miracles with the Sacraments, we have:

1. The Cana Wedding: Baptism

2. The Nobleman's Son: Confirmation

3. The Impotent Man: Confession.

Vs. 2. "Sheep Market"—Not right in Greek. It is a "Sheep Door" "Probätika"—προβατικῇ—Through which the sheep were driven into the Temple to be sacrificed. There is a hint in the background of the Passover, of the Lamb of God to be sacrificed. But it is only a hint.

"Bethesda"—Βηθεσδά—"Beth"—"house"; "Hesida"—"Grace." It is a picture of a place where the Graceful Powers are working to the aid of the fallen human being.

"Pool"—A pond probably with volcanic underground. In Jerusalem the city is underlaid with volcanic rock and fissures through which fire came. The emphasis here is on fresh water agitated by volcanic action.

"Five porches"—May have to do with the five signs, five dark, "underneath" signs of the Zodiac, as against the four signs of light above which are connected with the ego. The number four is the number of the ego. Thinking, Feeling, Willing, Ego = four.

Vs. 3. "Blind"—Connected with sight—the spiritual, the conceptual, thought sphere: Thinking.

"Halt"—Opposite pole—the will sphere, connected with limbs: Will, Action.

"Withered"—Lack the streaming, circulating, rhythmic life forces: emotion, feeling.

— These three types represent three aspects of the human being fallen from the divine, his illness.

— "Waiting for the moving of the water"—these people sought healing by turning back to the original powers that created the human being—a turning back to the etheric—a kind of nature-healing.

Vs. 4. "An Angel": A being from the etheric sphere, the angelic forces that create us out of the etheric sphere, from which we have come.

The etheric life forces of these people are consumed, and they await the return of these forces. But Christ heals the man from quite another side, from the ego side.

"troubled the water"—The boiling effect from volcanic action with a healing, nature effect.

"stepped in"—A reflection of the Jordan Baptism.

"first"—This represents the "unsocial principle" of natural healing. When Dr. Rudolf Frieling was a clergyman in Vienna, on Monday (the clergyman's holiday), he used to walk in the woods, and was always shocked by the papers and refuse from the Sunday crowds. There were no healing, restoring, etheric forces left in the woods at all. But day by day they would be built up again until another Sunday. And then whoever comes to get the benefit of them, well he or she comes, and the benefit is his or hers. So that is how unsocial, so to speak, this was here.

"Angel"—The supersensible force. Angels can incorporate in very fine mist or water in movement.

In the time of Julian the Apostate work on excavation of the Temple foundation stopped when Volcanic fire appeared.

"into the pool"—This "into" is a Greek form, and has the meaning "by aid of." It is incorporation in perception form "by aid of" the water. A materialization.

This is living water, water in movement. The elementary spirits can incarnate in it—a slight dematerialization.

Vs. 5. "a certain man"—This is a Judean miracle, hence of an individual nature, performed in Jerusalem. It happens to an individual (ego) person.

Vs. 6. "Jesus saw"—This "saw" is a creative looking. He saw through the man's whole karma. In this "seeing" of Christ, sense perception and inner revelation came together, at the same time. It is a reference also to the healing of the man born blind born.

"Wilt thou be made whole?"—This is the first speech of Christ in this scene. He speaks three times: verses 6, 8, and 14.

This passage is a deep question, "Have you the will (talo)—θέλω—to be made whole?" This is another word than "the will (talamä)—θέλημα—of the Father." He asks him if he wants to get well, so he can take part in the activities of humanity again. This points to a common psychological symptom of people who take to their beds to escape the activities, duties, etc., of humanity around them.

They use sickness as an escape device.

In this miracle Christ kindles the fire of the ego in the man once again. It is a changing of water into wine again—a reflection of the pattern miracle.

"The spirit blows where it wills" (talo)—θέλω—where there is a willingness! A reflection of the Nicodemus talk.

The key word of this whole miracle is this word "Wilt" (talos)—τέλος—

Vs. 7. "No man to put me into the pool"—This is like the German fairy story of the little boy who, worn out and tired, sits beside the road and says listlessly, "I wish something would come along and take me along with it!" So this man seeks for something not of his own willing, not of his own ego. He expects the whole salvation from the outside, as people take to mineral baths, seashore, mountains, or to nature for healing. But Christ comes from quite another side, from the ego, for the man to awaken his own inner fire.

"another steppeth down before me"—Illustrates the selfish, anti-social nature of "nature-healing."

Vs. 8. "Rise, take up thy bed and walk"—the second of the three speeches of Christ here.

This speech is in three parts:

1) "Rise": Points to the Resurrection—the resurrection of the ego of this man. He is to stand on his feet. It is an awakening of the will power in him.

2) "Take up": Bear. So to speak, to take up our baggage. It is a carrying, as in Greek architecture, the columns not only support, but also carry the load. It rather points to the reference to "columns" in the Apocalypse. He is to lift the load and carry it. It is a call to his ego.

3) "Walk"—In German, the word for walk (wandeln) is also the word for "Transubstantiation." So here, as in the Sacrament, the human being is to join the great movement of the world which goes onward.

Vs. 9. "The Sabbath"—This verse points to the first of the great Sabbath conflicts as recorded by John. This is the first reference to the problem. There are three Sabbaths in the Bible:

1. The Creative Sunday of the Father (Genesis)
2. The Resurrection Sunday of the Son (Easter)
3. The Whitsuntide Sunday of the Holy Spirit

In the time of Christ the Creative (Genesis) Sunday of the Father had become a mournful day, a day of death, a day of weariness, of Saturn chill and cold of great age. Nietzsche voiced this in his saying "God is Dead." They began to have this feeling—a Saturn (lead) feeling. The things of nature as created by God (Genesis) go on, but where is the impulse for fresh creation? God has "rested" unto death. This was the feeling, the mood of the Jewish Sabbath. And this was expressed, fulfilled outwardly, in the fact that God the Son lay in death within the tomb, the grave, during the Jewish Sabbath! And in the Resurrection, we see that this external (Genesis, Jewish-Sabbath) impulse now goes into the human being and comes forth through the ego and will, in his or her deeds on earth—the new creative impulse. God in the Son, Christ in us, God in us. And in this verse Christ breaks the Jewish Sabbath deliberately, not an accident, thus pointing to his final "breaking" of it in the great Resurrection, and pointing to the Whitsuntide (Holy Ghost) Sabbath of Humanity—when all human beings can share in this new creative "Sabbath" impulse through Christ. This is the basis of the "Sabbath controversy" of the Gospels, where Christ "breaks" the Jewish dead form of Sabbath and brings the new Christ-Sabbath in deeds.

So the ascent from the Imagination (Image) sphere to the Inspiration sphere is the key to this healing!

Vs. 11. "Take up thy bed and walk"—This is the key phrase—repeated three times: Verses 8, 11, 12. This is not an accidental repetition. It is the same with the phrase, "Thy son liveth," repeated three times in Chapter 5. The repetition is important.

Vs. 14. In this moment is the real healing of the man. Here Christ speaks for the third and last time in this scene.

"findeth"—This is like Christ's calling of the disciples (Chapter 1, John's Gospel). He found them, because he knew how to find them.

"Behold"—He brings something up to the level of the man's consciousness, an appeal to thought. A knowledge aspect.

"Sin no more"—He traces effect to cause. It is interesting to compare this reference to sin to that of the man born blind:

1) "Sin no more"—the impotent man—his sin lay in the past—it was a penalty.

2) "Neither" had this man sinned, nor his parents"—the man born blind, his sin lay in the realm of possibility—he had not sinned at all. His blindness was a possibility, represented a possibility for the future so the Christ could work on him.

This "sin no more" is not to be taken as the clergy so often represent it, as a kind of dire warning. It is an explanation of the relationship between the sin of the past and the healing in the present—it tells *how* the healing was done! In this verse, Christ sees through the karma, the destiny of this man, and simply points out the consequences of past deeds. It is not a warning—it is an explanation.

Vs. 17. "My Father worketh"—They objected to the breaking of the Sabbath of the Jews—and Christ pointed out that the Father's work (Genesis), extended "to this point" ("hitherto"), "until this moment," (As in the Angel in the Pool). The Father healed in the nature-healing, the creative nature (Genesis) impulses.

"and I work"—Greek "kägo ergätsomai"—κἀγὼ ἐργάζουαι—"I myself"—this has tremendous power when spoken by Christ! It is thus that Christ works as he worked in the healing of the Impotent

Man—in kindling the warmth, the fire of the man's ego, through love—and this is the inner core of the meaning of this miracle.

Vs. 18. "himself equal with God"—Points to selfhood of Christ. Dr. Steiner says that this selfhood principle lives in the Beatitudes: "Blessed are they which do hunger and thirst ... for they (in themselves—in their selfhood) shall be filled," etc.—And the same in all the Beatitudes.

The balance of this chapter is divided by content: Verses 19 through 30, one unit; and 31–40, another unit. These units contain very important points in theology and Christology.

Vs. 19. The mystical relationship of the Son to the Father, the interactivity of Christ with God—A supersensible experience. Christ draws aside the curtain and lets us see the relationship between himself and God.

"Verily, verily"—Greek, "Amen, Amen"—"it is so" "it is reliable"—confirming a reality. These words we use to close a prayer, but Christ begins with them! The Christ starts with the reality, from the reality to which we strive to rise in our prayers, and with which we conclude. Christ, in all statements beginning "Verily, verily," starts with a significant reality and descends to us, while we strive to rise to this height!

In the Apocalypse, we find Christ spoken of as "The Amen." Thus, He is the fulfillment of world evolution.

"What he seeth the Father do": The Christ works out of the sphere of the absolute truth, the real "I" which "sees."

1. "The Father does"—The picture of death and resurrection in nature—God's sphere.
2. "The Son does"—The picture of death and resurrection in the human being and of the human being—Christ's sphere.

In one of his poems, Schiller gives a picture of this death and rebirth in nature as the activity of God, but of death and resurrection of the human being as the activity of Christ.

Vs. 20. "The Father loveth the Son." This is not "loves" (agape), but "fela-o"—φιλέω—"likes", is "friendly toward" "a friend of the Son. God is a friend of the Christ!"

"will show him greater works": This is because his "hour is not yet come"—something for the future.

"greater works": this is a motif of John's Gospel—it reflects what has been said to Nathanael, and the Samaritan Woman—"the gift of life"—to the Son.

The Son of God—The Christ as part of the Trinity

The Son of Man—The Christ passing through human incarnation, through humanity.

Vs. 21. "Raiseth up the dead": Points to the resurrection of Lazarus.

"The Son quickeneth whom he will": This does not mean that the Son will enable those to reincarnate whom He chooses arbitrarily out a whim, or any caprice. It means that Christ will lift to the level of a Son, to the level of personality, those in whom he can kindle the will forces. This points to the healing of the Impotent Man: "Do you have the will to be healed?"—"whom he will": into whom he can pour his will, in whom he can kindle His willing power.

Vs. 22. "judgeth ... judgment": These are poor words for the Greek meaning. They raise a Roman, juridical thought, which is not meant here at all!

"Hath committed all judgment to the Son": The task of the human being on earth is to meet the Christ in the right way. So this "judgment" is a comparison, to see if we are connected with Him or not. It is not judgment in an external sense. The human being is compared with the Christ. Christ is held up as the ideal. Are you connected with Him or not?

"judgment": Greek "kresen"—κρίσιν—"divide, decide."

Christ is a decisive factor in human destiny—a positive or negative factor as the case may be. All destiny has to do with meeting with the Christ.

Every night in sleep we have a kind of "little judgment" when in our sleep we have to confront all the impulses which have arisen in our astral bodies during the day. But this is an unconscious judgment, an unconscious matter. Then at death we have another "judgment" in our review of our life activity, when that which we have done is reviewed in the light of Christ—and this is a conscious judgment.

Then at the end of world evolution, at the end of our earth-incarnations, we have a still greater "Last Judgment" when we are finally compared with the ideal, the Christ.

Vs. 23. "honor" temose—τιμῶσι—"Price," "value," "worth"—having a feeling for the value, the importance of the Son-principle in relation to the Father-principle.

"He that honoreth not the Son, honoreth not the Father. . . ." This is addressed first, primarily to the Jews. In other words, the Jews stuck to the idea of the Father only, to the Father-principle, and had no appreciation for the Son. And of course, since the Father-principle had come to a kind of standstill in the world, if they stuck to that alone, they would come the point where they would not take up the Father revealed as the Son, the Christ-impulse, and would only have Ahriman. They would come to the death of the "Father-principle" and would find only the devil. This is what Christ means later when he says "Ye are of your Father, the devil." In short, this verse can mean:

"He who loses the Son, loses the Father also, and finds only Ahriman, the Devil."

This verse is amplified in the Apocalypse, chapters 4 and 5.

Vs. 24. This is a continuation of Verse 23, now amplified, a clarification of it. The Father-Son mystery amplified.

"passed from death unto life": In Greek this means, "steps over from death to life" (metäbebaken)—μεταβέβηκεν.

Vs. 25. "Hour is coming and now is": This is a formula of John's Gospel: Already spoken of in the Samaritan Woman scene:

John 4:23 (page 56 of these notes), the possibility of the future wrapped in the present.

"the dead shall hear": this points to the Impotent Man who lay 38 years as one dead and who heard the voice of the Christ telling him to rise. Also points to Lazarus.

"shall hear the voice": This is another formula of St. John's Gospel (see the notes on page 40 of these notes), reference to "Bridegrooms voice," etc.—Ch. 2:9).

Vs. 26. "Father hath life in himself": The Father is the source of life, the self-existent life.

"given to the Son": This is a lending of life to the Son.

"to have life in himself": Dr. Steiner points out that we are not our body; I am not my physical body, but I have my physical body! So we have an Etheric body which, when it is transformed by our meeting with Christ, will become "life spirit" (buddhi). So all our members, if transformed by our meeting with Christ, will be taken through death and resolved into higher faculties. When these members are transformed by Christ, we no longer will say, "I have this," but will say, "I am this." What we have made our own through meeting Christ, we can take with us through death. It will no longer be "baggage." When we can say, "I am this," not, "I have this," we can take it through death with us. This verse points to the life spirit of Christ. (See John 6:57.)

John 6:57 explained:

1. "As the living Father hath sent me, (Father)
2. "and I live by the Father; (Son)
3. "so he that eateth me, even he shall live by me" (the community of the Christians)

This Verse explains the passing of the life spirit: the life (a) from the Father, (b) to the Christ, (c) to the Christians.

Vs. 27. Here the meaning is blocked by the Roman type of words "execute judgment," etc., which hides the Greek meaning.

John 5:1–47

"authority," etc.: Greek, "exuse-än"—ἐξουσίαν: the ego organization, points to the Exusiae, Spirits of Form which organize the human ego.

Christ is the ideal human being, the archetype of humanity, the model, the pattern for comparison, the basis for judgment, the great dividing point.

Vs. 28. This is a picture of the Second Resurrection. Note that it is all in the future tense, purely future.

1) Verse 25. The First Resurrection, the resurrection of the soul through the meeting with Christ. This meeting does not exclude the passing through death, for we all shall die.

2) Verse 28. The second Resurrection, purely in the future, the resurrection which extends to the body itself: the appearance of the "Resurrection Body," the transformed human body.

   "shall hear his voice": Shall come to a consciousness of what they have accomplished in the whole sum of their earthly incarnations—the picture of the Last Judgment.

Vs. 29. An amplification of Verse 28.

1) "The resurrection of life": In the Last Judgment, if they have met the Christ so that He has transformed them entirely in the course of their earth incarnations, this will be a Resurrection Body of "life."

2) "The resurrection of damnation": In the Last Judgment, if they come to a consciousness of having missed the meaning of their earth incarnations, they will find this a resurrection to "damnation"—they will embody the evil, the demonic powers.

Vs. 30. "I can of mine own self": This is a subjective statement. It is balanced by Verse 19: "The Son can do," etc., an objective statement. In this verse 30 the faculty of hearing is spoken of; in verse 19 the faculty of seeing is spoken of. These balance each other. This ends Christ's sermon.

Vs. 31. Here we have an apparent contradiction to Ch. 3 vs. 11—and people might think that John, being an old man, had forgotten what he had written before, but this is not a contradiction. It is evidence of the growing consciousness of the Christ.

The spirit cannot be proven, its existence cannot be proven by any material evidence. The spirit bears its own evidence. The existence of the divine is not dependent on material proofs—you can't prove the existence of the divine, the eternal, by any external proofs. The spirit proves itself entirely—it reveals itself in us—not externally.

Vs. 32. Reference to John.

Vs. 33. This is the last direct reference to John the Baptist by Christ. It is a necrologue—the last words of Christ about him. John the Baptist is mentioned once again in the John Gospel, just before the Lazarus miracle, and then the name "John the Baptist" disappears.

Vs. 35. "He was a burning and shining light": John the Baptist is now dead, and this is a necrologue of the Christ concerning him. But this reference to John the Baptist in this verse is a quotation from one of the Books of the Apocrypha: Ecclesiasticus, or the Wisdom of Jesus son of Sirach 48:1, "And Elias the prophet stood up, as a fire, and his word burnt like a torch"—here again, the name Elias is linked to John the Baptist!

Vs. 36. Another reference to "works"—a formula of John.

Vs. 37–38.

1) "Heard"—Inspiration
2) "Seen"—Imagination
3) "Abide"—Intuition

Vs. 39. "Search the Scriptures": This is not in the Imperative mode in the Greek. It should read "Ye search the Scriptures, for in them ye think ye have eternal life," etc. This is addressed to the Jews, who studied the old books and records so intently and narrowly. "Search": this is the infinitive of the verb, not the imperative—"ye search."

But it is as though these books are dead, not alive. It is as though he said, "You read too many books"—but it is not quite wrong, for at the same time, these books "are they which testify of me." It is not wrong to search the Gospels, for they are the bridge for finding the living Christ of today. On the other hand, if we only search the Gospels, as the Protestants do, this is a kind of Mohammedanism, a making of a Koran out of them.

We need to meet the Christ!

Vs. 40. "Ye [the Jews] will not come to me that ye might have life"—instead of life ye have dead books! (this is the end of this sermon of the Christ).

Vs. 41. "Honor": this is the Greek word "Doxän"—δόξαν—"Glory."

Vs. 43. "Name": The mystery of the name here.

Vs. 44. "Honor": Greek, "doxän"—δόξαν—"glory." See above, also reference Chapter 8.

Vs. 45. "Moses" the second figure again mentioned! In John 1:21, Elias-John, and in Ch. 1, Vs. 17, Moses are mentioned. In Ch. 5, Vs. 35, Elias is referred to (see page 74, these notes) and here, Moses, and the Christ, stands between them as a representative mediator, a balance. In the Old Testament we have (page 87):

1) Elias: The apocalyptic style of prophet, the pictures of judgment and catastrophe—the end of the world, the Last Judgment—World Dissolution.

2) Moses: The Law-Giver—the recorder of the Creation of the World. The Ten Commandments and the Laws generally are the last remnant of the creative Impulse, the nature impulse of the Father God—He was the recorder of the World Foundation.

And Christ is the balance between the two.

Another prophecy of the Transfiguration Scene.

Vs. 46. "He wrote of me"—Here he says they are not even Jews!—Moses wrote of Christ.

John 6:1–71

1. After these things Jesus went over the sea of Galilee, which is the sea of Tiberias.
2. And a great multitude followed him, because they saw his miracles which he did on them that were diseased.
3. And Jesus went up into a mountain, and there he sat with his disciples.
4. And the Passover, a feast of the Jews, was nigh.
5. When Jesus then lifted up his eyes, and saw a great company come unto him, he saith unto Phillip, Whence shall we buy bread, that these may eat?
6. And this he said to prove him, for he himself knew what he would do.
7. Phillip answered him, Two hundred pennyworth of bread is not sufficient for them, that every one of them may take a little.
8. And one of his disciples, Andrew, Simon Peter's brother, saith unto him,
9. There is a lad here, which hath five barley loaves, and two small fishes, but what are they among so many?
10. And Jesus said, Make the men sit down. Now there was much grass in the place. So the men sat down, in number about five thousand.
11. Now Jesus took the loaves; and when he had given thanks, he distributed to the disciples, and the disciples to them that were set down, and likewise of the fishes as much as they would.
12. When they were filled, he said unto the disciples, Gather up the fragments that remain, that nothing be lost.

13. Therefore they gathered them together, and filled twelve baskets with the fragments of the five barley loaves which remained over and above unto them that had eaten.

14. Then those men, when they had seen the miracle that Jesus did, said, This is of a truth that prophet that should come into the world.

15. When Jesus therefore perceived that they would come and take him by force, to make him a king, he departed again into a mountain himself alone.

16. And when even was now come, his disciples went down unto the sea,

17. And entered into a ship, and went over the sea toward Capernaum. And it was now dark, and Jesus was not come to them.

18. And the sea arose by reason of a great wind that blew.

19. So when they had rowed about five and twenty or thirty furlongs, they see Jesus walking on the sea, and drawing nigh unto the ship, and they were afraid.

20. But he saith unto them, It is I, be not afraid.

21. Then they willingly received him into the ship, and immediately the ship was at the land whither they went.

22. The day following, when the people which stood on the other side of the sea saw that there was none other boat there, save that one whereinto his disciples were entered, and that Jesus went not with his disciples into the boat, but that his disciples were gone away alone.

23. (Howbeit there came other boats from Tiberias nigh unto the place where they did eat bread, after that the Lord had given thanks.)

24. When the people saw that Jesus was not there, neither his disciples, they also took shipping, and came to Capernaum, seeking for Jesus.

25. And when they had found him on the other side of the sea, they said unto him, Rabbi, when camest thou hither?

26. Jesus answered them and said, Verily, verily, I say unto you, ye seek me, not because ye saw the miracles, but because ye did eat of the loaves, and were filled.

27. Labor not for the meat which perisheth, but for that meat which endureth unto everlasting life, which the Son of man shall give unto you, for him hath God the Father sealed.

28. Then said they unto him, What shall we do, that we might work the works of God?

29. Jesus answered and said unto them, This is the word of God, that ye believe on him whom he hath sent.

30. They said therefore unto him, What sign shewest thou then, that we may see, and believe thee? What dost thou work?

31. Our fathers did eat manna in the desert, as it is written, He gave them bread from heaven to eat.

32. Then Jesus said unto them, Verily, Verily, I say unto you, Moses gave you not that bread from heaven, but my Father giveth you the true bread from heaven.

33. For the bread of God is he which cometh down from heaven, and giveth life unto the world.

34. Then said they unto him, Lord evermore give us this bread.

35. And Jesus said unto them, I am the bread of Life: he that cometh to me shall never hunger, and he that believeth on me shall never thirst.

36. But I said unto you that ye also have seen me, and believe not.

37. All that the Father giveth me shall come to me, and him that cometh to me I will in no wise cast out.

38. For I came down from heaven, not to do mine own will, but the will of him that sent me.

John 6:1–71

39. And this is the Father's will which hath sent me: that of all which he hath given me I should lose nothing, but should raise it up again at the last day.

40. And this is the will of him that sent me: that every one which seeth the Son, and believeth on him, may have everlasting life, and I will raise him up at the last day.

41. The Jews then murmured at him, because he said, I am the bread which came down from heaven.

42. And they said, Is this not Jesus, the son of Joseph, whose father and mother we know? How is it then that he saith, I came down from heaven?

43. Jesus therefore answered and said unto them, Murmur not among yourselves.

44. No man can come to me, except the Father which hath sent me draw him, and I will raise him up at the last day.

45. It is written in the prophets, And they shall be all taught of God. Every man that hath heard, and hath learned of the Father, cometh unto me.

46. Not that any man hath seen the father, save he which is of God, he hath seen the Father.

47. Verily, verily, I say unto you, he that believeth on me hath everlasting life.

48. I am that bread of life.

49. Your fathers did eat manna in the wilderness, and are dead.

50. This is the bread which cometh down from heaven, that a man shall eat thereof and not die.

51. I am the living bread which came down from heaven: If any man eat of this bread, he shall live forever; and the bread that I will give is my flesh, which I will give for the life of the world.

52. The Jews therefore strove among themselves, saying, How can this man give us his flesh to eat?

53. Then Jesus said unto them, Verily, verily, I say unto you, except ye eat the flesh of the Son of man, and drink his blood, ye have no life in you.

54. Whoso eateth my flesh, and drinketh my blood, hath eternal life; and I will raise him up at the last day.

55. For my flesh is meat indeed, and my blood is drink indeed.

56. He that eateth my flesh, and drinketh my blood, dwelleth in me, and I in him.

57. As the living Father hath sent me, and I live by the Father, so he that eateth me, even he shall live by me.

58. This is the bread which came down from heaven: not as your fathers did eat manna, and are dead. He that eateth of this bread shall live forever.

59. These things said he in the synagogue, as he taught in Capernaum.

60. Many therefore of his disciples, when they had heard this, said, This is a hard saying, who can hear it?

61. When Jesus knew in himself that his disciples murmured at it, he said unto them, Doth this offend you?

62. What if ye shall see the Son of man ascend up where he was before?

63. It is the spirit that quickeneth; the flesh profiteth nothing; the words that I speak unto you, they are spirit, and they are life.

64. But there are some of you that believe not. For Jesus knew from the beginning who they were that believeth not, and who should betray him.

65. And he said unto them, Therefore said I unto you, that no man can come unto me, except it were given unto him of the Father.

John 6:1–71   81

66. From that time many of the disciples went back, and walked no more with him.

67. Then said Jesus unto the twelve, Will ye also go away?

68. Then Simon Peter answered him, Lord, to whom shall we go? Thou hast words of eternal life.

69. And we believe and are sure that thou are the Christ, the Son of the living God.

70. Jesus answered them, Have not I chosen you twelve, and one of you is a devil?

71. He spake of Judas Iscariot the son of Simon: for it was he that should betray him, being one of the twelve.

This is the longest chapter in this Gospel. It deals with the first references to the Last Supper, and to "mystical food" in general.

Vs. 1. "over the sea of Galilee": Dr. Steiner has said that between 1794 and 1806, the circle around Goethe and Schiller prefigured Anthroposophy. This was the time when Anthroposophy became a reality in the Etheric sphere above the physical—when it was reflected there—and became a possibility for entrance into the physical sphere.

"sea": etheric cosmic forces pictured.

In the same manner, the Last Supper is reflected, mirrored in the Sea of Galilee a whole year before it was to take place in the physical sphere. And this chapter gives a more cosmic, more universal picture of the Last Supper, mirrored in the etheric sphere (Sea of Galilee).

"Galilee": Is always the etheric world.

Vs. 3. "went up into a mountain": This scene is impressive—the Christ ascends the mountain above the lake—then he descends to the 5,000. Then in Vs. 15, he ascends the mountain again! It is like

Lohengrin, starting at a high level, then descending, then ascending at the end.

"sat with his disciples": a picture of meditation—Christ and his disciples in meditation.

Vs. 4. "the Passover": Second reference to this event—the Jewish New Year begins. This is the beginning of the next to the last year—thus the events here open the last year of Christ's activity upon earth and prefigure the last Passover which was to include the Event of Golgotha, but especially the Last Supper.

Vs. 5. "lifted up his eyes": This is a formula of John's Gospel, indicating a higher experience, a higher "seeing."

"a great company coming": We could think that he sees not only those then present but also humankind of the future coming to him.

"Philip" and "Andrew": Second mention of these two. (see ch. 1) and the third mention is in Ch. 12:21-22, where these two introduce Christ to the Greeks. John's Gospel, written especially for the Greeks, is the only Gospel which names these two in this "Feeding of the 5,000" scene. And it is interesting that only these two of all the Disciples have Greek names!

Vs. 9. "a lad": Greek (pais—παῖς—boy) "paidäre-on"—παιδάριον—a diminutive form—a "little boy" is meant—refers to the building, increasing, growing powers of childhood, of the increasing powers of the etheric life forces of growth, and this scene takes place on the east (morning, dawn, growing) side of the Sea of Galilee (etheric).

"five barley loaves, two small fishes": Total equals completeness—seven! But there is a greater amount of bread, and lesser of fish. These two substances:

1) Bread: related to the earth, physical, solid.
2) Fish: related to the sea, the waters, the cosmic, universal spheres.

These are the two preparatory substances—preparatory of the Bread and Wine of the Last Supper.

Vs. 10. "Jesus said": The first of the three speeches of Christ in this scene. The other two are in vs. 11 and vs. 12.

"Much grass": In the Mark Gospel account it says "green grass"— emphasis on the etheric, on the growing, multiplying power of the place. Another reference to the child forces.

Vs. 11. "took the loaves": This is the special style of the Words of the institution of the Last Supper—a style which is nearly the same in all the Gospels. In this connection, there are twelve references to the Last Supper in the New Testament:

The Last Supper: Matthew, Mark, Luke (3)

The Last Supper: 1 Corinthians:11 (Protestant version) (1)

Feeding of the 5,000: Matthew, Mark, Luke, John (4)

Feeding of the 4,000: Matthew, Mark (2)

Emmaus Scene: Luke, Ch. 24 (1)

Morning Meal: John, Ch. 21 (1)

A total of twelve.

There is also a kind of thirteenth in the account of St. Paul, when, on the ship after the thunderstorm, he broke bread and gave thanks, but it is not the same in reality.

It is interesting that all four Gospels give the account of the Feeding of the 5,000 (Matthew, Ch. 14; Mark, Ch. 6; Luke, Ch. 9; John, Ch. 6). Refer to Dr. Steiner's lectures on the Matthew Gospel and to the John Gospel in connection with the Feeding of the 5,000, especially in regard to the Zodiac signs, etc.

Compare the four accounts of the Feeding of the 5,000—the four ways this is described in the four Gospels—a very interesting comparison because of the revealing differences and similarities in style and information.

"Fish": there is no symmetry of balance between the amount of fish and bread. Likewise, there is no balance of dignity between the words spoken about the bread and the wine in the scene of the holy meal: The Last Supper. There is more dignity to the bread—more is said of the bread, and the wine falls short.

"Took the loaves":   first step

"gave thanks":   second step

"distributed":   third step

Compare John 21:31, with "cometh," "taketh," "giveth"— three steps.

This is the same formula-style of the Last Supper.

"as much as they would": Of the cosmic element, they had the element of will—A reference to the Healing of the Impotent Man: "Wilt thou be made whole?" (See pages 65-66] of these notes and see also page 87—These words are a part of the Last Supper and the Act of Consecration.

In the Mass more words are added in the Institution, and this should be studied and compared.

The Church says this is because the text of the Mass is older than the Gospels, having been developed by Peter and Paul in Rome before the Gospels were written! And in the Mass more words are said about the Wine than in the Gospels, hence there is more balance between the words spoken about the Bread and the Wine.

"giving thanks": Greek, "oischärestasäs"—εὐχαριστησας—"thanking Thee" (related to "schäres"—χάρις—"life")—grace, blessing, special manifestation of the divine presence.

"Uniting His soul (blessing) with it": Greek: "Benedicti" (related to Logos—"word")

"To Thee, His Father": these words are in the Mass, but not the Gospel. Also in the Act of Consecration.

John 6:1–71

More of a cosmic, universal aspect of the Lord's Supper is given in this sixth chapter of John.

In the Feeding of the 5,000, one substance is used, and the second (fish) is only a "bud."

In the Last Supper, two substances are used, and the third is indicated as a "bud."

In the Act of Consecration, three substances are used—Bread, Wine, and Thinking.

"Lifted up His eyes": these words are not a part of the Last Supper in the house in Jerusalem. They belong to the etheric sphere of Galilee.

Passing of the Last Supper (Mass) from Evening to Morning:

In Galilee	Feeding 5,000	From Day to Night
Nightfall	Bread and Fish	John 6
		Eating with Disciples
Holy Thursday—Last		Bread and Fish
Supper—Night—	In Galilee	From Night to Day
	Dawn	John 21

Thus the Last Supper (Feeding of the 5,000) at nightfall evolved further through the Lord's Supper at night. Then came the Resurrection—at dawn—and the post-Resurrection meal was held at dawn—and in the Mass and the Act of Consecration, the Last Supper is celebrated, but in the light of the Resurrection—Dawn. So the Protestant celebration of the Lord's Supper at Night—(as is frequently done) is not quite right if the Resurrection is taken into account.

The Death—an Evening Event (Twilight—the darkening hours), Golgotha

The Resurrection—a Morning Event (Dawn—the lightening hours)

- And the Mass and Act of Consecration are connected with the Resurrection, not the Death of Christ.

"Semai-on"—σημείων—("miracle," "sign"). See page 23, these notes.

This word means token, signs of something, but it is not the thing in itself. It only points to something. If it is only a token, then what is it a token of? It is a preparation, a representation of what will come—a preparation for Golgotha and Resurrection. It is a representation of what Christ will mean for the whole world after the Mystery of Golgotha. Outwardly today we can feel little connection with a man who was healed 2,000 years ago by Christ! But these "signs" represent different archetypal aspects of Christ spread out before our eyes—before the Mystery of Golgotha. But really they represent "pre-Christianity" for us today—because they were all done before His "hour had come." Only with the Death and Resurrection of Christ does Christianity begin!

Vs. 12. "Fragments"—"Breaking the Bread": Matter must be broken up to become the bearer of something higher. A kind of sacrifice of an earthly thing for something higher. That which is physical must be broken, opened up, so it can be the bearer of etheric forces, an opening so the etheric fullness, the fullness of the stars, can stream in.

In early Christian times, they broke the round loaves (coronae) in the Mass—they broke the circular, self-enclosed physical form, so the spiritual forces could stream in.

Breaking the bread in the Mass and the Act of Consecration, is connected with the mystery of alchemy which stands behind—the Breaking and the Immersing.

Transubstantiation: When they asked Dr. Steiner when the actual Act of Transubstantiation took place in the Act of Consecration, he took a pencil and drew a waving line down the margin of the page of the original manuscript of the Act of Consecration. He began at the Word of Institution and continued to the Elevation. He Said: "From here to here the act of Transubstantiation is taking place."

Vs. 13. "filled": This is the Greek word "plaromä"—πλήρωμα—as used earlier in the Gospel of John (1:16).

"twelve Baskets": See Dr Steiner's lectures referred to above (page 83, these notes).

The fish: "As much as they would" (Vs. 11). The cosmic element. This is not so spoken of the bread, that there is the element of will in it. The fish points to the future.

1) The Wine: The Cup—A more apocalyptic picture which points to the future—The Elias theme.

2) The Bread: the Host—A picture from the olden time, pointing to the past, the Moses theme.

The Christ unites both the Elias and the Moses themes.

Vs. 14. "A Prophet": The expected, they looked forward to the coming of this Prophet, hence they recognized Him, and He accepted this.

Vs. 15. "A King": they wished to tie Him to the past, and this He rejected.

> The Prophet : For the future—accepted
>
> The King: For the past—rejected.

"Into a Mountain": The theme ends as it started, from the mountain, and now returning to the mountain (page 81, these notes).

Act of Consecration:

1) "Take with the bread ..."
2) "Take with the wine ..."
3) "Take this into your thinking. ..."

"A King": this is the principle of Judas, earthly power.

"Himself alone": Greek "autos monos"—αυτὸς μόνος—a state of meditation. Through this meditation, he becomes visible, a vision, for the disciples who are in another place.

Vs. 17. "Into a ship": Denotes a change of mind, more into the sphere of spiritual imagination.

Vs. 18. "sea arose": A physical possibility, but at the same time an etheric, inward experience also.

Vs. 19. "see": tha-oroosin—θεωροῦσιν—from which theory is derived. Theory is a "seeing something."

The change of tenses—first and last parts in past tense, then the middle part in present tense—as in this verse, is special for St. John. He so lived within the thing as a present reality, that he wrote thus.

Vs. 19. Should read, "I AM, have no fear."

Vs. 20. "Saith": "says."

"It is I": This is not correct. "Ago aime"—Ἐγώ εἰμι: "I AM."

This is the second "I AM" statement in John. The second in a series of twelve. The first to the Samaritan Woman in the full day, sunlight—the second at night. Christ has now entered the night sphere. He enters the etheric and astral world of Imagination. Christ is now working into this sphere, in his supersensible figure. The old night visions, etc., are ended.

In the Bible, the night following a scene is very important—one sees another aspect of the scene just before. The Parable of the Sower is such a moment, given after a day scene.

In *Tristan and Isolde* (Act 3), Tristan lies wounded, and has a vision of Isolde walking over the sea, a sea of flowers: "Full of grace and loving mildness, floating o'er the oceans's wildness; by billows of flowers lightly lifted, gently toward the land she's drifted. . . ." Also Plato in *The Symposium*, near the end of the speeches to Tistema, speaks of walking on the billow of beauty.

In Luke 5, Christ is described as being further out in the middle of the sea. He appears fully in his Cosmic Being. The liquid sphere of the sea: to make liquid is to open something to the influence of the etheric forces coming from above. The watering of plants permits something of the etheric forces to enter into them.

The Question of the Nets: In Luke, Chapter 5, the net breaks under the draught of fishes. In John 21:11, it is specifically stated that the net did not break. This is like a dream—the dream cannot be caught—the net is broken. But in John 21, Christ now makes the dreams, the night experience fruitful—after Golgotha Christ is connected with the earthly world, is connected with our night experiences. So the net in John 21 is not broken! Note that John 21 takes place near the shore.

The sea: Through this experience, the disciples saw an aspect of the etheric being of Christ. Thus Christ makes the night experience fruitful. They see Him in his supersensible figure.

Vs. 21. "Willingly received him": This does not make sense as translated. In the Greek, "they received him in their wills." Echo of the healing of the Impotent Man. They have to catch him through the activity of their will forces. This is like the Emmaus scene where He would have continued his journey, but they had to become active to get Christ to stop with them. At the end of the Grimm fairy tales, the speaker speaks about the mouse who runs across the floor, and whoever catches him will have a fur hat for himself—an active "catching" of the intuition of the story just told! Of course, it is on another level of thought, but the idea is similar. Here they have to catch Him, to catch the movement. Like the fishes in the Feeding of the 5,000—that which they "were willing to take."

"the ship was at the land": coming to the land, the shore, is always awakening.

"Immediately": a dream and awakening.

Dr. Steiner indicated that in earlier times the descent through the etheric into the physical was a slower process upon awakening, hence pictures and dreams were more real. Today we pass through the etheric into the physical very rapidly, hence our dreams and awakening are not as fruitful as in earlier times.

This Walking on the Sea was only possible in Galilee. It had a dream character. And so does Chapter 21 especially. Note Ch. 21, Vs 7: This "knowing" and "not knowing" is especially related to the world of dreams. And here we experience something of the "aroma of dreams."

Peter being "naked" (not clothed in a physical body) puts on his coat (etheric body) and plunges into the sea (etheric)—Vs 7, Ch. 21—is typical of dream experience—such a putting on of a garment then plunging into the sea, does not make sense physically, otherwise. Peter is beginning his incorporation, coming to the etheric sphere.

In the medieval figures in sculpture, the vertical is the main line. The vertical is the line of devotion. You cannot imagine yourself praying with your feet wide apart and your hands on your hips, because that goes too much into the horizontal. In the seventeenth-century paintings (especially Flemish), the emphasis is on the physical—the human being has spread out, has conquered the physical, earth sphere. This is especially clear in the Flemish paintings with their dramatic coloring, their movement and huge size of figures.

The scene of Walking on the Sea is in Matthew and Mark, as well as here in John 6.

In Luke 9, Vs. 11, Christ *receives* the people.

In this scene of John 6, there is a progression:

1) They see Him (6:19)

2) They hear Him (6:20)

3) They receive (take) Him (6:21)

Vs. 22. "The day following": A clear indication of the return to day consciousness.

In the first part of this chapter we are in the Imaginative sphere—the sphere of pictures (Feeding of the 5,000—Walking on the Sea). With Verse 22, we go into the Inspiration sphere—the sphere of teaching, speaking, the sphere where decisions are made—the will sphere. Here we have Peter's confession and the departure of some of the followers (vs 66).

Vs. 23. "Where they did eat bread after that the Lord had given thanks." Here the Greek word that is used is "Oischäristasäntos"

John 6:1–71

—εὐχαριστήσαντος—(related to "Eucharist," Vs 11. "Giving thanks"). Dr. Steiner correctly translates this verse: "Through his giving thanks, they had eaten the bread."

Vs. 26. "the miracles": In Greek, "Semai-on" —σημεῖον—: "Tokens," signs, pointing to reality. They represent the window through which one sees the reality. These people did not see these miracles as Imaginations – they had only the experience of the feeding, but they did not see the star forces descending through the praying of Christ.

(Study: The reference to the Stigmata in the Cycle on Mark's Gospel by Dr. Steiner)—The Stigmata is a breaking through into the physical, of something which ordinarily would remain in the etheric realm of the picture consciousness. The etheric and physical bodies are connected in the palms, the side and the feet, hence the possibility for the manifestation of the Stigmata in those places.

Vs. 27. "Labor not for the meat": The word which has been translated as "meat" is, in the Greek, "Brosen"—βρῶσιν—"food"—"that which is eaten."

"everlasting life": In Greek, "Life which goes through the aeons."

"shall give": Points to the future after Golgotha.

Note: "Labor ... shall give": the thought is that that which starts as work ends in a gift; through work one becomes capable of receiving divine grace.

"him hath God the Father sealed": This is a picture shown later in the Apocalypse: the spiritual brought down into the bodily (physical) sphere, pressing itself right into the sphere of the etheric and physical bodies. In the Apocalypse the human being bears the seal, the impress, the mark, of either the beast or of Christ. Thus, the time will soon come when it will not be possible to hide the possession of real spirituality, and materialists will have the proof of the spiritual in the beauty of the bodies of the spiritually imbued. (See Dr. Steiner's Nüremburg Cycle on the Apocalypse.)

Vs. 28-29. Note Vs 28: "Works" (Plural) Vs 29: "Work" (singular). There is a great depth of meaning in this contrast. Here in this reply we are unified with the source of the Communion.

1) The Jews: "many good works"—"many sins."

2) Christ: "One work"—"one sin."

   The first (Jewish) is the realm of the Creative Father.

   The second (Christ) is the realm of the Son.

The "many sins" versus the "one sin"—see John 16:8-10.

These people were not in contact with the higher ego—such a "work" as to "believe on him whom he hath sent"—must come out of our contact, our connection with Christ.

Deeds which we do have spirit, soul, and body just as we ourselves do.

"believe": Greek, "Pistoisate"—πιστεύσητε—that which is done with the blood—that which enters into the Ego—this word denotes that which has its connection in the heart.

Vs. 30. "sign": "Semai-on"—σημεῖον—(see above). Note that their reply is now in the singular: "sign" and "what ... work."

Vs. 31. This verse represents a suggestion on the part of the disciples, a kind of a tentative idea that they are putting out as an answer.

Vs. 33. "World": In Greek, "cosmo"—κόσμῳ—"that which has fallen away from God" (see John 4:42 and page 58, these notes.) It points to the earthly world in need of redemption, that which we call "the dying earth existence."

Vs. 35. This is the first of the "I AM" statements of Christ: The first of the series of seven. Note that it is in three parts:

1) "I Am the Bread of Life."

2) "He that cometh to me shall never hunger."

3) "He that believeth on me shall never thirst."

John 6:1–71

The twofoldness of "hunger" and "thirst" is a pointing to the twofoldness of the Last Supper—"bread and wine," "hunger and thirst."

Chapter 6 is divided into three main sections, and these sections are divided into seven sub-sections:

Main Divisions: Verses 1–21, 22–59, 60–71.

Sub-divisions: Verses 1–15, 16–21, 22–41, 42–51, 52–59, 60–66, 67–71.

Thus, there are three sections in seven parts, and this is repeated later in the composition of other chapters of this Gospel.

The first Main Division (Vs 1–21)—Sphere of Imagination

The second Main Division (Vs 22–59)—Sphere of Inspiration

The third Main Division (vs 60–71)—Sphere of Destiny, Decision, Communion, Excomunication

In other words, parts 60–71, especially, deal with the great problem of Communion and Excomunication.

Rhythms: In this 6th Chapter, there are certain rhythms, which weave backward and forward, moving like waves through the chapters. These are in the form of certain special themes which weave and move as in the Buddhistic texts. It would be good to take a colored pencil and underline these, giving each its own color, thus identifying the wave-movement through the chapter. Some of these themes follow:

1) "Descending from heaven" ("coming down")
2) "Raise it up in the last day"
3) "Life"
4) "Living Father"

Vs. 39. "all": In the Greek, "everything."

"raise it up again": Note that this "it" will change to "him" in Verse 40.

"seeth" and "believeth"

"eats" and "drinks"

"bread" and "wine"

"body" and "blood"

The body represents the shaping forces of the picture of the archetype. The blood is deepened, developed later.

The formula "raise him up" is repeated three times. Verses 39, 40, 41.

Vs. 41. "murmured": Greek, "egoggootson"—ἐγόγγυζον—note the heavy guttural sounds in this word. It is a picture in sound of "murmuring." Later (Vs 52) they "strove"—a more active sense, introducing the next division in the chapter.

Vs. 42. Evidence of the "heritage thinking" of the Jews. They are bounded by the physical (horizontal) line, and the vertical line of descent is hidden from them.

Vs. 44. "No man can come to me except the Father which hath sent me draw him: and I will raise him up at the last day." The Father draws the world of karma from the realm of the Cherubim and Seraphim. In the Greek, the "Father draws *and teaches.*"

Vs. 46. This verse refers to the Prologue and to the Farewell Discourse of Christ. In Greek it is correctly translated: "Who has the Father as the source of his being, he has seen the Father."

Vs. 48. This is a repetition of the first "I Am" Statement, but now there is a metamorphosis in it—it is not quite the same. This statement is repeated three times, and there is a distinct clarification and metamorphosis in it:

1) "I Am the bread of Life." (Vs 35)

2) "I Am that bread of life." (Vs 48)

3) "I Am the living bread." (Vs 51, most "acting")

Vs. 49–50. Following this repetition of the "I AM" statement, come three little sentences:

John 6:1–71

1) "Your fathers did eat manna in the wilderness, and are dead."
2) "This is the bread which cometh down from heaven. . . ."
3) ". . . that a man may eat thereof and not die."

The manna is a prophecy, a forecast—that which comes from the Father, the creative Source.

Vs. 51. Following this third repetition of the "I AM" statement, comes three little sentences again:

1) "If any man eat of this bread, he shall live forever."
2) "And the bread that I will give is my flesh."
3) "Which I will give for the life of the world . . ."

Note the following words:

Vs. 35. "hunger and thirst": A soul condition, astral, problem of longing and fulfillment.

Vs. 48. "dying and living": The Father world, the physical, which ends in death.

Vs. 51. "live and life" The pure etheric world of the Christ.

Verse 51 presents the cosmic meaning, the universal meaning of the Last Supper. It is shown as a living process.

Vs. 52. "flesh": the same word as used in the Prologue, now used again here. This verse introduces the realm of "flesh."

"strove": the Jews gain activity now.

Vss. 53, 54, 57. Note the progression in the three pronouns as Christ speaks:

1) "eat the flesh of the Son of Man, and drink his blood"
2) "eateth my flesh and drinketh my blood"
3) "eateth me, shall live by me"

Vs. 55. "is meat indeed": The word "meat" in Greek is "food"—note.

Vs. 56. "eateth . . . drinketh": There is a kind of reciprocity in it. "dwelleth in me and I in him": like the door and the knock. This is the same pattern found in the Apocalypse.

Vs. 57. There is a sequence here:

1) The living Father

2) I live

3) He shall live.

Vs. 58. "dead . . . live": The contrast: The manna and the "Bread of Life."

This whole section (verses 52-59) is an excellent meditation for Communion.

In connection with the Communion—the eating and drinking—"flesh and blood"—remember:

1) Goethe said "The Archetype is not first in time (history)."

2) The original is not the barbaric, the cannibal—the "cannibal" came after the Last Supper, so to speak.

Vs. 53. "Body"—"fragete": Here the word is "särkä"—σάρκα—a more radical word for body.

Note that this verse is in the third person, a more objective presentation. Refers to Verse 14 of the Proglogue in Chapter 1. This is continued in Verse 54 which follows.

Vs. 55. "My flesh is the true food and my blood is the true drink." It is as though he said:

"My body is the truth of all food,"

"My blood is the truth of all drink."

"flesh": "särkä"—σάρκα—same word in Prologue.

"meat" in Greek should be translated "food."

Note the rhythms in these verses which again are found in Chapter 15.

Eating is sometimes thought to be bestial, despite modern conventions. Actually the eating of the animals is a reflection of a reflection. The sacrament is the real eating, and the eating of our every day life is symbolic eating. The order really is:

1) The Last Supper: Real Eating: Sacrament
2) The common daily human eating
3) The eating of animals

All the previous acts of eating of Christ with the disciples is in one line leading to the Last Supper.

Vs. 56. "Dwell": To be eternal, belongs to the eternal light. Refers to Prologue, Ch. 1:39.

Dwell in the privacy of the ego. This verse continues the rhythms, and all these are repeated in Chapter 15 about the wine.

Vs. 57. "I am living by the Father."

"He lives by me." The "me" and "my" (vs 54) are related.

Vs. 58. Completing the whole. Contrast of "dead" and "live."

Vs. 59. This is a well-known synagogue. It is said to have been build up by the Centurion mentioned in Luke. The ruins of this synagogue remain today, and it is well known for its Greek bas-reliefs with wheat and grapes prominently figuring in them. This verse ends this section.

Vs. 60. This may be thought of as the "Section of Decisions"—the will impulse plays a great role here. The feeling that destiny plays a role beginning here. There are two parts:

1) Vs 60–66: The wider circle of the disciples.
2) Vs 67–71: The smaller circle of the disciples.

"hard": Greek "Sklaros"—Σκληρός—to do with death, with the bones, the physical structure. The early Gnostics could not comprehend the death on Golgotha, nor the words about the "flesh."

They considered these things too materialistic and sought a more spiritual way. In this sense, the word "hard" is meant in this verse.

Vs. 61. "Knew in himself": this is a formula of St. John's Gospel. Means: "knew in his own self"—intuition.

"offend": In Greek, "skändäletsai"—σκανδαλίζει—"a trap"

"skändäletso"—σκανδαλίζω—scandalize—to offend.

"Doth this scandalize you?"

Vs. 62. "ascend up": The key to the understanding of the Last Supper. Ascension is the knowledge. Key for Transubstantiation and for the Transfiguration.

The Ascension Formula of St. John's Gospel:

"Glory"—"One with the Father"—"Ascend"

1) Nicodemus scene: 3:13

2) "Ascend up": 6:62

3) "I ascend unto": 20:17

"Änäbainontä"—ἀναβαίνοντα—from "änäbai-o" ἀναβαίνω—"Ascend" —always used in the John Gospel.

Vs. 63. This famous verse was cause of one of the most famous disputes in Protestant Theology: between Luther and Zwingli regarding the *Presence* in Communion. Luther thought there was a mystical element in Transubstantiation, and Zwingli and Calvin thought there was not—that there was only the thought—and the latter used this verse as proof of their point of view.

Proper Translation: "The spirit is that which creates life; the flesh as such cannot be of any use (cannot help anything)—the words that I have spoken unto you are spirit and are life."—Refers to the words just spoken regarding the Communion.

The physical alone has no power—is maya—illusion—but when the spirit touches the physical sphere it has more power—it shows more power. When God touches the physical, it shows greater

John 6:1–71

power, because the power to enter another sphere is a greater power.

"Words": From the middle region, the sphere of the etheric. The bridge for the spirit to come into the physical, the sacramental words. They are "life" into the etheric world—they can connect the spirit with the body.

Vs. 64. "Knew": The sovereignty of Christ—Gethsemane—the Judas-motif.

Vs. 65. "given to him of my Father": the necessary result of his former doings—his karma.

Vs. 67. this is the first verse of the last part—"the twelve": this is repeated three times in this section: Vs. 67, 70, 71.

Vs. 68. This is an echo of Verse 63. Now it is more personal.

"Peter" here balances "Judas" in Verse 71.

"the words of eternal life": In Greek there are two forms of the term "Word":

1) "Logos"—λόγος: more of the thought aspect.

2) "hramätä"—ῥήματα: (from "hra-o"—ῥέω—("flow"): More of the etheric, life, active side or aspect. It is the more "magical" side. "Magic" means entering the physical sphere. The Christ power to enter a sphere that is not his own.

Vs. 69. Correct translation: "We have believed and we have known"—the two aspects:

1) "believed": the warmth aspect

2) "known": the light aspect

"thou art the Saint, the Holy One of God": The word is, in Greek, "Häge-os"—ἅγιος—not "Christ."

This statement represents the answer of Peter to the Communion. Christ overcomes the cleft, the abyss between God and human being. Acknowledgment of "the Holy One" by the human being (as in Peter's case) is necessary in Communion. So in Communion, something comes from God and something else comes from the human being.

"Son of the Living God": This phrase is put in here by the translators to help establish "the Harmony of the Gospels"—to make this verse agree with one in Matthew.

Vs. 70. "Devil": Greek "De-äbolos"—διάβολός—Luciferic side. The Judas, the Golgotha theme.

The three formulae of John's Gospel (see page 107, these notes):

1) "Devil"—three times
2) "Satan"—three times
3) "Prince of the World"—three times.

Vs. 71. "Iscäre-oton"—Ισκαριώτον: "Ish": "human being," and "Cariot": a place in Judea. Judas was the only Judean among the Disciples. The rest were Galileans.

"should betray": One of the typical Johannine reflections, recollections—a peculiarity of John not found in the other Gospels.

"one of the twelve": (Twelve in Greek is "Dodekä"—δώδεκα). Here we have the Disciples as a twelve-hood. There is a complete framework of the figure 12 for the whole chapter.—At the beginning of Chapter 6, there are twelve baskets and twelve disciples, and here at the end are twelve disciples—and the figure "12" is mentioned three times at the end of the chapter.

In Chapter 6, the whole Christian year is outlined. All the Christian festivals of the Holy Year are grouped around the Last Supper, Golgotha, Resurrection and Ascension. Grouped around the Sacrament of Communion are all the other Sacraments.

A peculiarity of John's Gospel is that John selected events from the life of Christ which were grouped around certain Jewish feasts and festival times. There was a certain exaltation of mood then. Thus Chapter 7 through Chapter 10, verse 21, is grouped around the autumnal feast, the Michaelmas time—the Feast of the Tabernacles. This is related to the Feast of the Renewing of the Tabernacle—the Temple. In 168 B.C. Antiochus set up a Hellenistic God in the Temple on December 25—"the Day of the Rising Sun"—and in 165 B.C. (after three years) the Temple was restored (Feast of the Tabernacles) by Judas Maccabeus. (See Maccabees, Chapters 3 and 4.)

1) Passover: the spring: Ch. 6:4

2) Tabernacles: the fall: Michaelmas: Chs. 7–10:21

3) Rising Sun: the winter: Dec 25: Christmas: Ch. 10:22

4) Passover: Lazarus: Near Easter.

(the whole Christian Year in this last year.) The Christ's time is in the spring, the Passover Time.

John 7:1–53

1. After these things Jesus walked in Galilee: for he would not walk in Jewry, because the Jews sought to kill him.
2. Now the Jews feast of tabernacles was at hand.
3. His brethren therefore said unto him, Depart hence, and go into Judea, that thy disciples may see the work that thou doest.
4. For there is no man that doeth anything in secret and he himself seeketh to be known openly. If thou do these things, shew thyself to the world.
5. For neither did his brethren believe in him.
6. Then Jesus said unto them, My time is not yet come, but your time is always ready.
7. The world cannot hate you; but me it hateth, because I testify of it, that the works thereof are evil.
8. Go ye up unto this feast. I go not up yet unto this feast, for my time is not yet full come.
9. When he said these words unto them, he abode still in Galilee.
10. But when his brethren were gone up, then went he also up unto the feast, not openly, but as it were in secret.
11. Then the Jews sought him at the feast, and said, Where is he?
12. And there was much murmuring among the people concerning him, for some said, He is a good man; others said, Nay; but he deceiveth the people.
13. Howbeit no man spake openly of him for fear of the Jews.

14. Now about the midst of the feast Jesus went up into the temple and taught.
15. And the Jews marveled, saying, How knoweth this man letters, having never learned?
16. Jesus answered them and said, My doctrine is not mine, but his that sent me.
17. If any man will do his will, he shall know of the doctrine, whether it be of God, or whether I speak of myself.
18. He that speaketh of himself seeketh his own glory: but he that seeketh his glory that sent him, the same is true, and no unrighteousness is in Him.
19. Did not Moses give you the law, and yet none of you keepeth the law? Why go ye about to kill me?
20. The people answered and said, Thou hast a devil. Who goeth about to kill thee?
21. Jesus answered and said unto them, "I have done one work, and ye all marvel.
22. Moses therefore gave unto you circumcision (not because it is of Moses, but of the fathers), and ye on the Sabbath day circumcise a man.
23. If a man on the Sabbath day receive circumcision, that the law of Moses should not be broken, are ye angry at me, because I have made a man every whit whole on the Sabbath day?
24. Judge not according to the appearance, but judge righteous judgement.
25. Then said some of them of Jerusalem, Is not this he, whom they seek to kill?
26. But lo, he speaketh boldly, and they say nothing unto him. Do the rulers know indeed that this is the very Christ?

27. Howbeit we know this man whence he is, but when Christ cometh, no man knoweth whence he is.
28. Then cried Jesus in the temple as he taught, saying, Ye both know me, and ye know whence I am; and I am not come of myself, but he that sent me is true, whom ye know not.
29. But I know him for I am from him, and he hath sent me.
30. Then they sought to take him: but no man laid hands on him, because his hour was not yet come.
31. And many of the people believed on him, and said, When Christ cometh, will he do more miracles than these which this man hath done?
32. The Pharissees heard that the people murmured such things concerning him; and the Pharisees and the chief priests sent officers to take him.
33. Then said Jesus unto them, Yet a little while I am with you, and then I go unto him that sent me.
34. Ye shall seek me, and shall not find me, and where I am, thither ye cannot come.
35. Then said the Jews among themselves, Whither will he go, that we shall not find him? Will he go unto the dispersed among the Gentiles, and teach the Gentiles?
36. What manner of saying is this that he said, Ye shall seek me, and shall not find me, and where I am thither ye cannot come?
37. In the last day, that great day of the feast, Jesus stood and cried, saying, If any man thirst, let him come unto me, and drink.
38. He that believeth on me, as the scripture hath said, out of his belly shall flow rivers of living water.
39. (But this spake he of the Spirit, which they that believe on him should receive: for the Holy Ghost was not yet given; because that Jesus was not yet glorified.)

John 7:1–53

40. Many of the people therefore, when they heard this saying, said, Of a truth this is the Phrophet.
41. Others said, This is the Christ. But some said, Shall Christ come out of Galilee?
42. Hath not the scripture said that Christ cometh of the seed of David, and out of the town of Bethlehem, where David was?
43. So there was a division among the people because of him.
44. And some of them would have taken him; but no man laid hands on him.
45. Then came the officers to the chief priest and Pharisees and they said unto them, Why have ye not brought him?
46. The officers answered, Never a man spake like this man.
47. Then answered them the Pharisees, Are ye also deceived?
48. Have any of the rulers or of the Pharisees believed on him?
49. But this people who knoweth not the law are cursed.
50. Nicodemus saith unto them (he that came to Jesus by night, being one of them),
51. Doth our law judge any man, before it hear him, and know what he doeth?
52. They answered and said unto him, "Art thou also of Galilee? Search, and look: for out of Galilee ariseth no prophet."
53. And every man went into his own house.

Vs. 1. What Jesus did in Galilee is not told.

"sought to kill him": The mood of Michaelmas—the mood of killing and death.

Vs. 2. "Feast of the Tabernacles": See above page 101, these notes.

Vs 6. "My time is not yet come": In Greek, "Kairos"—καιρὸς—"Time," but in a qualitive sense—points to a special moment.

Vs. 8. "go up": There is a double meaning in the Greek here. The word "Änäbaino"—ἀναβαίνω—(see page 98 of these notes)—"ascend"—refers both to going up to the Feast at the Temple, and to Golgotha and Ascension. It is not yet the moment for Him to ascend to God.

"My time": The Ego, the I AM

"Full come": "Is not yet fulfilled"

Vs. 10. "in secret": In Latin, "in occult"—In Greek, "Kroopto"—κρυπτῶ—(see below).

Vs. 12. The dangerous atmosphere stressed.

The first part of the Chapter stresses the word "secret;" Christ is not visible. He is in "secret," so to speak. Then he appears and speaks in Verse 14.

Vs. 14. "The midst of the midst of the feast"—The Feast of the Tabernacle lasts eight days. On the fourth day, therefore, Christ shows Himself. He comes out of the "secret" and manifests Himself—He teaches. The order is:

1) First three Days—He is present but not manifested.
2) The fourth Day—He is manifested—enters the Temple.
3) The seventh Day—"The Last Day: The Great Day—(See Verse 37)—the Apocalyptic fulfillment.

— This is a picture of the Passion Week also.

— It may also be thought of as connected with the *processes of evolution:*

1) Saturn, Sun, Moon Stages: Christ present but not manifested.
2) Earth Incarnation—the fourth Stage — The manifestation of the Christ.
3) "The Last Day"—The Vulcan Stage—Seventh Stage.

— Again, one could think of this in connection with the Great Cultural Periods:

1) Ancient Indian, Persian, Egyptian: The Christ working but not visible.
2) The Graeco-Latin: The Incarnation of Christ.
3) The Last four Periods: Christ unites Earth and us with Himself.

Vs. 15. They realized He was "self-made"—that He had never studied in the official Rabbinical Schools. Their interest was in the intellect, in books and studies in the official form. It doesn't mean He didn't go to school.

(Dr. Rudolf Frieling recommended the books of Rudolf Kittel on Old Testament history.)

Vs. 17. Will comes into the sphere of knowledge, a fundamental idea of Dr. Steiner. Points to the will sphere in contradistinction to the intellect.

Vs. 19. "Kill": This word "Kill" is repeated three times: Verses 19, 20, 25. This "Kill" is the motif of Chapter 5. Points to the increasing tension here.

Vs. 20. "a devil": "daimone-on"—δαιμόνιον—"evil spirit." (more fully explained in Notes to Ch. 12:31)

Vs. 22. "circumcision of the fathers": The ritual of circumcision was given to Abraham, who performed it upon Isaac. But it was Moses who made it part of the law. Always in Jewish practice, circumcision was performed on the octave of the birth—8 days after birth—even if that day fell upon a Sabbath. It was about the only ritual act permitted on the Sabbath.

This is a real rabbinistic discussion, typical of the Jews—showing John's intimate knowledge of Jewish customs. This is the Michael way of argumentation and battle.

Vs. 23. "I have made a man every whit whole": Refers to the 5th Chapter—Healing the Impotent Man.

Vs. 24. "Do not judge on the surface of things"

Vs. 25. "Kill": The Good Friday mood. Michael mood.

Vs. 27. In looking for the Messiah, the Jews had borrowed the ideas of the Babylonians and Hindu folklore, where the great 'parentage, background and ancestry was shrouded in mystery. Eastern Kings' ancestry was a spiritual mystery. They were "born in a garden," etc. And so the Jews came to think that their Messiah would be one whose ancestry was quite mysterious and unknown. Therefore, they rejected Jesus because they knew his ancestry—another example of John's intimate knowledge of Jewish official ideas.

Vs. 28-29. Note the threefold reference to "know." The "knowing" role. The Michael sphere. This "know" is preparatory for the opening of the eyes of the Man Born Blind (Chapter 9).

Vs. 29. Jesus never says, "You know" the Father—He says, "I" know"—this points to the special relation of Christ to the Father. The word "Father" is used very carefully and sparingly in the Apocalypse.

John's Gospel, Chapters 5, 7, 8, 9, and half of Chapter 10, contain "The Theory of Knowledge of the Christ."

Vs. 30. "His hour was not yet come": This motif is heard for the first time in the Cana Wedding. It occurs eight times: then three times we hear the motif, "Mine hour is come." And between these two motifs (eight times and three times) is the Raising of Lazarus.

Vs. 33. "A little while": Greek, "schronon"—χρόνον—indicates quantative time.

John 7:1–53

Vs. 34. You cannot reach the sphere where the "I Am" is at home.

Vs. 35. "Dispersed": Greek, "de-äsporän"—διασπορὰν—the dispersal. The dispersal of the Jews throughout the world was a great help to early Christianity. Many non-Jews had adopted Judaism throughout the world because of the simplicity of the religion. It consisted of (1) Monotheism, (2) the Ten Commandments and (3) Circumcision. It was to the Jewish communities throughout the world that the first Christian teachers went.

Vs. 36. Note the stress in this verse, the rhythm, a kind of formula or motif of John's Gospel.

Vs. 37. "Now on the last day, the great day of the festival, Jesus stood up and cried out, If anyone is thirsty, let him come to me and drink."

"The last day": Greek "Eschäta hamarä"—ἐσχάτῃ ἡμέρᾳ—apocalyptic character—same word as in the Apocalypse.

"great day": In Greek, "Magic, spiritual, powerful."

Believing, cup, wine, blood. Thirst.

Vs. 38. A reference to the Samaritan Woman scene—the speech at the well (see page 53, these notes).

"belly": in Greek, "ko-ele-äs"—κοιλίας—most powerful forces—the forces connected with digestion and will—the higher hierarchies can work there.

"the scripture": reference unknown.

"Believeth on me": "ho pistoi-on ais ama"—ὁ πιστεύων εἰς ἐμέ.

This motif of John's Gospel appears seven times:

(1)	6:35		(5)	12:44
(2)	7:38		(6)	12:46
(3)	11:25		(7)	14:12
(4)	11:26			

It illustrates the power of faith.

The Mystery of the Last Day—points to the sphere of generation—the primeval overcoming of death on the earth. In the midst—the high point of the Festival of the Tabernacles was when a great Act of Purification took place. With singing of Psalms, the priests, led by the High Priest, walked in procession to the Pool of Siloa near the Temple. Water was drawn and carried in great golden vessels into the Temple. Then it was poured out as a solemn act by the priests as a cleansing process or ritual. Behind the ritual is the thought that the body is a vessel, an organ releasing spiritual forces of blessing on the earth. In the Last Day—the Great Day—the body will be like a golden vessel, pouring out joy and blessing for humanity—a kind of water process.

It was in the presence of this Pouring of Water as a Ritual Act that Christ made this statement about the flowing of the "living water," (Ch. 7:38).

— Also, near the end of the Feast of the Tabernacles came a moment when a great bonfire was built in the Temple precincts as a Ritual Act. In the light or against the background of this fire, Jesus says, "I Am the Light of the World!"

— So there is a balance:

1) Water: Life (Water of Life)
2) Fire: Knowledge (Light)

Vs. 39. "He meant by this the Spirit which those who believed in him were to receive—for the Spirit had not yet come, because Jesus had not yet been glorified."

The Holy Ghost was not yet working in the sphere of the human being.

"Glorified"—"revealed in his divinity." This is the second word used by John to represent Golgotha and Resurrection. (Dr Steiner translated this as "manifested.")

Vs. 40. "Prophet": This was a popular idea but different aspects were held by different people.

Vs. 49. "These common people (worldly ones) who do not know the Law are doomed!": This is a genuine Pharisaical idea—typical.

Vs. 50. The second appearance of Nicodemus. The third is when he appears with the group under the cross on Golgotha. Here Nicodemus comes out, disassociates himself from the group soul.

Vs. 51. Here Nicodemus has the courage to announce the commonplace.

Vs. 52. "They answered, Are you from Galilee too? Study and you will find that no prophet is to appear from Galilee." They show that they despise the nature forces of the Galileans.

John 8:1–59

1. Jesus went unto the mount of Olives.
2. And early in the morning he came again into the temple, and all the people came unto him; and he sat down and taught them.
3. And the scribes and Pharisees brought unto him a woman taken in adultery; and when they had set her in the midst,
4. They say unto him, Master, this woman was taken in adultery, in the very act.
5. Now Moses in the law commanded us, that such should be stoned, but what sayest thou?
6. This they said, tempting him, that they might have to accuse him. But Jesus stooped down, and with his finger wrote on the ground, as though he heard them not.
7. So when they continued asking him, he lifted up himself, and said unto them, He that is without sin among you, let him first cast a stone at her.
8. And again he stooped down, and wrote on the ground.
9. And they which heard it being convicted by their own conscience, went out one by one, beginning at the eldest, even unto the last, and Jesus was left alone, and the woman standing in the midst.
10. When Jesus had lifted himself up, and saw none but the woman, he said unto her, Woman, where are those thine accusers? Hath no man condemned thee?
11. She said, No man, Lord. And Jesus said unto her, Neither do I condemn thee: go, and sin no more.

12. Then spake Jesus again unto them, saying, I am the light of the world: he that followeth me shall not walk in darkness, but shall have the light of life.

13. The Pharisees therefore said unto him, Thou bearest record of thyself; thy record is not true.

14. Jesus answered and said unto them, Though I bear record of myself, yet my record is true, for I know whence I came, and whither I go; but ye cannot tell whence I come, and whither I go.

15. Ye judge after the flesh; I judge no man.

16. And yet if I judge, my judgment is true, for I am not alone, but I and the Father that sent me.

17. It is also written in your law, that the testimony of two men is true.

18. I am one that bear witness of myself, and the Father that sent me beareth witness of me.

19. Then said they unto him, Where is thy Father? Jesus answered, Ye neither know me, nor my Father. If ye had known me, ye should have known my Father also.

20. These words spake Jesus in the treasury, as he taught in the temple, and no man laid hands on him; for his hour was not yet come.

21. Then said Jesus again unto them, I go my way, and ye shall seek me, and shall die in your sins. Whither I go, ye cannot come.

22. Then said the Jews, Will he kill himself? because he saith Whither I go, ye cannot come.

23. And he said unto them, Ye are from beneath, I am from above; ye are of this world: I am not of this world.

24. I said therefore unto you, that ye shall die in your sins: for if ye believe not that I am he, ye shall die in your sins.

25. Then said they unto him, Who art thou? And Jesus saith unto them, Even the same that I said unto you from the beginning.

26. I have many things to say and to judge of you, but he that sent me is true; and I speak to the world those things which I have heard of him.

27. They understood not that he spake to them of the Father.

28. Then said Jesus unto them, When ye have lifted up the Son of man, then shall ye know that I am he, and that I do nothing of myself; but as my Father that taught me, I speak these things.

29. And he that sent me is with me: the Father hath not left me alone, for I do always those things that please him.

30. As he spake these words, many believed on him.

31. Then said Jesus to those Jews which believed on him, If ye continue in my word, then are ye my disciples indeed,

32. And ye shall know the truth, and the truth shall make you free.

33. They answered him, We be Abraham's seed, and were never in bondage to any man. How sayest thou, Ye shall be made free?

34. Jesus answered them, Verily, verily, I say unto you, whosoever committeth sin is the servant of sin.

35. And the servant abideth not in the house for ever, but the Son abideth ever.

36. If the Son therefore shall make you free, ye shall be free indeed.

37. I know that ye are Abraham's seed; but ye seek to kill me, because my word hath no place in you.

38. I speak that which I have seen with my Father, and ye do that which ye have seen with your father.

39. They answered and said unto him, Abraham is our father. Jesus saith unto them, If ye were Abraham's children, ye would do the works of Abraham.

40. But now ye seek to kill me, a man which hath told the truth, which I have heard of God; this did not Abraham.

41. Ye do the deeds of your father. Then said they unto him, We be born not of fornication; we have one Father, even God.

42. Jesus said unto them, If God were your Father, ye would love me; for I proceeded forth and came from God; neither came I of myself, but he sent me.

43. Why do ye not understand my speech? Even because ye cannot hear my word.

44. Ye are of your father the devil, and the lusts of your father ye will do. He was a murderer from the beginning, and abode not in the truth, because there is no truth in him. When he speaketh a lie, he speaketh of his own; for he is a liar and the father of it.

45. And because I tell you the truth, ye believe me not.

46. Which of you convinceth me of sin? And if I say the truth, why do ye not believe me?

47. He that is of God heareth God's words; ye therefore hear them not, because ye are not of God.

48. Then answered the Jews, and said unto him, Say we not well that thou art a Samaritan, and hast a Devil?

49. Jesus answered, I have not a Devil; but I honor my Father, and ye do dishonor me.

50. And I seek not my own glory; there is one that seeketh and judgeth.

51. Verily, Verily, I say unto you, if a man shall keep my saying, he shall never see death.

52. Then said the Jews unto him, Now we know that thou hast a devil. Abraham is dead, and the prophets; and thou sayest, If a man keep my saying, he shall never taste of death.

53. Art thou greater than our father Abraham, which is dead? And the prophets are dead. Whom makest thou thyself?

54. Jesus answered, If I honor myself, my honor is nothing: it is my Father that honoreth me; of whom ye say, that he is your God;

55. Yet ye have not known him; but I know him, and if I should say, I know him not, I shall be a liar like unto you, but I know him, and keep his saying.

56. Your father Abraham rejoiced to see my day, and he saw it, and was glad.

57. Then said the Jews unto him, Thou art not fifty years old, and hast thou seen Abraham?

58. Jesus said unto them, Verily, verily, I say unto you, before Abraham was, I am.

59. Then took they up stones to cast at him: but Jesus hid himself, and went out of the Temple, going through the midst of them, and so passed by.

Chapter 8 is "The Light Chapter"—Chapter of the Ego—"I AM" appears three times 8:24, 28, 58.

Story of the Woman taken in Adultery: This story was held back by the early Christian Fathers, because, according to them, there were three sins which were considered to be absolutely unforgivable:

1) Apostasy

2) Adultery

3) Murder

Therefore, they did not wish to show Christ's forgiveness of one of these three forms of sin. But this is in the earliest Greek texts.

Chapter 8 is noted for its typical Michaelmas, autumnal mood. It is filled with very sharp discussions, a severe, hard mood of battle and clash of swords—typical Michael mood.

The word "friend" in the Gospels:

This word increases in the Gospels as one advances through them. In Matthew it is used only three times: "The Laborers in the Vineyard"; "The Wedding Garment"; Gethsemane, Judas called "friend."

Then in John's Gospel: "I have called you friends." First they are called servants, now "friends."

The Lazarus scene represents the awakening of friendship.

Vs. 6. The phrase "as though he heard them not" does not appear in the Greek text. This is an attempt of the King James translators to rationalize the text. The meaning of the writing in the earth was lost on them. By this writing, the objective guilt of this deed was written into the earth.

Vs. 9. "convicted by their own conscience": This does not appear in the earliest Greek texts. The word "conscience" does not appear until St. Paul obtains it from the Greeks.

Vs. 6-10. Special motif: "stooped down," "lifted up himself"—special action. The repetition is important. Christ did not take this sin of the woman lightly—He united this sin with the earth that was later to be His body—with which He was later to unite Himself. He took her sin upon Himself in the deepest sense of the word!

Note on composition of Chapter 8:

1) Section 1: Verses 12-20: Christ speaks three times
2) Section 2: Verses 21-30: Christ speaks four times
3) Section 3: Verses 31-59: Christ speaks seven times.

This chapter deals with a "Theory of Knowledge."

This chapter deals with the Michael (fall) festival.

Vs. 12. Another "I AM" statement. In three parts:

1) "I Am the light of the world."

2) "He that followeth me shall not walk in darkness."

3) "... but shall have the light of life."

Vs. 14. A spiritual being carries his own support. This is the second speech of Christ.

Vs. 16. This is related to Vs 29, below.

Vs. 17. He stands outside their law because of his spiritual origin. It is a bit strange at first to hear him say that. They require two witnesses for their law.

Vs. 18. Here are his two witnesses:

1) The "I AM"

2) The "Father"

This is a kind of metamorphosis of the two testimonies of the lower world. This is a preparation for Ch. 10:30, "I and the Father are one."

Vs. 19. The third speech of Christ. The higher self of Christ cannot be separated from the Father forces. Note the word "known" (knowledge)—special for this chapter.

Part II of the Chapter

Vs. 20. "treasury": Not an accidental reference. Perhaps the thought of "shining" is behind it—the mystery of metals—"light of the world."

"hour not yet come": Greek, "horä"—ὥρα—this word for "hora" is counted in John's Gospel. It is given three times:

1) Ch. 2:4—Cana Wedding

2) Ch. 7:30—Feast of Tabernacles

3) Ch. 8:20—the Treasury

Vs. 21. This is the first of four speeches of Christ in this section. He indicates that these Jews do not have the possibility of lifting themselves up to the sphere of the Mystery of Golgotha—there "they cannot come." This "whither I go ye cannot come" is a counted formula of John's Gospel. It has already appeared in Ch. 7:34.

Vs. 22. In German, suicide is called "Freitod"—a "free death." The Christ will die a "free death," but not yet—the Mystery of Golgotha has yet to come!

"Kill": This is a motif of John's Gospel. This statement of the Jews is a kind of Ahrimanic caricature of the "free death" on Golgotha. It is a kind of Ahrimanic distortion of the facts.

Vs. 23. "World": In Greek, "cosmoo"—κόσμου—Indicates that which is separated from the divine (see explanation of John 4:42; page 58 of these notes).

"from beneath": You are entangled in the earth karma.

"from above": Christ can help, because He comes from outside—from above. At this moment, Christ is not united with the world. This is a speech which makes a great distinction between His state at this point and what His relation to the world will be later.

They are entangled in their sins. They have started things they cannot get out of or stop the consequences of—except with the help of Christ.

Vs. 24. "die in your sins": They are so entangled in their sins that it can end only in death, the karmic consequences for human doings. We today are entangled—we can't realize the far-reaching consequences of what we do, of our deeds.

"if ye believe not that I am": The "he" in the King James Version is to be omitted. You must believe on the "I Am," to be freed of your sins. Through faith and confidence in the higher I AM of Christ, humankind is taken out of the consequences of sins—and only thus!

Vs. 25. The third statement of Christ in this section.

Special Words of John's Gospel:

(1) Light; (2) know; (3) knowledge; (4) I Am; (5) gnosis.

Vs. 28. "Lifted up": This is the second repetition of this formula of John's Gospel. In Greek, "hupsosate—ὑψώσητε—to lift up: (1) Ch. 3:14; (2) Ch. 8:28; (3) Ch. 12:32.

"ye shall know that I Am": No "he" in the Greek. Here the believing (versus Vs 24) changes into "Knowing"—the "I Am."

The last part of the verse refers to the mystical relationship between Christ and the Father who "teaches" Christ.

Vs. 29. there is a relationship between this verse and Vs 16 above. The things that Christ does "please" the Father.

Vs. 31. This opens the third section of this chapter. Here the Christ speaks seven times. This section represents the great discussion with the Jews.

The Three Sections of Chapter 8:

1) The problem of knowledge: light, knowledge, knowing—The Holy Spirit—(the caricature of the Holy Spirit is Lucifer).

2) Salvation interest—Christ as the savior of the World—human beings die in their sins if they do not know the I Am—the Son.

3) Conversation with the Jews—Abraham as the father—the Father. The caricature of the Father is Ahriman—Satan—who holds the place of the Father for the Jews without Christ.

These form a kind of trinity.

In Verse 31, he points out that knowledge of the "I Am" is the basis for discipleship, the basis for freedom.

Vs. 32. Note the future tense: "shall know," and "shall make."

This is the Gnosis.

It represents a "Theory of Knowledge."

"becoming free" and "becoming known": This is the Philosophy of Freedom.

Here the Christ points to the pride of the Jews: they think they are free, whereas he says they are not, but they can become free.

Vs. 33. They take up his challenge on the question of their freedom. They think they are free already.

Vs. 34. He says that through committing sin, freedom is lost. This is because of the karmic consequences of sin. For example, if in this life you do wrong to a man, you become dependent on him in the next life. In the story of Joseph and his brothers (Genesis)—when they wronged him, they later became dependent upon him, they came within his power. This is a perfect, pattern example of karmic balance—shown in one lifetime.

Vs. 35. "the house": this is the house of the body. By becoming sinful, the human being becomes mortal.

"abideth ever": In the resurrection-body. This points to the Resurrection.

Vs. 36. Only in connection with Christ is there freedom.

Vs. 37. Literally, "hath no good in you."

Vs. 38. Contrast of "my" and "yours": God the Father and Satan (Ahriman) their father.

Contrast of "seen" (Verse 38) with "taught" (Verse 28).

The last part is incorrectly translated—should be "that which ye have heard with your father." They are inspired (inspiration, hearing) by their father: Ahriman, Satan.

Vs. 39. He specifically says Abraham is not their father! Ahriman, Satan, is their father. The word "Abraham" mentioned three times. This is the third speech of Christ in this section.

Vs. 40. "kill": The motif of death. This "killing" is a leading motif of John's Gospel. This "heard" points to their "heard" in verse 38 above.

Vs. 41. They now twist away from Abraham and try to point to God as their Father.

Vs. 42. Jesus explains to them why God is NOT their Father. This is the fourth speech of Christ is this section.

Vs. 43. "ye cannot hear my word":—because you have no room for it!

Vs. 44. "a murderer": In Greek. "änthropoktonos"—ἀνθρωποκτόνος—means "a killer of the human being," "a crusher of the human being." The enemy of that which is human in the world.

"the devil, and the lusts of your father will ye fulfill"—"accomplish": The great passion (lust) and emotion of the devil is to bring down the values of human dignity into the mud. A lust, an emotion for destruction, "a lie": Ahriman, Satan, is the father of the lie. And this first great lie of Satan is to give the material aspect of the world, to show things as they are not.

Vs. 46. This verse points to their relationship with the woman taken in adultery (beginning of the chapter). Christ is not with sin because he is from "above." He is not entangled in it. This is a kind of enlightening of his death.

Vs. 47. "He that is of God": This is typical of the style of St. John—a typical phrase.

Vs. 48. "devil": This introduces the word "daimone-on"—δαιμόνιον—to be possessed of a devil—the characteristic of the Samaritans in the eyes of the Jews.

There are three numbered words for "Devil" in John (see Notes to 12:31; 6:70; 7:20; 8:48):

1) "De-äbolos"—διάβολος—occurs three times
2) "Sätänäs"—Σατανᾶς—occurs one time
3) "Prince of this World"—occurs three times

This makes the Evil seven!

Vs. 51. "Keep": In Greek, "tarasa"—τηρήση—"observant"—related to the Hebrew word "nazan" (observe). This verse is in the style of the Apocalypse! It is in the style of a living spiritual exercise—pointing to a regulated, rhythmical spiritual life. It is like the work of a gardener, who regularly cultivates, tends his or her garden. The culture of meditation. To take the word which comes out of the "I Am" into his or her meditative culture.

"see death": This points to the last verse of chapter 3 with John the Baptist. The theme there being "see life." Another related motif is: "see the kingdom of God." All of these three in the distinct style of John.

Vs. 52. "a devil": this is the Greek "daimone-on"—δαιμόνιον.

"taste": A metamorphosis of the "see" death in Verse 51. A going deeper. In Lazarus "stinketh" is the "smell" of death. Sensory pictures.

Vs. 53. "greater than our Father Abraham": this is the same theme which was touched by the Samaritan woman who asked: "greater than our father Jacob?"

Vs. 54. This is the sixth speech of Christ in this last (third) section.

Vs. 55. "known": This word repeated three times in this verse. Refers to Prologue—"know." Here is the contrast between "seeing" and "knowing." Note—the Word was. The human being became.

"keep": Christ cultivates the living Logos of the Father in his Ego.

"I know him": This points to the Prologue.

Vs. 56. "Abraham exulted (rejoiced) to see the day (my day) of the I Am": the word "rejoiced" is too weak here.

"it"—not in the Greek text. "He saw and was glad." "Glad"—points to the verse where the disciples were "glad" to see the Lord.

Abraham saw the Akashic picture of the Christ in the sphere of the Sun (Dr. Steiner).

Vs. 57. This verse is trivial unless understood as it is. Like the Nicodemus question about birth and youth. In ancient times, by the very process of growing old, people became wise. At each stage of growth more knowledge was revealed to them. Thus, when seven cycles of seven years each had elapsed, people were considered sufficiently mature to have a direct vision of the Patriarchs. Therefore, when the Jews, to whom this was a fact, pointed out that Christ was not yet fifty years old (7 x 7 = 49), they meant, how could he have this vision of the Patriarchs—of the spirit of the Fathers, the great spirit of Abraham—since he had not yet attained an age when that kind of vision was considered possible? This is a kind of balance to the Nicodemus question regarding youth, for here is a question regarding age.

Nicodemus—too old, seeking youth; Christ—too young—seeking age; in the estimation of the Jews.

Vs. 58. The seventh speech—the great climax of this Chapter 8. This is the seventh speech of the third section. The correct translation is:

"Before Abraham became—I Am."

In other words, Abraham became, but the Christ is "I Am." The Christ is beyond the future and the past, and reaches into the realm which is free from time.

The I Am of Christ is older than that developed by Abraham. The Word was; the human being became.

The Sections of Chapter 8:

1) Section 1: "Light"

2) Section 2: "I Am"

3) Section 3 "Judgment"

The Frame is "I Am":

1) Verse 12: "I Am the light of the World"

2) Verse 58: "Before Abraham became, I Am"

And midway between these two are: "believe the I Am" and "Know the I Am."

Vs. 59. "Stones": These are typical of the hardened etheric body of the Jews, under the influence of their father, Ahriman.

John's Gospel is exact to the last physical detail. This verse is an example. Here they "took up" the stones, from the rubble of the Temple court, since the Temple was still in the process of construction. They snatched them from the workmen's rubbish. However, in Ch. 10:31, the word "took up" is not correctly translated. The Greek there is "ebästäsän"—ἐβάστασαν—and means "carried," "brought," "fetched"—in other words, in that scene, they carried the stones into Solomon's Hall, where, since the construction was finished, nothing was lying about, as in Verse 59 of Chapter 8.

Chapters 7, 8, 9, to 10:21 take place in the Fall—occupying a space of 8 or 9 days, continuing around the Autumn Festival.

In Chapter 10:22, we jump from fall to Christmas time. Chapter 10:39 begins the spring (Passover) time.

John 9:1-41

1. And as Jesus passed by, he saw a man which was blind from his birth.
2. And his disciples asked him, saying, Master, who did sin, this man, or his parents, that he was born blind?
3. Jesus answered, Neither hath this man sinned, nor his parents, but that the works of God should be made manifest in him.
4. I must work the works of him that sent me, while it is day: the night cometh, when no man can work.
5. As long as I am in the world, I am the light of the world.
6. When he had thus spoken, he spat on the ground, and made clay of the spittle, and he anointed the eyes of the blind man with the clay,
7. And said unto him, Go, wash in the pool of Siloam, (which is by interpretation, Sent.) He went his way therefore, and washed, and came seeing.
8. The neighbors therefore, and they which before had seen him that he was blind, said, Is this not he that sat and begged?
9. Some said, This is he; others said, He is like him, but he said, I am he.
10. Therefore said they unto him, How were thine eyes opened?
11. He answered and said, A man that is called Jesus made clay, and anointed mine eyes, and said unto me, Go to the pool of Siloam, and wash: and I went and washed, and I received sight.
12. Then they said unto him, Where is he? He said, I know not.
13. They brought to the Pharisees him that aforetime was blind.

14. And it was the Sabbath day when Jesus made the clay and opened his eyes.
15. Then again the Pharisees also asked him how he had received his sight. He said unto them, He put clay upon mine eyes, and I washed, and do see.
16. Therefore said some of the Pharisees, This man is not of God, because he keepeth not the the Sabbath day. Others said, How can a man that is a sinner do such miracles? and there was a division among them.
17. They say unto the blind man again, What sayest thou of him, that he hath opened thine eyes? He said, He is a prophet.
18. But the Jews did not believe concerning him, that he had been blind, and received his sight, until they called the parents of him that had received his sight.
19. And they asked them saying, Is this your son, who ye say was born blind? How then doth he now see?
20. His parents answered them and said, We know that this is our son, and that he was born blind,
21. But by what means he now seeth, we know not; or who hath opened his eyes, we know not. He is of age, ask him: he shall speak for himself.
22. These words spake his parents, because they feared the Jews: for the Jews had agreed already, that if any man did confess that he was Christ, he should be put out of the synagogue.
23. Therefore said his parents, He is of age, ask him.
24. Then again called they the man that was blind, and said unto him, Give God the praise, we know that this man is a sinner.
25. He answered and said, Whether he be a sinner or no, I know not: one thing I know, that, whereas I was blind, now I see.

26. Then said they unto him again, What did he do unto thee? How opened he thine eyes?

27. He answered them, I have told you already, and ye did not hear: wherefore would ye hear it again? Will ye also be his disciples?

28. Then they reviled him, and said, Thou art his disciple, but we are Moses' disciples.

29. We know that God spake unto Moses; as for this fellow, we know not from whence he is.

30. The man answered and said unto them, Why herein is a marvelous thing, that ye know not from whence he is, and yet he hath opened mine eyes.

31. Now we know that God heareth not sinners, but if any man be a worshipper of God, and doeth his will, him he heareth.

32. Since the world began was it is not heard that any man opened the eyes of one that was born blind.

33. If this man were not of God, he could do nothing.

34. They answered and said unto him, Thou wast altogether born in sin, and dost thou teach us? And they cast him out.

35. Jesus heard that they had cast him out; and when he had found him, he said unto him, Dost thou believe on the Son of God?

36. He answered and said, Who is he, Lord, that I might believe on him?

37. And Jesus said unto him, Thou has both seen him, and it is he that talketh with thee.

38. And he said, Lord, I believe. And he worshipped him.

39. And Jesus said, For judgment I am come into his world, that they which see not might see and that they which see might be made blind.

40. And some of the Pharisees which were with him heard these words, and said unto him, Are we blind also?

41. Jesus said unto them, If ye were blind, ye would have no sin, but now ye say, We see; therefore your sin remaineth.

This Chapter is divided into seven parts:

1) The healing of the man born blind, Vs 1–7
2) The Neighbors of the man born blind, Vs 8–12
3) The Pharisees and the man born blind, Vs 3–17
4) The Jews and the parents of the man born blind, Vs 18–23
5) The Jews and the man born blind, Vs 24–34
6) Jesus and the man born blind, Vs 35–38
7) Jesus and the Pharisees from 8:39 to 10:21

John 10:1–42

1. Verily, verily, I say unto you, he that entereth not by the door into the sheepfold, but climeth up some other way, the same is a thief and a robber.
2. But he that entereth in by the door is the shepherd of the sheep.
3. To him the porter openeth: and the sheep hear his voice, and he calleth his own sheep by name, and leadeth them out.
4. And when he putteth forth his own sheep, he goeth before them, and the sheep followeth, because they know his voice.
5. And a stranger will they not follow, but will flee from him, for they know not the voice of strangers.
6. This parable spake Jesus unto them, but they understood not what things they were which he spake unto them.
7. Then said Jesus unto them again, Verily, verily, I say unto you, I am the door of the sheep.
8. All that ever came before me are thieves and robbers, but the sheep did not hear them.
9. I am the door, by me if any man enter in, he shall be saved, and shall go in and out, and find pasture.
10. The thief cometh not, but for to steal, and to kill, and to destroy. I am come that they might have life, and that they might have it more abundantly.
11. I am the good shepherd: the good shepherd giveth his life for the sheep.
12. But he that is an hireling, and not the shepherd, whose own the sheep are not, seeth the wolf coming, and leaveth the

John 10:1–42

sheep, and fleeth, and the wolf catcheth them, and scattereth the sheep.

13. The hireling fleeth, because he is an hireling, and careth not for the sheep.

14. I am the good shepherd, and know my sheep, and am known of mine.

15. As the Father knoweth me, even so know I the Father, and I lay down my life for the sheep.

16. And other sheep I have, which are not of this fold: them also I must bring, and they shall hear my voice; and there shall be one fold: and one shepherd.

17. Therefore doth my Father love me, because I lay down my life, that I might take it again.

18. No man taketh it from me, but I lay it down of myself. I have power to lay it down, and I have power to take it again. This Commandment have I received of my Father.

19. There was a division therefore again among the Jews for these sayings.

20. And many of them said, He hath a devil, and is mad; why hear ye him?

21. Others said, These are not the words of him that hath a devil. Can a devil open the eyes of the blind?

22. And it was at Jerusalem the feast of the dedication, and it was winter.

23. And Jesus walked in the temple in Solomon's porch.

24. Then came the Jews round about him, and said unto him, How long dost thou make us to doubt? If thou be Christ, tell us plainly.

25. Jesus answered them, I told you, and ye believed not: the works that I do in my Father's name, they bear witness of me.

26. But ye believe not, because ye are not of my sheep, as I said unto you.
27. My sheep hear my voice, and I know them, and they follow me,
28. And I give unto them eternal life; and they shall never perish, neither shall any man pluck them out of my hand.
29. My Father, which gave them me, is greater than all; and no man is able to pluck them out of my Father's hand.
30. I and my Father are one.
31. Then the Jews took up stones again to stone him.
32. Jesus answered them, Many good works have I shewed you from my Father; for which of those works do ye stone me?
33. The Jews answered him, saying, For a good work we stone thee not, but for blasphemy; and because that thou, being a man, makest thyself God.
34. Jesus answered them, Is it not written in your law, I said ye are Gods?
35. If he called them Gods, unto whom the word of God came, and the scripture cannot be broken;
36. Say ye of him, whom the Father hath sanctified, and sent into the world, Thou blasphemest, because I said, I am the Son of God?
37. If I do not the works of my Father, believe me not.
38. But if I do, though ye believe not me, believe the works: that ye may know, and believe, that the Father is in me, and I him.
39. Therefore they sought again to take him, but he escaped out of their hand,
40. And went away again beyond Jordan into the place where John at first baptized; and there he abode.

41. And many resorted unto him, and said, John did no miracle, but all things that John spake of this man were true.
42. And many believed on him there.

Vs. 21. "Can a devil open the eyes of the blind?"

devil: In Greek, "daimon"—δαίμων—this is a formula of John's Gospel.

Vs. 40. Here begins the spring (Passover) season.

John 11:1–58

1. Now a certain man was sick, named Lazarus, of Bethany, the town of Mary and her sister Martha.
2. (It was that Mary which anointed the Lord with ointment, and wiped his feet with her hair, whose brother Lazarus was sick.)
3. Therefore his sisters sent unto him saying, Lord, behold, he whom thou lovest is sick.
4. When Jesus heard that, he said, This sickness is not unto death, but for the Glory of God, that the Son of God might be glorified thereby.
5. Now Jesus loved Martha, and her sister, and Lazarus.
6. When he heard therefore that he was sick, he abode two days still in the same place where he was.
7. Then after that saith he to his disciples, Let us go into Judea again.
8. His disciples say unto him, Master, the Jews of late sought to stone thee; and goest thou thither again?
9. Jesus answered, Are there not twelve hours in the day? If any man walk in the day, he stumbleth not, because he seeth the light of this world.
10. But if a man walk in the night, he stumbleth, because there is not light in him.
11. These things said he, and after that he saith unto them, Our friend Lazarus sleepeth; but I go, that I may awake him out of sleep.
12. Then said his disciples, Lord, if he sleep, he shall do well.
13. Howbeit Jesus spake of his death, but they thought that he had spoken of taking of rest in sleep.

14. Then said Jesus unto them plainly, Lazarus is dead.

15. And I am glad for your sakes that I was not there, to the intent ye may believe; nevertheless let us go unto him.

16. Then said Thomas, which is Didymus, unto his fellow disciples, Let us also go, that we may die with him.

17. Then when Jesus came, he found that he had lain in the grave four days already.

18. Now Bethany was nigh unto Jerusalem, about fifteen furlongs off,

19. And many of the Jews came to Martha and Mary, to comfort them concerning their brother.

20. Then Martha, as soon as she heard that Jesus was coming, went and met him, but Mary sat still in the house.

21. Then said Martha unto Jesus, Lord, if thou hadst been here, my brother had not died.

22. But I know, that even now, whatsoever thou wilt ask of God, God will give it thee.

23. Jesus saith unto her, Thy brother will rise again.

24. Martha saith unto him, I know that he shall rise again in the resurrection at the last day.

25. Jesus said unto her, I am the resurrection and the life: he that believeth in me, though he were dead, yet shall he live,

26. And whosoever liveth and believeth in me shall never die. Believest thou this?

27. She saith unto him, Yea, Lord, I believe that thou art the Christ, the Son of God, which should come into the world.

28. And when she had so said, she went her way, and called Mary her sister secretly, saying, The Master is come, and calleth for thee.

29. As soon as she heard that, she arose quickly, and came unto him.
30. Now Jesus was not yet come into the town, but was in that place where Martha met him.
31. The Jews then which were with her in the house, and comforted her, when they saw Mary, that she rose up hastily and went out, followed her, saying, She goeth unto the grave to weep there.
32. Then when Mary was come where Jesus was, and saw him, she fell down at his feet, saying unto him, Lord, if thou hadst been here, my brother had not died.
33. When Jesus saw her weeping, and the Jews also weeping which came with her, he groaned in the spirit, and was troubled,
34. And said, Where have ye laid him? They said unto him, Lord, Come and see.
35. Jesus wept.
36. Then said the Jews, Behold how he loved him!
37. And some of them said, Could not this man, which opened the eyes of the blind, have caused that even this man should not have died?
38. Jesus therefore again groaning in himself cometh to the grave. It was a cave, and a stone lay upon it.
39. Jesus said, Take ye away the stone. Martha, the sister of him that was dead, saith unto him, Lord, by this time he stinketh, for he hath been dead four days.
40. Jesus saith unto her, Said I not unto thee, that, if thou wouldst believe, thou shouldst see the glory of God?
41. Then they took away the stone from the place where the dead was laid. And Jesus lifted up his eyes, and said, Father, I thank thee that thou hast heard me,

John 11:1–58

42. And I knew that thou hearest me always, but because of the people which stand by I said it, that they may believe that thou hast sent me.

43. And when he thus had spoken, he cried with a loud voice, Lazarus, come forth.

44. And he that was dead came forth, bound hand and foot with grave-clothes, and his face was bound about with a napkin. Jesus saith unto them, Loose him, and let him go.

45. Then many of the Jews which came to Mary, and had seen the things which Jesus did, believed on him.

46. But some of them went their way to the Pharisees, and told them what Jesus had done.

47. Then gathered the chief priests and the Pharisees a council and said, What do we? For this man doeth many miracles.

48. If we let him thus alone, all men will believe on him, and the Romans shall come and take away both our place and our nation.

49. And one of them, named Caiaphas, being the high priest that same year, said unto them, Ye know nothing at all,

50. Nor consider that it is profitable for us, that one man should die for the people, and that the whole nation perish not.

51. And this spake he not of himself, but being high priest that year, he prophesied that Jesus should die for that nation;

52. And not for that nation only, but that also he should gather together in one the children of God that were scattered abroad.

53. Then from that day forth they took counsel together for to put him to death.

54. Jesus therefore walked no more openly among the Jews; but went thence unto a country near to the wilderness, into a city called Ephraim, and there continued with the disciples.

55. And the Jews' Passover was nigh at hand, and many went out of the country up to Jerusalem before the Passover, to purify themselves.

56. Then sought they for Jesus and spake among themselves, as they stood in the temple, What think ye, that he will not come to the feast?

58. Now both the chief priests and the Pharisees had given a commandment, that, if any man knew were he were, he should shew it, that they might take him.

The Lazarus-Miracle

Vs. 1. "Now someone was ill—Lazarus": This is the correct translation from the Greek.

In the repetition of the name "John" three times—in Ch. 10:40-41—we have the special emphasis on John the Baptist (see the notes on page 11 of these notes).

The Lazarus-Miracle is the story of the man who wrote the Gospel of John!

John the Baptist identified with Bethany east of the Jordan. In this Bethany, Christ remains (Ch. 10:40), taking in something of the atmosphere of John the Baptist. The Lazarus-Bethany is west of the Jordan. So the movement is from one Bethany to the other.

Note the sequence: (1) Lazarus, (2) Mary, (3) Martha. From the most intimate to the most external. (Compare with Vs. 5.)

Vs. 2. John presupposes his readers know this story, though he doesn't tell it until later (Ch. 12). He probably felt they would have read it in Luke's Gospel—chapters 7 and 8.

"Lazarus": this is the second mention of the name.

John 11:1–58

Vs. 3. Here, instead of the logically expected mention of the name "Lazarus," we find a new name for him—"he whom thou lovest!" This name reappears at the Last Supper, Chap 13:23.

Vs. 4. "Glory": In Greek,—"doxas"—δόξης. This is correctly translated in the sense of "manifestation"—not an abstract light, as is often trivially associated with the word "glory" but with "meaning" (see page 26 of these notes).

In a sense, we are Lazarus. The human being is, in truth, the crown of creation, but the human being is sick; something is wrong!

Vs. 5. Here John reverses the previous order, and goes from the more external to the more inward: 1) Martha, 2) Mary, 3) Lazarus. From the most external to the most intimate.

There are two words commonly translated as "loved" in John's Gospel. They are:

(1) "fela-o"—φιλέω—"like"

(2) ägäpa—ἀγάπη—"love"—"divine love"—the main word of St. John.

In Vs 3: the translation is "whom you like"—(φιλέω—fela-o).

In Vs 5: The translation is "Jesus Loved"—(ἀγάπη—ägäpa).

One should check the use of "ägäpa"—ἀγάπη—and "fela-o"—φιλέω. In Chapter 21:15–17, Christ uses "ägäpa" and Peter uses "felao," until the last questioning. It is as though Peter is afraid to accept the high goal and comes to it only by degrees. Check this in a Greek text of John's Gospel. Also, see Chapter 21 of these notes.

Vs. 6. "abode"—"remained": In Greek "emainen"—ἔμεινεν—It is the same word as in Ch. 10:40. Christ deliberately remained in "the other Bethany," in the spiritual atmosphere of John the Baptist for a time, deliberately allowing three and a half days to pass before setting out on the eight-hour-long walk to the Bethany of Lazarus. This walk is a passing from John the Baptist to John the Evangelist—through Lazarus!!

It makes the relation of the two Bethanys very clear.

Here we should realize the Gospel of John is divided into two parts:

1) Ch. 1:1 to 10:39—The Circle of John the Baptist
2) Ch: 10:39 to 21:35—the Circle of the Beloved Disciple

We can understand part two only if Christ performs the Lazarus miracle upon us!

John the Baptist was the last and mightiest of all the prophets. "John" means "The Grace of God."

Vs. 7. "Then after that": This is a kind of releasing of the action. He holds them there in Bethany, east of the Jordan, till three days are past, then he "lets them go"—"Let us go"—a releasing, pointing perhaps to his remarks (Vs 44)

"Let him go": It is as though he had a special purpose in this incongruous waiting, and only after this purpose was accomplished, would he let them go.

Vss. 8-11. "to stone": Refers to Ch. 10, Vs 31.

"Twelve hours in the day"—It is as though "the day" represents the earth sphere, the destiny of Christ on earth. He has the feeling that his earth life is not over, hence the threat of the Jews to stone him has no power.

"light, darkness": A leading motif of John. The life with Christ (light) and without Christ (darkness).

Vs. 9. The twelve hours represent the "Day" of the Christ—the span of his earthly destiny. This "Day and Night" theme refers to the Prologue of John's Gospel, the theme of the "Light" and "Darkness."

Vs. 12. "friend": (felos)—φίλος—the same theme, "friend of the Bridegroom;" "I have called you friends." This is the second in a series of three:

1) "Friend of the Bridegroom"
2) "Our friend Lazarus"
3) "Called you friends"

It is the shading of "the disciple whom the Lord loved" behind it, but only a shading.

"sleepeth": literal Greek "has fallen asleep."

"awake him": In Greek, "exoopneso auton"- ἐξυπνίσω αὐτόν—"Awake him"—This word is ex-hypnosis!

This is in contrast to the usual Greek word "egairo"—ἐγείρο—"to wake up."

So the situation is that he deliberately waits three and a half days before going to Lazarus. Why? This was the length of time of an initiation, because the Greeks thought the soul was bound to the body for this length of time by "a silver cord" which was severed only at the end of this period, and then the soul could no longer be recalled to the body. So Christ leaves and walks the 8 hours to Bethany, arriving on the fourth day.

Vs. 13. "taking of rest in sleep"—"koimasa-os hoopoo"—κοιμήσεως ὕπου—literal translation: "of the rest of sleep"—"Committed to hypnosis."

Vs. 16. "die": Word of Thomas. "Called Didymos" "Dedoomos"—Δίδυμος—Didymus means "Twin," a doubting person. John is especially interested in Thomas—and stresses him. He is not spoken of in the other Gospels—only by name. But John is interested in him, because Thomas represents intellectual knowledge—and how the intellectual person comes to Christ. This is a problem of our time, and so, it is of interest to John, since his is the Gospel for our time.

    Thomas—Intellectual Knowledge

    John—Spiritual Knowledge

The difference between the two is seen in Leonardo's *The Last Supper*, where John leans aside, letting the full light from the window behind him pour into the room, while Thomas, with his finger upraised, pointing slightly to his own head—the intellect—almost completely shuts out the light from the window behind him.

"die": Thomas later became the apostle to India and is shown to be akin to the Hindu preoccupation with death.

Vs. 17. This introduces the second part of the Lazarus story.

Vs. 18. fifteen furlongs —Jerusalem was two and three quarters kilometers, or about one and a half miles from Bethany. Bethany is still deeply associated with Lazarus, even today being called by the Arabs "El Lazarea." It was at Bethany that pilgrims bound for Jerusalem (at Passover, for instance) robed themselves for triumphant entries into the city. The great pilgrim road to Jerusalem passed through Bethany.

Vs. 20. Martha: She is the more external of the two sisters. More outside activity. She talks with Christ in words, while Mary's meeting is almost wordless, because her connection and conversation is much more inward. She doesn't need words to communicate with Christ!

Martha is active; Mary is passive. Thus they carry out the qualities they have in Luke 10.

Rainer Maria Rilke was repelled by the Lazarus-miracle, because he saw no sense in it. It appeared to him to be a very great act of partiality on the part of Christ. He found the whole thing physically repellant. He felt, why should a single man be restored like this when perhaps others, needed more by their families, remained dead? Why not restore a father to his wife and children who needed him for support, for example?

However, we must remember that the purpose of this miracle is resurrection, not restoration. It is an external picture of the great deed which Christ will perform later: his own resurrection. This is a far greater thing than regarding the Lazarus miracle as a single sign or miracle, unrelated to anything else. If the latter sense were true, then Rilke's estimation would be right.

The Greek word for "resurrection" used in Vs 23 is "Änästasetai"— Αναστήσεται.

Vs. 24. Her disappointment is evident. She uses the future tense, pushing the event into the future, the far future.

John 11:1–58

"In the Last day":

This is a formula of John's Gospel:

1) Chapter 6: It is used four times
2) Chapter 7: "Last Day of Feast"—one time
3) Chapter 11: In Vs 24, one time

This is a kind of mystic inwardness, where mysticism is united with an historic point of view—and is one of the key points of anthroposophy.

Vs. 25. Here is the fifth of the "I Am" statements of the Christ. It is in three parts:

1) "I Am the resurrection and the life"
2) "He that believes on me, though he die, yet shall he live"—(the application to the individual)
3) "And everyone who lives and believes on me shall die in no wise forever"—The key word here is "everyone," a fuller expansion.

Martha: brings out of Christ this recognition of himself, his divine nature. She calls forth his recognition of his possibility for resurrection! It is as though a part of the future is present in the present.

Christ regains the heavenly knowledge of himself through the "I Am" statements. All the "I Am's" are events within himself; they are steps on the way to Golgotha.

He becomes aware of his own power of resurrection.

Vs. 27. Martha's confession is threefold:

1) "Thou art the Christ"
2) "The Son of God"
3) "Who comes into the world"

Vs. 28. Martha's calling Mary begins Part Three of the drama.

Vs. 32. Mary's attitude to Jesus is very different from that of Martha. Martha does not fall at his feet, but Mary does.

Note Mary's confidence in Christ.

Martha uses a Greek word "had not died" "ook än epethnakai"—οὐκ ἂν ἐπεθνήκει—(Vs 21), which is a perfect completion—a final word.

Mary uses the Greek word, "had not died" "ook än äpethänen"—οὐκ ἂν ἀπέθανέν—which is much more delicate. When correctly translated, it is, "had not crossed over."

Mary uses the Greek word "moo"—μου—(my) in a much sweeter, more tender way than Martha. Mary says "moo ho ädelfos"—μου ὁ αδελφός—(my brother), while Martha says "ho ädelfos-moo"—ὁ αδελφός μου—(brother my)—much less tender.

Mary surrenders to Christ. She stops short outwardly in her speech. She cannot find the outer words the way Martha does.

Here we have one of the great keynotes of John's Gospel, one of his great gifts: his ability to depict personalities down to the last, exact psychological detail.

Vs. 33. "he groaned in the spirit": This is the Greek verb, "enebremasäto"—ἐνεβριμήσατο—and it is repeated in Vs 38.

This groaning is a kind of inner uproar of forces, a kind of magical power, a prayer, an assembling of his forces. Dr. Rittlemeyer spoke of this as, "He strengthened himself in the spirit." It is a creative inner moment in the spirit of Christ.

"troubled": this is the Greek word "etäraxen"—ἐτάραξεν—and appears three times in this part of the Gospel: in Chapters 11, 12 and 13.

— This groaning and troubling is where the whole body is brought into the action. Here he is shaken with the first stirring of the force which will bring him into Easter. It is like a kind of earthquake in the soul.

Vs. 35. "Jesus wept": "Wept" in the Greek, "edäkroosen"—ἐδάκρυσεν—(from the Greek word "däkroo-on")—δάκρυον—"the tear."

There is another Greek word, "klai-o"—κλαίω—meaning "to cry"—with a noise, in other words, "to sob." This kind of crying is an expression of the emotions, of the astral.

"edäkroosen"—ἐδάκρυσεν—(used in Vs 35) meaning "to weep" is a nobler word, a depiction of a state ruled more by the ego. It is not emotion in the usual sense; something in the body participates in inner movement. But it is usually taken only in the common way, and this is an error. Dr. Steiner said tears are an evidence we are in the body—in earth. It is like Faust, weeping after the suicide thoughts at Easter. In the resurrection scene, Mary "weeps" before the tomb, but here the word is "clai-o"—κλαίω—"sobs"—more emotion.

Vs. 36. "Loved": This is not correct. The Greek verb is "efelai"—ἐφίλει—liked—Remember, Lazarus is the disciple whom the Lord loved. In the eyes of the Jews, this is only "liked"—a significant difference. This points to the Lazarus-John mystery.

Vs. 37. "opened the eyes of the blind": This is not a casual or trivial reference. It is a bridge, leading from the sixth to the seventh sign (miracle). "semai-on"—σημεῖον. It is a distinct pointing to the theme.

In the case of Lazarus, it is an echo of an old saying of the Jews. "He who sees God, dies"—BUT he dies in order that he may resurrect—as in the Lazarus sign.

This is the ninth mention of this formula:

1) In Chapter 9: "Open the eyes"—seven times

2) In Chapter 10: Verse 21 "Open the eyes"—one time

3) In chapter 11: Verse 36 "Open the eyes"—one time

Vs. 38. "Groaning": See the explanation of Verse 33 above.

"Stone," "Cave": A parallel with the burial of Christ after Golgotha. The stone represents the pressing into the earth, the final judgement of matter.

Vs. 39. "him who has died": A formula relating to what is to come in Chapter 12.

"stinks": the figure of St. John is the Eagle, and the Eagle is a transfigured Scorpion. To the Scorpion belong smells explicitly! In Chapter 12, we are to have the sweet smell of the precious nard oil ointment. This is the counterpart to the smell of putrifaction. The stink of putrifaction is contrasted to the sweet smell of consecration. In the stink of putrifaction, we feel the shame of the human being after the Fall.

Vs. 40. "Glory of God": "doxä"—δόξα—"Glory"—this is a bridge from Verse 4, explaining it and calling it to memory.

Vs. 41. "I thank": In the Greek, "oischäristo"—εὐχαριστῶ—"I thank"—and our word "eucharist" is derived from it.

This is the first of the three prayers in John's Gospel:

1) Ch. 11:41–42

2) Ch. 12:27–28

3) Ch. 17:1–26 (the High Priestly Prayer)

This Prayer of Chapter 11 forms a Trinity:

1) "Father, I thank Thee that thou hast heard me"—To the Father

2) "And I knew that thou hearest me always"—the ego, the Son

3) "But on account of the crowd who stand around I said, that they may believe that thou hast sent me."—The congregation, held together by the Holy Spirit.

Vs. 42. "thou me didst send": This formula is repeated four times in the High Priestly Prayer (Ch. 17).

This prayer reveals the inner mystical life of Christ in his connection with the Father. All the movements of Christ—of the soul of Christ—have an echo, a resonance, in the spiritual worlds. This is a much deeper thing than is generally thought of. "Thou hast heard me." The whole inner life of Christ is heard by God.

"I knew": Greek, "ago adain"—ἐγὼ ᾔδειν—In John's Gospel, the Christ never "believes" God. "I know"—(Ch. 8). In the Gospel of John, he "sees" the Father, and he "knows" him.

"That you might believe": A dawning of knowledge in the devout feelings of the sisters and disciples.

Vs. 43. "With a loud voice": This "loud" is not quite accurate. The Greek word is "Megäla"—μεγάλη—and should be translated: "great." Our word "magic" is derived from it. This voice of Christ is heard in the other world, the world of the dead.

"Voice": In the Greek, "ekraugäsen"—ἐκραύγασεν—"shout"—that which is "powerful."

The Greek word for "out" is "exo"—ἔξω.

"Lazarus, come forth": "out" and "exo"—Greek, "Läzära doiro exo"—Λάζαρε δεῦρο ἔξω—"Lazarus, come out!"

Vs. 44. "came forth": Greek, "exelthen"—ἐξῆλθεν—"came out."

"Who had been dead": In Greek, "Ho-tethnakos"—ὁ τεθνηκώς—Indicates a kind of suspense. He is not quite back in earth existence. It is as though he is under a veil.

In the first Chapter of the Apocalypse, we have the key to this Lazarus-miracle. There we have the picture of John who dies upon seeing Christ, and is resurrected.

"napkin": Greek, "soodäre-o"—σουδαρίῳ—This is the same word used in Chapter 20, of John's Gospel, Verse 7, where it is lying aside by itself, folded.

In one of the Catacombs at Rome, there is a depiction of the Raising of Lazarus. It is not naturalistic, but deeply symbolic. The gigantic figure of the Christ stands with his arm extended and in his hand is a long staff—the extension of his will through his arm—the principle of the King's scepter. It is like Moses striking the rock with his staff. (The King's crown represents his thoughts; his robe, his emotions, his feelings). The arm of Christ points toward the entrance of a little temple, and before this Temple, leading upward to it, are seven steps. On the seventh step, at the top, stands a tiny figure in the entrance. The figure is like a chrysalis in appearance: this is Lazarus. The steps make us feel, this is a Temple of Initiation, and only the one who has gone through these seven steps can enter this grave.

"bound": In Greek, "Dedemenos"—δεδεμένος—Indicates something not yet finished. It is like the Faust Epilogue, where Faust is an infant in the beginning of the heavenly journey, but grows toward maturity as the journey progresses.

"Loose him": In Greek, "loosäte auton"—λύσατε αὐτὸν—"free," "unbind," "dissolve." "loosis"—λύσις—separation, dissolution—in German, "entbinden" = "to give birth."

And now we come to a mystery—the abrupt ending. The Lazarus story and the Healing of the Man Born Blind are the longest stories in the New Testament. In the most intimate details, they are perfect. But just at the very point where we expect more details—having had very many extremely precise ones—at the very highest pitch of interest, the story suddenly ends—abruptly. The veiled Lazarus stands there: the face of Lazarus is a secret. In the future, every Christian should see his or her own face. But just as we are about to see the face of Lazarus, and experience the joy of his restoration to the two sisters, to the awe of the disciples, etc., there is the abrupt ending! A great secret stands behind this break.

Vs. 47. "a council": In Greek, "Soonedre-on"—συνέδριον—Sanhedron.

"miracles": In Greek, "semai-ä"—σημεῖα—"signs"—that which is translucent. An incorporated imagination for something which stands behind.

John 11:1–58

"Saducees": This group, this large family, were descendants of Sadok, the High Priest under Solomon. They were an old, aristocratic priest-family. They represent the genuinely Ahrimanic line of the Jews—they were first, and merely, politicians. They performed the ceremonies in a completely cold, matter-of-fact way, a routine. Their attitude was entirely superficial. They were very unsocial, removed, detached, disliking, and refusing to mingle with other sections of society. They celebrated the cult, but there was no spiritual responsibility behind it. They had a kind of cynical connection with the Romans.

The Pharisees: This group believed in resurrection, the last judgment, angels (spirits)—see the Acts of the Apostles 23:8. Their ideas were possibly connected with the Persian Zarathustra worship. After the Babylonian exile, the Jewish religion was greatly enriched by many borrowings from the Persians. At this time the Pharisees appeared.

John's description here (Vs 47 et Seq.) exactly follows the precise conditions in Palestine in this time. It is another evidence of the genuineness of this Gospel. The Saducees are described exactly.

Vs. 48. "the place": In Greek, "Topon"—τόπον—In Hebrew, "markarone." A mystery word used for "Temple." In the Zohar, this word is even used for God—a kind of reticence.

"Nation":—Greek "ethnos"—ἔθνος—the usual Greek word.

Vs. 49. "Of that year": Means "Of that decisive year." The High Priest was, of course, not changed every year. This is no criticism of John—it does not indicate that he did not know this fact. It is a pointing out of that particular, fateful year.

Vs. 50. "Profitable": Greek, "useful."

"for us":—Greek, "for you."

"the people":—Greek, "lä-oo"- λαοὺ—A cultic word, in contrast to the usual Greek word for "nation" (ethnos). It carries the meaning of, "the sacred people"—the nation as a carrier of a divine being, of a special spirit. It is a solemn word for a nation as the carrier of a god, a divine being and destiny.

In the third chapter of Kings is the description of a King who was willing to sacrifice his son on the walls of a city in order to save it. The sacrifice was not carried out, but the implication is plain.

A lower stage is the sacrifice of criminals.

Ritual murder is a decadence of a very noble ideal, one of the highest of all ideals.

Vs. 52. This is another special Johannine insertion. It reflects the old idea that with the office of the spirit came also the spirit of prophecy, for example, with that of the High Priest. In this prophecy of Caiaphas we have a last remainder of something once great. He was inspired, but who inspired him?

"prophesied": Greek "eproifatensen"—ἐπροεφήτευσεν.

Vs. 52. "Gather together": Greek "soonägäga"—συναγάγη—"sun" or "syn"—together—"again"—lead.

(This is the source of the word "synagogue.")

"in one": Greek, "ais en"—εἰς ἕν—(oneness)—The neuter form. "Into a oneness" This is mentioned seven times in John's Gospel. In Chapter 10, it is first mentioned, and in Chapter 17, the High Priestly Prayer.

"the children of God": Greek, "tä teknä too Tha-oo"—τα τεκνα τοῦ θεοῦ. A birth out of death, "not out of the flesh, but out of God." This is a reflection of the Prologue. It is Lazarus who first received this new birth.

Vs. 53. "Kill": The motif of death reappears. It is a counterpoint of what has already appeared in Ch. 5. He gives life, but is brought to death—a reaction.

Vs. 54. This is the aftermath of the event of the Lazarus miracle. Lazarus disappears into the Desert of Juda, with the other disciples, in order to rest and to digest all that had happened. This

Desert of Juda was later the home of the early Christian hermits and Essenes. There is something behind this word "continued."— It is the same Greek word, "emainen,"—ἔμεινεν;—and "meno,"— μένω—and "koma-o"—κομεώ—All translated "tarry," "remain," "abide."

Vs. 55. "The Passover of the Jews": This is the third mention of this in John's Gospel. Passover was the old spring sacrifice, overcoming the effects of the winter. The Passover is associated with:

1) Wine—After Cana Wedding—"Passover of the Jews"

2) Bread—Feeding of the 5,000—"Passover of the Jews"

3) Resuscitation—Lazarus Miracle—"Passover of the Jews"

4) Golgotha and Resurrection—Christ—"Passover of the Jews"

"Purify themselves": In Greek, "hägnesosin"—ἀγνίσωσιν— "sanctify" themselves.

John 12:1-50

1. Then Jesus six days before the Passover came to Bethany, where Lazarus was which had been dead, whom he raised from the dead.
2. There they made him a supper, and Martha served, but Lazarus was one of them that sat at the table with him.
3. Then took Mary a pound of ointment of spikenard, very costly, and anointed the feet of Jesus, and wiped his feet with her hair, and the house was filled with the odor of the ointment.
4. Then saith one of his disciples, Judas Iscariot, Simon's son, which should betray him,
5. Why was not this ointment sold for three hundred pence, and given to the poor?
6. This he said, not that he cared for the poor; but because he was a thief, and had the bag, and bare what was put therein.
7. Then said Jesus, Let her alone: against the day of my burying hath she kept this.
8. For the poor always ye have with you; but me ye have not always.
9. Much people of the Jews therefore knew that he was there, and they came not for Jesus' sake only, but that they might see Lazarus also, whom he had raised from the dead.
10. But the chief priests consulted that they might put Lazarus also to death;
11. Because that by reason of him many of the Jews went away, and believed on Jesus.

12. On the next day much people that were come to the feast, when they heard that Jesus was coming to Jerusalem,

13. Took branches of palm trees, and went forth to meet him, and cried, Hosanna: blessed is the king of Israel that cometh in the name of the Lord.

14. And Jesus, when he had found a young ass, sat thereon; as it is written,

15. Fear not, daughter of Sion: behold, thy King cometh, sitting on an ass's colt.

16. These things understood not his disciples at the first, but when Jesus was glorified, then remembered they that these things were written of him, and that they had done these things unto him.

17. The people therefore that was with him when he called Lazarus out of his grave, and raised him from the dead, bare record.

18. For this cause the people also met him, for that they heard that he had done this miracle.

19. The Pharisees therefore said among themselves, Perceive ye how ye prevail nothing? Behold, the world is gone after him.

20. And there were certain Greeks among them that came up to worship at the feast.

21. The same came therefore to Philip, which was of Bethesda of Galilee, and desired him, saying, Sir, we would see Jesus.

22. Philip cometh and telleth Andrew, and again Andrew and Philip tell Jesus.

23. And Jesus answered them, saying, The hour is come, that the Son of man should be glorified.

24. Verily, verily, I say unto you, except a corn of wheat fall into the ground and die, it abideth alone, but if it die, it bringeth forth much fruit.

25. He that loveth his life shall lose it; and he that hateth his life in this world shall keep it unto life eternal.

26. If any man serve me, let him follow me; and where I am, there shall also my servant be: if any man serve me, him will my Father honor.

27. Now is my soul troubled, and what shall I say? Father, save me from this hour: but for this cause came I unto this hour.

28. Father, glorify thy name. Then came there a voice from heaven, saying, I have both glorified it, and will glorify it again.

29. The people therefore, that stood by, and heard it, said that it thundered; others said, An angel spake to him.

30. Jesus answered and said, This voice came not because of me, but for your sakes.

31. Now is the judgment of this world; now shall the prince of this world be cast out.

32. And I, if I be lifted up from the earth, will draw all men unto me.

33. This he said, signifying what death he should die.

34. The people answered him, We have heard out of the law that Christ abideth forever, and how sayest thou the Son of man must be lifted up? Who is this Son of man?

35. Then Jesus said unto them, Yet a little while is the light with you. Walk while ye have the light, lest darkness come upon you: for he that walketh in darkness knoweth not whither he goeth.

36. While ye have light, believe in the light, that ye may be the children of light. These things spake Jesus, and departed, and did hide himself from them.

37. But though he had done so many miracles before them, yet they believed not on him.

38. That the saying of Esaias the prophet might be fulfilled, which he spake, Lord, who hath believed our report? And to whom hath the arm of the Lord been revealed?

39. Therefore they could not believe, because that Esaias said again,

40. He hath blinded their eyes, and hardened their heart; that they should not see with their eyes, nor understand with their heart, and be converted, and I should heal them.

41. These things said Esaias, when he saw his glory, and spake of him.

42. Nevertheless among the chief rulers also many believed on him; but because of the Pharisees they did not confess him, lest they should be put out of the synagogue.

43. For they loved the praise of men more than the praise of God.

44. Jesus cried and said, He that believeth on me, believeth not on me but on him that sent me.

45. And he that seeth me seeth him that sent me.

46. I am come a light into the world, that whosoever believeth on me should not abide in darkness.

47. And if any man hear my words, and believe not, I judge him not: for I came not to judge the world, but to save the world.

48. He that rejecteth me, and receiveth not my words, hath one that judgeth him: the word that I have spoken, the same shall judge him in the last day.

49. For I have not spoken of myself; but the Father which sent me, he gave me a commandment, what I should say, and what I should speak.

50. And I know that his commandment is life everlasting: whatsoever I speak therefore, even as the Father said unto me, so I speak.

Vss. 1-2. Out of the loneliness of the desert of Juda, out of Ephraim, Christ appears for the entrance into Jerusalem.

The Bethany scene takes place on the Saturday before Palm Sunday. He comes to Bethany and has a thanksgiving meal there with Lazarus and his sisters in thanks to him for raising the brother.

"raised from the dead": in Greek, "hon agairen ek nekron"—ὅν ἤγειρεν ἐκ νεκρῶν—"raised from among dead." This formula appears three times in Chapter 12.

Martha, Mary, and Lazarus all have the same characteristics as cited before in the Gospel. (See above, notes to Chapter 11.)

Note that Lazarus reclines at the table with Christ"—Christ is now the higher life in which Lazarus lives. This moment is like a kind of picture of the Table of the Holy Grail.

Vs. 3. "pure nard ointment": Greek, "närdoo pistikas"—νάρδου πιστικῆς—translates as "genuine," not as "pure." This was a most costly ointment. Nardus is a Hindu word for the plant. This Nard came from the Orient, from India, via Persia by means of caravans. It is very precious indeed.

This scene is the Epilogue of the Lazarus Chapter.

The breaking of the vessel filled the house with the perfume—it was a foretaste, a prophecy of the earth filled with the aroma of Christ when the body of Christ was broken.

Parallel reference in II Corinthians: "the smell of life and smell of death"—A special Oriental point. (II Cor. 2:15)

After the Deluge, God smells the sacrifice of Noah.

(The life ether is connected with smell, as is Old Saturn).

Vs. 4 and 5. Now the note of discord breaks into the harmony of the scene. There is an atmosphere of Thanksgiving.

(Note: There is a kind of "luxury" in John's Gospel.—The large amount of wine at Cana, and here the costly ointment. This is a kind of reflection of the "Plaromä"—πλήρωμα—the fullness of Christ.)

This points out the right of the existence of luxury in spiritual things. The argument of Communism in regard to luxury in the churches, that it ought not to be, and the money should be given to the poor since Christ was "poor," may be logically right, but it destroys the spiritual in the world.

Vs. 6. "Thief": In Greek, "kleptas"—κλέπτης—(see the Epistle to the Phillippians)—did not think it robbery to be "equal to God"—"ison to Tha-o"—Ἴσον τῷ Θεῷ—but not by way of a thief, but by way of *sacrifice*. Christ is an Ego-like God, a personality in the highest sense. The contrary, the opposite, is Judas. A thief has always to do with the ego. It is to take part of the world and claim it for me and mine, private. The word for "property" in Latin means "to steal." However, *property* balanced by *sacrifice* ceases to be stolen, and is not against God.

In Judas lives the ego in the lower sphere. Judas is the unique Judean, the only one among the disciples. He is more awake in the earthly world. The others live in the etheric sphere of the Galilean lakes and hills, more dreaming in nature. The Judas-type, the city people, are more awake, more ego-conscious, more Ahrimanic.

Christ gave Judas the cash, the money, in order to give him the opportunity to put his special faculties at the service of the spiritual. Children of the city are generally more adept at handling money—know more about it—than country children.

Vs. 7. "day of my burial": one week from this day, Christ will be in the grave!

Vs. 8. "poor"—There will never be a really adequate solution to the social life—it will be always fluid—because of the matter in the world.

There is a difference in the details of the accounts of the Temptation in Matthew and Luke. Note that the Luke account ends with the words: "äschre kairoo"—ἄχρι καιροῦ—"For a time." Ahriman cannot be overcome for all times as long as there is matter in the world. Tragedy is connected with matter, and we can't fix material things once and for all, we can't make these things permanent. There will always be difficulty as long as we deal with matter.

"me ye have not always": His bodily presence will cease.

Anointment (Extreme Unction) belonged to the mystical death. It was a part of the ritual of the mysteries. Mary did the right thing, ignorantly perhaps, but nevertheless the right thing for Christ.

Vs. 9. "Raised from among the) dead": Second mention of this formula in this chapter (see 12:1).

Vs. 10. The high priesthood extended this idea of "killing" (see Ch. 11:53) even to Lazarus.

Vss. 12–13. The spirit of Nathanael echoed by the Jews. It is the real spirit of Israel speaking.

The Entrance into Jerusalem:

This is connected with the resuscitation of Lazarus. It is because of the Lazarus event that the people recognized Christ's greatness. There is a logical inner connection between the event of Bethany and the rejoicing upon Christ's Entry into Jerusalem.

"Hosanna" = Hebrew word "Ho-sha-ah-na" = "help" plus "ana," "in the highest." The literal translation is, "Help, Thou Being in the heights!" "O-sana" is a mantric form in the Mass.

"King of Israel": This is the Nathanael spirit. The people, the nation's representatives, come together here, and become the bearer for the real folk spirit. This is the last moment of the manifestation of the true folk spirit of the Jewish people, the "lä-oo"— λαοῦ—(see explanation of 11:50, above). After this they became Ahrimanic, a collective, a crowd, a mob. Then they cried "Crucify him!" Later, the phrase, "King of Israel," plays a great role in the trial before Pilate.

Vs. 14–15. Matthew's Gospel gives the details of the finding of the colt. John expected people to already know these details from having read the Matthew Gospel. John sees this event on one side, more from the point of view of the spiritual heights, and on the other side, he sees more the physical events. In the first instance, it is more ego-like. On the physical side, he gives the chronological frame for the events and is more exact than the other Gospel writers in the description of the physical events, more outlined.

Vs. 16. Another "note" of John, pointing to the events following Golgotha and the Resurrection.

"Glorified": In Greek, "edoxästha"—ἐδοξάσθη: John's secret expression for Golgotha. The prophecies represent the eternal necessities for Christ. It is like the external writing. The first writing signs were outlines of the constellations. The original books were the stars. In the Apocalypse we see heaven is the original book—the signs are heavenly pictures. Christ looks to the necessities and fulfills them with, and in, his life. Prophecies are not something "thought out in advance" by the prophets.

Verse 16 means that Christianity began with a fact which was later understood.

Vs. 17. This frames the whole account of the entry into Jerusalem with the Resuscitation of Lazarus.

Vs. 18. This is the third mention of the formula, "raised him from among (the) dead." Thus note how John connects this event with Lazarus.

The Ass: Is connected with the physical body. St. Francis called his body, "brother ass."

Here we see how Christ now enters fully into the physical body. Thus the event of Golgotha is prepared!

In a German fairy tale, four animals are mentioned: the cock (ego), cat (astral), bear (etheric) and ass (physical).

Vs 19. "the world": In Greek, "kosmos"—κόσμος. This word is a bridge leading to the Greeks who appear in Verse 20. It is a door for the Greek spirit.

The Ass: represents the old physical body of Christ which is going to die.

The Colt: represents the new body which appeared after the Resurrection.

The Entrance into the City: Now Christ enters the physical sphere fully. He is now in touch, in immediate contact with the physical sphere, and death already awaits him.

The World: In Greek, "kosmos"—κόσμος—represents "the earthly world" and "humankind." Here It is used, as often by John, in a double sense.

In the scene with the Greeks, Christ speaks three times:

1) Vs 23-28

2) Vs 30-32

3) Vs 35-36

Vs. 20. "coming up": In Greek, "Änäbaino"—ἀναβαίνω: This is a physical and a spiritual ascent.

Vs. 21. Phillipus: this is a true Greek name.

"Sir" They say "Koore-a"—Κύριε—(usually translated as "Sir")—but the Greek word used is that usually used in referring to Christ, means "Lord." This is not a usual address. He (Phillip) reflects some of the dignity they feel for Christ.

"Would see": In Greek it is more emphatic—"we will see" the Christ. The Greeks live more in the eyes—as Dr. Rittlemeyer stressed.

Phillipus: One of those small characters who appears only in John. He is hesitating, slow in mind and in nature.

Andreas: The disciple of the East. He corresponds to Petrus in the West. He is the link between Christianity and the Greek world. He has had great influence in the Russian Orthodox Church (see notes on Ch. 1:40). He is the brother of Peter.

Vs. 23. Christ speaks for the first time of three times. Christ realizes he has to gain another existence not limited to place through material sense. "Glorification" is his transfer to a higher stage of existence, getting rid of the limitations of the physical body.

"The hour has come": In Greek, "Elaloothen ha horä"—Ἐλήλυθεν ἡ ὥρα.

This is the first of three times for this formula:

John 12:1–50

1) 12:23
2) 13:1
3) 17:1

Now we have entered the sphere of the Mystery of Golgotha.

"Glorified"—Transfigured for the whole earth, universal for all people.

Vs. 24. "Grain": In Greek, "kokkos"—κόκκος—"seed." Christ is the archetype of the Seed. He has to be laid in the earth to gain the omnipresence.

"abideth alone": In Greek, "autos monos menai"—αὐτὸς μόνος μένει—it alone abides. This is in contrast to "much fruit." This verse in His own case, literally!

Vs. 25. "Loves": In Greek, "felon"—φιλῶν—"likes" (see notes on Chapter 11:5).

"his life": In Greek, "psooschen"—ψυχὴν—"soul."

— Here is a picture of the terror in the soul of Christ when He confronts, faces physical death. A Gethsemane experience.

— "loves" = "likes" too much, so he may ruin the soul.

— "hates" = Costs Christ an effort. It is a reflection of the physical zone before Golgotha, and the whole verse is a precursor of the Gethsemane "hate."—To throw down, cast aside what comes out of His own astrality as likes, dislikes, etc. An effort is needed to push this away, aside.

Vs. 26. "me": In Greek, "emoi"—ἐμοὶ—a streaming of the *me*—like a spelling in capital letters—"He who serves the Higher Ego is represented in me."

"My servant"—In the Greek: "ho deäkonos ho emos" ὁ διάκονος ὁ ἐμὸς = "my *pupil*" = the *pupil* of the Higher Ego.

"Where I am"—In Chapters 7 and 8, He says, "Where I am you *cannot* come"—three times. Three times in the *negative*. *Now* He says this three times in the *positive*—Chapters 12, 15, and 17. "Where" = "At this level—this spiritual sphere."

"Honor"—In the Greek: "timasai"—τιμήσει (from "timä-o"— τιμάω) = Give the right value to, the right weight in the world. The highest hierarchy.

Vs. 27. This is the second prayer of Christ in John's Gospel.

The first prayer is in the Lazarus scene. Here in this Verse 27, we come to the critical, the problematic prayer. He is struggling for his *Sonship*. In the first prayer, (Lazarus) he is more desirous that it should become manifest for those standing around—like the Holy Spirit. In the third prayer Christ confronts the idea that he is going to die. There is a reticence before speaking of the God facing death. The third prayer is addressed more to the Father.

"Now": This word is stressed. "Now"—"in this moment."

"Troubled": In Greek, "Tetäräktai"—τετάρακται: "shook"

In the Lazarus scene, "etäräxen"—ἐτάραξεν—"shook himself."

In Ch. 13:21—He is "shaken in spirit"—"etäräschtha"—ἐταράχθη.

This is a three-time repeated formula, passing through three regions of the Christ:

1) Lazarus Prayer = "shook himself" = bodily sphere.

2) Chapter 12 Prayer = "soul shaken" = "soul sphere"

3) Chapter 13:21 Prayer = "shaken in spirit" = "spirit sphere"

— All of this is a picture of what the Mystery of Golgotha means to Christ. This shock, this being shaken in body, soul and spirit—to the foundations of his being.

This prayer is divided into three parts:

1) "Father take me out of this hour": He sinks down in contemplation of the Father.

2) "But on account of this I came to this hour": out of contemplation of the Father, He grasps himself—He finds his ego.

3) "Father, glorify Thy Name": He asks this for the people—more like the Holy Spirit.

All three Prayers of Christ begin with the word "Father."

In this second prayer (Ch. 12) he finds his purpose.

What is wrong in his prayer is corrected.

Another analysis of this prayer:

1) Father: an escape to the Father
2) Son: He grasps Himself as the Son—comes to Himself out of praying to the Father
3) Holy Ghost: "doxa"—"glory"—Revelation of the Father God as he is known. A prayer that the depth of the Father God (the Name) should come out and be known, be manifested to all human beings.

Vs. 28. "I have revealed (manifested, "edoxäsä)—ἐδόξασα—my name, and again will reveal it"—"doxäso"—δοξάσω.

There is an echo of this verse in Ch. 17:26 of John's Gospel in reference to the "Name."

The voice was not heard alike by all. It was received as each group was able to receive it: to some as thunder, to others as an angelic voice.

Vs. 29. The voice was the result of Christ's overcoming the temptation of this hour in his soul.

He sends away the devil and overcomes the temptation of the desire to be "taken out of this hour." It is a decisive moment for Christ, and results in a kind of earthquake in his soul.

This prayer of Christ is a deed, and it has an effect.

The hearing of the people was a different kind of hearing from the ordinary. It was according to their inner degree of spiritual preparation.

Vs. 30. This is the beginning of the second speech of Christ in this section.

Vs. 31. "Now": In Greek, "Noon"—νῦν—a special, flashing emphasis. Like lightning, the present moment, now! A kind of apocalyptic moment. This word has already appeared in Verse 27.

"judgment": In Greek, "kreses"—κρίσις—division—"crisis" is the word used here. Means a "decisive decision." The path is dividing.

"now": again, the special "Now."

'prince": In Greek, "ärschon"—ἄρχων—"ruler."

"cast out": In Greek, literally, "thrown out"—The Mystery of Golgotha is prepared. Dr. Steiner said in this moment, Christ has thoroughly cleared out his etheric body.

— That God has withdrawn His power to make the Mystery of Golgotha possible—this is a Christian idea.

— That God alone is omnipotent—this is a Jewish idea.

— God gives up part of His omnipotence in favor of human freedom. We learn to give back that which he has resigned to us.

— In 2 Corinthians, Chapter 15, it is said that, in the end (the future), God will be All in All.

In John's Gospel, the words for Devil (see also notes to 6:70; 7:20; 8:48):

1) "De-äboloo"—διαβόλου: Used three times: Ch. 6:17, 13:2—more Luciferic.

2) "Ärschon too kosmoo"—ἄρχων τοῦ κόσμου: Used three times, but only in the sphere of the Mystery of Golgotha. Christ has entered the earth, and the earth opens for him.

The ruler of this world:—the Ahrimanic world which brings out of a world of its own, this world. This term is connected with death. This term is used three times:

1) "Will be"—future—12:31.
2) "Has no hold in me;" "Approaches"—present—14:30.
3) "Has been judged"—The Paraclete—the half spirit—past tense—16:11.

#3) "ho Sätänäs"—ὁ Σατανάς—used one time. Chapter 13, Vs 27.

— Therefore he speaks of the adversary seven times, and presents three aspects of this adversary.

Vs. 32. "lifted up from the earth": this is the third and last time this formula is used:

1) Nicodemus—Ch. 3:14
2) To the Jews—Ch. 8:28
3) To the People—Ch. 12:32

This is a being lifted up in exaltation.

"me": In Greek, "emauton"—ἐμαυτόν—"to my self."

"will draw": The human being can resist if this is done outwardly, but this is done by a gentle way, by an inner way.

"all": In Greek, "päntäs"—πάντας: The resistence is not on His side.

Through death, Christ obtains the new existence of omnipresence on the earth! This is the meaning of the verse.

Vs. 33. this is another note, and interpolation of John.

Vs. 35. "the light is in you" (not "with")

Verses 34 and 35 are more in the sphere of the Holy Ghost—the problem of "Knowing" and "not Knowing." The "light" and "darkness." This "knowing" is an aspect of the Holy Ghost.

Verse 35 introduces the third speech of Christ in this section.

"that the darkness may not come upon you"—(not "overtake").

Vs. 36. " that the sons of light ye may become"—(not "children," nor "be"). They are to be conscious representatives of the light—witnesses of the Christ, out of full responsibility as sons, not as little children. Fully responsible "sons," witnesses of the Holy Ghost.

— These are the last words of Christ, spoken directly to the people, with Christ physically and visibly present.

Vs. 37–38. This is a note, a meditation, of the Evangelist. In a sense, even the loss of a consciousness of heaven has good in it.

The reference to Esaias is from Chapter 53 of Isaiah.

Vs. 39. This is a remark, a note of John. This reference is to Chapter 6 of Esaias. What Esaisas saw, and the Seraphim adored, was the Christ. This also is a reference to the Prologue of John's Gospel.

Vs. 40. "I could heal them"—(not "should").

Vs. 41. "when he saw His glory"—a formula of John.

"spoke concerning Him"—the "him"—"autoo"—αὐτοῦ—is very strongly stressed here.

This verse is one of the evidences that Isaiah saw the pre-existent Christ. One of the leading evidences of the Pre-existence of Christ.

Three pictures of the Pre-existence of Christ as recorded in the Old Testament:

1) Isaiah, Ch. 6: the Seraphim—The Christ is carried by the Seraphim, who pass the word to each other concerning Him. This is the knowledge aspect. This is the aspect of the Holy Spirit.

2) Ezekiel, Ch. 1: the Vision of the Merkhabah—The Cherubim. The aspect of Christ as the Son of Man—carried by the Cherubim. This is the Logos aspect. This is the Christ seen from the aspect of the Son.

3) Daniel, Ch. 7: The Thrones. This is the Christ seen from the Father aspect.

a) In Chapters 4 and 5 of the Apocalypse, these three pictures are mixed and brought more into a unity. In other words, in Verse 41 John says that one could see the glory of Christ before his incarnation.

Vss. 42–43. This introduces the longest note or interpolation of John in his Gospel.

"Glory of men": contrasted with the "Glory of God"—(the word "doxän"—δόξαν—used twice). See Chapter 5:41, 44—when the word "honor" is the Greek word "Doxa" and is "Glory."

— With this meditation of John, now completed, the curtain falls on the drama. This curtain was raised in John 1:19.

— This is the end of the public work of Christ in the Gospel of John. From here, we pass into the more esoteric sphere of the Mystery of Golgotha, worked out in the circle of the disciples.

— After the curtain falls, we hear a voice—no person appears, only a voice—a bodiless voice, speaking an Epilogue which corresponds with the Prologue at the beginning of the Gospel, balances it. This Epilogue is a summing up of all that stands behind the public life and teaching of Christ.

Vs. 45. "beholds": In Greek, "sees"—refers to Chapter 6 of John's Gospel.

Vs. 46. "I . . . a light": Greek, "ago fos"—ἐγὼ φῶς. See Chapter 8:12—Greek "Ago aime to fos"—Ἐγώ εἰμι τὸ Φῶς—(I Am the light), and in Chapter 9:5—upon seeing the man born blind, he says "fos aime"—φῶς εἰμι. And here in Ch. 12:46, in the Epilogue, these two are brought together in this "ago fos"—ἐγὼ φῶς.

Vs. 47. This refers to the Nicodemus chapter of the Gospel of John.

"and not believe": In Greek, this is, "and not keep them."

Vs. 48. "has him who judges": In Greek, this is "has his judge."

"In the last day": Again, this is a formula of John (see Chapters 6 and 7). These words point to the reality of the Last Day. They will be a reality then. His words are a reality. Christ has created these words, and out of these words of Christ, we shall be judged. When confronted with them, we shall be judged (see Chapters 6–7).

Vs. 49. "I spoke": indicates that his speaking is now in the past—is finished.

"Father": he finishes on the note of the Father.

"commandment": This is not correct. It is a Roman form. The Greek word is "entolan"—ἐντολὴν—and means "goal," "aim," "purpose." It is a goal entrusted to him. Certainly eternal life is not a commandment; it is an aim, a goal!

Thus, the public work of Christ is finished, and the curtain falls. Thus, we are at the end of the first section of John's Gospel. This is not the mathematical half of the Gospel. The mathematical middle of the Gospel is the Lazarus story. But we are at the natural division of the Gospel. We now enter into a more intimate sphere, as into a chapel, from the out-of-doors.

And from Chapter 12, verse 36 to verse 50, we are in the sphere of a meditation of the Evangelist John.

John 13:1-38

1. Now before the feast of the Passover, when Jesus knew that his hour was come that he should depart out of this world unto the Father, having loved his own which were in the world, he loved them unto the end.
2. And supper being ended, the devil having now put into the heart of Judas Iscariot, Simon's son, to betray him;
3. Jesus knowing that the Father had given all things into his hands, and that he was come from God, and went to God;
4. He riseth from supper, and laid aside his garments; and took a towel, and girded himself.
5. After that he poureth water into a basin, and began to wash the disciples' feet, and to wipe them with the towel wherewith he was girded.
6. Then cometh he to Simon Peter, and Peter saith unto him, Lord doest thou wash my feet?
7. Jesus answered and said unto him, What I do thou knowest not now; but thou shalt know hereafter.
8. Peter said unto him, Thou shall never wash my feet. Jesus answered him, If I wash thee not, thou hast no part with me.
9. Simon Peter saith unto him, Lord, not my feet only, but also my hands and my head.
10. Jesus saith to him, He that is washed needeth not save to wash his feet, but is clean every whit: and ye are clean, but not all.
11. For he knew who should betray him, therefore said he, Ye are not all clean.
12. So after he had washed their feet, and had taken his garments, and was set down again, he said unto them, Know ye what I have done to you?

13. Ye call me Master and Lord, and ye say well, for so I am.
14. If I then, your Lord and Master, have washed your feet, ye also ought to wash one another's feet.
15. For I have given you an example, that ye should do as I have done to you.
16. Verily, verily, I say unto you, the servant is not greater than his Lord; neither he that is sent greater than he that sent him.
17. If ye know these things, happy are ye if you do them.
18. I speak not of you all, I know whom I have chosen: but that the scripture might be fulfilled. He that eateth bread with me hath lifted up his heel against me.
19. Now I tell you before it come, that, when it is come to pass, ye may believe that I am he.
20. Verily, verily, I say unto you, he that receiveth whomsoever I send receiveth me; and he that receiveth me receiveth him that sent me.
21. When Jesus had thus said, he was troubled in spirit, and testified, and said, Verily, verily, I say unto you, that one of you shall betray me.
22. Then the disciples looked one on another, doubting of whom he spake.
23. Now there was leaning on Jesus' bosom one of his disciples, whom Jesus loved.
24. Simon Peter therefore beckoned to him, that he should ask who it should be of whom he spake.
25. He then lying on Jesus' breast saith unto him, Lord, who is it?
26. Jesus answered, He it is, to whom I shall give a sop, when I have dipped it. And when he had dipped the sop, he gave it to Judas Iscariot, the son of Simon.

27. And after the sop Satan entered into him. Then said Jesus unto him, That thou doest, do quickly.

28. Now no man at the table knew for what intent he spake this unto him.

29. For some of them thought, because Judas had the bag, that Jesus had said unto him, Buy those things that we have need of against the feast, or that he should give something to the poor.

30. He then having received the sop went immediately out: and it was night.

31. Therefore when he was gone out, Jesus said, Now is the Son of man glorified, and God is glorified in him.

32. If God be glorified in him, God shall also glorify him in himself, and shall straightway glorify him.

33. Little children, yet a little while I am with you. Ye shall seek me, and as I said unto the Jews, Whither I go, ye cannot come; so now I say to you.

34. A new commandment I give unto you, that ye love one another, as I have loved you, that ye also love one another.

35. By this shall all men know that ye are my disciples, if ye have love one to another.

36. Simon Peter said unto him, Lord whither goest thou? Jesus answered him, Whither I go thou canst not follow me now, but thou shalt follow me afterward.

37. Peter said unto him, Lord, why cannot I follow thee now? I will lay down my life for thy sake.

38. Jesus answered him, Wilt thou lay down thy life for my sake? Verily, verily, I say unto thee, the cock shall not crow, till thou hast denied me thrice.

This new section of the Gospel opens with a Prologue, just as does the beginning of the Gospel. It consists of Verses 1 through 3. (All a Mediation—Note of John).

Where the Prologue to the Gospel uses the word "Logos," the "Little Prologue" speaks of the incarnated Christ who has made His disciples into individuals, and has loved them to the end. In the Prologue, "darkness" is spoken of. Here "Judas" is spoken of.

The Prologue to the Gospel says he "came to the world and the world knew him not." Here it says he came from the Father and goes to the Father. Then the Creator kneels before the fallen creatures to Wash the Feet.

Vs. 1. "Knowing": In Greek, "aidos"—εἰδὼς—This is a participle. The word "idea" comes from it. It is a word typical of John's Gospel record of the Passion. Christ is conscious of the Passion.

"the hour has come": This is a formula of John's Gospel. It is used three times.

"Depart": In Greek, "Metäba"—μεταβῇ—"pass over"—a passing over. It is also used in Chapter 5. The Christ is about to "pass over" to the Father. [Note: Passover = "pässchä" = πάσχα]

"his own": These are the "ego-bearers."

"He loved them unto the end": The Greek word here is "telos"—τέλος = "End"—points far to the future—an apocalyptical word. The whole phrase in Greek is, "Telos hagäpasen autoos"—τέλος ἠγάπησεν αὐτούς.

"Telos"—τέλος: Greek, for "end," "goal," "aim." It also means "tax" or "toll," and is so translated often in the Gospel.

In the Prologue in Chapter 1 of the Gospel, the word "ärscha"—ἀρχῆ—(beginning) appears. In this Prologue, the word "Telos"—τέλος—(end) appears. This is a linking of "beginning" and "end" as in the Apocalypse, the "Alpha" and "Omega."—Note the relationship between:

"knowing" ("aidos")—εἰδὼς—Tree of Knowledge

"loved" ("Agäpasen")—ἠγάπησεν—Tree of Life as in the first Prologue of John's Gospel.

Vs. 2. "devil": In Greek, "de-äbolon"—διαβόλον.

"put into the heart": Greek, literally, "thrown into the heart."

Vs. 3. "Knowing": Greek, "aidos"—εἰδὼς—(see Vs 1). Note the position of this word in the verse. It is stressed.

"Into his hands": See Chapters 3 and 10.

"he came out from God . . . and goes to God": Note the movement, the rhythm in these words. There is a pressing forward, a flowing in them, and this is continued into the first word of Verse 4: "egairetai"—ἐγείρεται—"He stands up"—and we are literally "flowed" into the scene of the Washing of the Feet.

This "came out . . . going to" is the theme for the Farewell Address:

"Comes from God": theme for first part of John's Gospel

"Goes to God": theme for second part of John's Gospel.

The Washing of the Feet is the beginning of a new creation. Once the Word had created the universe, but the chief creatures whom He created in his image had fallen away. Now, with unbounded love, the Creator has begun to integrate this fallen creature into the universal harmony—to "redeem" him. The first creation, based on unlimited power—the new creation based on unlimited service. Here the human being enters into cooperation. Where we truly serve, we are creative. Where we serve beast, plant and stone, we grow into co-workers, into His image once more.

Vs. 4. "He rises": In Greek, "egairetai"—ἐγείρεται—the present tense. The intermingling of the past and present tenses in a free way, as in John's Gospel, is apparently not according to any preconceived plan, but it is excellent because it brings life into the whole. The Washing of the Feet is an act of humiliation which is connected with certain aspects of Eternity.—"rises," "lays aside," "having taken," "girded," "pours," "began," etc.

Between the 5th and 6th Verse, there is a pause—a creative silence. Christ washes the feet of the other disciples in silence. They are astonished, and cannot speak.—Then in Verse 6, Peter breaks the silence.

Vs. 6. "Lord": In Greek, "Koore-a"—Κύριε—Peter here uses a very high and lofty term.

Vs. 7. The Christ speaks seven times in Chapter 13:1-30. Verses 7, 8, 10, 12, 21, 26, 27 (seven speeches in all).

Vs. 11. "He knew": In Greek, "adai"—ᾔδει (from "oidä"—οἶδα = to know): an aspect of "knowing"—Typical of John's Gospel. "Gnosis"—γνῶσις—(Knowledge). There will be a deeper knowledge. This opens the door to the deeper understanding in the future. Their present state of "not knowing" is not forever. It is a fundamental point of Christianity that first there is a deed accomplished, something is done, and then there is a growing into a knowledge, an understanding of this deed in the future. First the deed, then the understanding of the deed.

One characteristic of Peter is that he is always either too enthusiastic or too modest.

The feet indicated the human being's relationship to what is below himself or herself. If this relationship is established in the right way, then the whole is right. Indicates a correct relationship to human beings and to the earth.

Vs. 12. This is the longest saying of the seven. It presents the theology, the meaning of the act which has just been performed.

"Do you know": Greek, "Ginoskete"—Γινώσκετε—Here is the contrast between "knowing" and "doing." It is as though he says, "I know whom I select" (vs 18).

Vs. 13. "well ye say": Literally in Greek, "And you are right."

Vs. 16. "bondman": literally in Greek, "servant."

"messenger": literally in Greek, "apostle."

John 13:1–38

Vs. 19. "it": The Mystery of Golgotha. And when this "it" comes to pass, you should have confidence in my Higher Ego (the I AM). But they did not have the confidence!

Vs. 21. This is the problematic saying. The world is in need of such a deed. "Shaken" (not "troubled")—in the "spirit" (This completes the "body," "soul," and now, "spirit." He is "shaking" for the knowledge of having such an insight into the Mystery of Golgotha as a deep necessity of world evolution. It is a shaking experience of the spirit, not a trivial thing.

Vs. 23. "him whom Jesus loved": The first mention of this deep formula of John's Gospel.

"kolpo":—κόλπῳ—appears again from the Prologue ("bosom").

Vs. 24. Note that it is Peter who makes the sign.

Vs. 26. "Takes and gives": Greek, "lambänai kai dedosin"—λαμβάνει καὶ δίδωσιν. It is like a communion. Not "sop" but "morsel." "Iscariot" = "Ish" = "man", "Cariot" = a town in Judea. So it means, "the man of Cariot."

Vs. 27. "Satan": In Greek, "Sätänäs"—Σατανᾶς.

"What thou doest, do more quickly"—(the comparative form). Here is the directing sovereignty of the Christ. He directs what is now to come upon him.

Vs. 28. "wherefore he spoke to them": literally, "what he meant."

Vs. 29. "thought": literally in Greek, "edokoon"—ἐδόκουν—"believed." And here even the misunderstandings of the people are important. All these misunderstandings are important in the Gospel of John! (Vs 29, another Johannine note.)

Vs. 30. "And it was night": This is one of the little typical Johannine indications, so important, so significant. The darkness devours Judas when the door opens. It is a coincidence of the outer and the inner events.

This verse 30 completes this section.

In this section, The Christ has spoken seven times: see above, under Vs. 7. These are a kind of balance, like the seven-branched candlestick.

Thus:

1) Vs 7: The subject of "doing," "knowing," and "not knowing."

7) Vs 27: "doing," "more quickly."

Above two represent the will sphere—Simon Peter.

2) Vs 8: partaking of the Christ, having part of the personal Christ

6) Vs 26: the giving of the Sacrament

Above two represent the etheric sphere—sacramental sphere.

3) Vs 10: all are not clean, not pure

5) Vs 21: one will betray; the Judas theme

Above two represent the astral sphere—the emotion.

4) Vs 12: In the midst of these stands the meaning, the whole symbol of the mystical act. The indication of the betrayal is not as clear as in the fifth Saying (Vs. 21). This is the longest of the sayings and presents the bad, the evil counter-picture of the Communion.

Vs. 31. And now comes a great high point of the Gospel. In contrast to the "night"of the moment before, the darkness which swallowed up Judas when he went out, now "light," "Glory" (Doxa), bursts out! A mighty spiritual sunrise takes place! This is one of the most impressive places of the whole Gospel of John. Here we have three examples of the Zarathustra-struggle of light with darkness. "Glorification"—"Doxa"—A great threefold outburst of Glory—A great moment of Transfiguration! Three kinds of Glorification:

1) "The Son of Man"—The inner glory comes out and transfigures him.

2) "The Father"—The Father has been made manifest, has been revealed in him, in the perfection of the human being.

3) "The human is revealed in God"—Has been manifested in the Father God. Here is a revelation of what is God and what is the human.

The perfect revelation of the Son of God in the human being is the perfect revelation of the human being.

The perfect revelation of God within the human being is at the same time the perfect revelation of the human being within God.

When the human receives the divine, the divine receives its humanity.

All this is like a threefold sunrise after the "night" motif. It is like the rising of three suns at once!

Vs. 31. A kind of entry into the sphere of the Farewell Address. It is the "beginning" of the Farewell Address. It begins with the Motif of Transformation.

In John's Gospel, the whole Passion is painted in the major tone—not in the minor key or tone. In the other Gospels, the Passion is painted in the minor tone. Bach caught this fact, and his *St. Matthew Passion* is in a minor key, and has the choral opening of "Weep, Daughters of Zion", while his *St. John's Passion* is in the major key, and opens with "O Lord, our Lord, how excellent is Thy Name" from Psalm 8.

Vs. 32. "Immediately": In Greek, "oithoos"—εὐθὺς—literally, "straightway." This "oithoos" is full of will, and is very often used in Mark's Gospel. It is a leading motif of Mark's Gospel.

The way of Christ is the straight way of destiny, not a meandering way, as ours so often is.

Vs. 33. "Little Children": In Greek, "tekne-ä"—τεκνία—a special diminutive, meaning, "very little children." He sees how little they are developed, sees all this is but a tiny germ in them, but he addresses this germ.

Vs. 34. Note the negative here: Where he goes, they cannot come. This is in contrast to the where he goes, they can come.

Vs. 35. "A new commandment": In Greek, "Entelan kainen"—ἐντολὴν καινὴν—This "entolan" is from "na-os"—νέος—"different" and is related to "kainos"—καινός—the word of the Apocalypse—"newness"—as in "All things new." This refers to the sphere of originality, creative originality—connected with qualities of the Ego—with the Archai, the "beginnings." Those who are Spirits of Personality, thus establishing a new beginning in the world. The whole world goes through the personality of the Ego, the I Am, and through this, takes on a new quality. Thus, this verse points to a "commandment," a "goal," an "aim," which has the quality of "newness," the Christ-substance.

"Entolen"—ἐντολὴν—"aim," "goal," "commandment."—That which is connected with the Ego, which comes out of the Ego.

This thought in this verse takes the form of the other Commandments, but in itself, it is NOT the 11th Commandment. It actually marks the END of the Commandments, because it is connected with the development of the Higher Ego. The sphere of the Ego is higher than the sphere of the Commandments.

This verse 34 of "aim" is threefold:

1) "A new aim I give you that you should love one another": This is the sphere of the Father God. The authoritative form.

2) ". . . like (käthos)—καθώς—like I loved you that also you should love one another."—This is pointing to himself as the Archetype. The sphere of the Son, the Christ.

3) "By this shall all know that my disciples you are, if you have love among yourselves."—The sphere of "knowing" (gnosontai)—γνώσονται—the sphere of the Holy Ghost. This

is a conditional phase, where they have the possibility to become the disciples of the Higher Ego ("I") of the Christ. The "my" should be "MY" (amoi)—ἐμοὶ—The sphere of true freedom is here indicated.

Special Note: In the Old Testament, Abraham is always connected with trees. Isaac is always connected with wells; Jacob, with stones.

Vs. 36. Peter always speaks too soon, too hastily, and he always makes too much "talk"—too impetuous. Here he uses the famous, "Quo Vadis"—Related to Rome.

Vs. 37. "my life": Greek, "psooschen"—ψυχήν—should read "My soul . . ." I will put down (not lay down). This is a formula which was contained before in Chapter 10:15, regarding the Good Shepherd. It is interesting that Peter comes in here (13:37) and again is connected with the shepherd theme in 21:15-17. This is another link also with Rome, and with Peter's death.

Vs. 38. "Your soul" again as in Vs 37. This is a kind of repetition of Peter's words, as though to say, "Are you conscious of what you have said?"

The "Let not your heart," etc., of 14:1 can be considered as a continuation of his comfort to them all, just following his prophecy of Peter's denial. It is really a continuation, and not necessarily a completely new saying. The chapter beginning should be disregarded entirely.

John 14:1-31

1. Let not your heart be troubled: ye believe in God, believe also in me.
2. In my Father's house are many mansions: if it were not so, I would have told you. I go to prepare a place for you.
3. And if I go and prepare a place for you, I will come again, and receive you unto myself; that where I am, there ye may be also.
4. And whither I go ye know, and the way ye know.
5. Thomas saith unto him, Lord, we know not whither thou goest; and how can we know the way?
6. Jesus saith unto him, I am the way, the truth and the life: no man cometh to the Father, but by me.
7. If ye had known me, ye should have known my Father also: and from henceforth ye know him, and have seen him.
8. Philip saith unto him, Lord shew us the Father, and it sufficeth us.
9. Jesus saith unto him, Have I been so long time with you, and yet hast thou not known me, Philip? He that hath seen me hath seen the Father; and how sayest thou then, Shew us the Father?
10. Believest thou not that I am in the Father, and the Father in me? The words that I speak unto you I speak not of myself; but the Father that dwelleth in me, he doeth the works.
11. Believe me that I am in the Father, and the Father in me, or else believe me for the very work's sake.
12. Verily, verily, I say unto you; he that believeth in me, the works that I do shall he do also, and greater works than these shall he do; because I go unto my Father.

13. And whatsoever ye shall ask in my name, that I will do, that the Father may be glorified in the Son.
14. If ye shall ask anything in my name, I will do it.
15. If ye love me, keep my commandments.
16. And I will pray the Father, and he shall give you another Comforter, that he may abide with you for ever;
17. Even the Spirit of truth; whom the world cannot receive, because it seeth him not, neither knoweth him, but ye know him; for he dwelleth with you, and shall be in you.
18. I will not leave you comfortless; I will come to you.
19. Yet a little while, and the world seeth me no more; but ye see me: because I live, ye shall live also.
20. At that day ye shall know that I am in my Father, and ye in me, and I in you.
21. He that hath my commandments and keepeth them, he it is that loveth me: and he that loveth me shall be loved of my Father, and I will love him, and will manifest myself to him.
22. Judas saith to him, not Iscariot, Lord, how is it that thou wilt manifest thyself unto us, and not unto the world?
23. Jesus answered and said unto him, If a man love me, he will keep my words: and my Father will love him, and we will come unto him, and make our abode with him.
24. He that loveth me not keepeth not my sayings: and the word which ye hear is not mine, but the Father's which sent me.
25. These things have I spoken unto you, being yet present with you.
26. But the Comforter, which is the Holy Ghost, whom the Father will send in my name, he shall teach you all things, and bring all things to your remembrance, whatsoever I have said unto you.

27. Peace I leave with you, my peace I give unto you: not as the world giveth, give I unto you. Let not your heart be troubled, neither let it be afraid.

28. Ye have heard how I said unto you, I go away, and come again unto you. If ye loved me, ye would rejoice, because I said I go unto the Father, for my Father is greater than I.

29. And now have I told you before it come to pass, that when it is come to pass, ye might believe.

30. Hereafter I will not talk much with you, for the prince of this world cometh, and hath nothing in me.

31. But that the world may know that I love the Father; and as the Father gave me commandment, even so I do. Arise, let us go hence.

Vs. 1. "Let not your heart be troubled": spoken to all, but especially to Peter, in view of that which has just gone before.

"Tärässetho,"—ταρασσέθω—not "troubled", but "shaken"—The same verb as before when the Christ was "shaken" in body, soul and spirit, successively.

"kärde-ä"—καρδία—"heart"—the mystery of the heart.

"Believe on God, also on me believe": This is the literal order in the Gospel. Note how the two words "believe" frame the thought. There is an imperative used twice (not "ye" believe). This word is "pistoi-ete"—πιστεύετε—"believe," "confidence," "faith"—"have confidence." Here Christ puts himself beside God in a very radical way.

Vs. 2. "many mansions": In Greek, "monai Pollai"—μοναὶ Πολαι—This "monai" derived from "mona"—μονη; "meno"—μένω—to "remain," "abide," "tarry." The phrase can be best translated "many abodes." (Same word, "mona"- μονη—used before in the Gospel of John—special for John). In the sphere of the Father God there are many chances to be guaranteed eternal life.

John 14:1–31

"I go": In Greek, "Poroi-omai"—πορεύομαι—"I travel." But this is a very high and exalted word here—not trivial.

"A place": In Greek, "topon"—τόπον—(Our word "topography" comes from this). The word is repeated in Vs. 3.

Vs. 3. "I am coming": (This is the literal Greek) This is first announcement of his coming again. Up to now he has (1) come from God, and (2) is going to God, and now (3) is coming again! This is a complete rhythm. Note the rhythm in the order of verbs: (1) "I go;" ". . . prepare;" (2) "I am coming;" and (3) "will receive;" "I am" . . . ye may be."

"will receive": In Greek, "Pärälampsomai"—παραλήμψομαι.

"To myself": The strongest form of "Myself." "I will receive you into the sphere of my I Am" (aime ago)— εἰμι ἐγω.

1) In Ch. 12:26 the verse is, "where I am, my servant shall also be."—This is more the Father aspect. He speaks more as a master to servants. (Father).

2) In Ch. 14:3, the verse is, "where I am also ye may be." This is more the Son aspect. He speaks to them in a person-to-person way. "ye" (Son).

3) In Ch. 17:24, this verse is, "where I am they also may be with me." This is more the aspect of the Holy Spirit. He speaks of "they"—in this High Priestly Prayer. (The Holy Spirit).

Vs. 4. "Whither": Echo of the Peter "Quo Vadis"—13:36).

"the Way": "The Path"—the key word for Thomas—later the disciple who came to India. For the Indian, "Path" is the key. The "Thomas-Christians" in India were deeply interested in the "Path"—the "Way."

Vs. 5. Here Thomas speaks, as he might be expected to do, of the "way," the "path."

Vs. 6. Here is one of the seven great "I Am statements":

"I Am myself, the way, the path, leading to the Truth and the Life (älathe-ä kai ha tsoa)—αλήθιεα καὶ ἡ ζωή of the Lost Paradise.

"No man cometh unto the Father but by me":—Only through the development of the Higher Ego. Through the I Am of the Christ, is the only way one can come to the Father God.

Vs. 7. The problem of "knowing": In Greek, as in John's Gospel, there are two verbs for "knowing":

1) "Gegnoskete"—γιγνώσκετε = "knowing"—connected with "Gnosis" and with "Genesis" and "Generation"—in a sense, with Adam. In other words, knowledge connected with the "generative." A Knowledge which points backward to the origin of things, the creation of things.

2) "Oidä"—οἶδα: "knowing"—connected with "wisdom"—but with the wisdom of the sight—with that which is learned through the eyes. Therefore, this is like the "willing" pole and the "knowing" pole.

Vs. 8. Philip, as a typical Greek, is intimately connected with "sight," "seeing," "showing" (see Rittlemeyer on John's Gospel), "show": (Greek, "daixon"—δεῖξον). This is not the simple verb "to show" in Greek. This verb meant rather, "Lead us to have a vision." And in this sense, the verb really pertains to much deeper meaning, and the whole stature of Phillip is increased thereby.

In the Greek mysteries and early Christianity there are three nouns of greatest importance:

1) "Dyknoemenon" (phonetically) (From ("Dyknoome" (phonetically)—"I show")—"that which is shown"—like the Monstrance. A "showing" of that which is sacred to the people. As the "showing" of holy pictures, images, etc. Also sacred "acts" in the cult, as picture.—the sphere of Imagination.

2) "Legominin" (phonetically)—(Related to "lego"—λέγω and to "logos"— λόγοσ—"that which is said"—Related

to "the-ologe-ä"—θεολογία—"theology"—also to "hiero-logos"—ἱερο-λόγοσ—("the word of the Priest")—the saying of the sacred deed. The sphere of Inspiration.

3) "Drominon" (phonetically)—related to "Drä-o"—δράω—(Drama)—"That which is done." An actual "doing," the "effect," the "performance" of the sacred cultus. The sphere of Intuition.

Vs. 9. "known" and "seen": Refers to the Prologue (1:10) and to 6:46. So there is a step-by-step development in these three verses, a metamorphosis.

Vs. 10. Contrast 10:38—"Know" and 14:10—"Believe." This is like "light" and "warmth"—two poles.

a) "I am in the Father"—he abandons Himself to the Father

b) "The Father in me"—sphere of knowledge

There is a turning, a reversal in:

a) "In me is the Father, and I in Him"—10:38

b) "I am in the Father, and the Father in me" 14:10

"in" me: Greek "en"—ἐν—in. A formula of John. Points to inner-ness—(innerlichkeit)—inwardness—connected with having an ego. Thus the human being is able to create a sphere of his or her "tä aide-ä—τὰ ἀίδια. This use of "in" grows in the second half of the Gospel, and reaches a climax in the High Priestly Prayer (Ch. 17). In Chapter 6 it begins to play a great role in connection with the Communion. Then in Chapter 10 it reaches a still greater height and emphasis. It points to that person in whom that which is spiritual can remain—a reciprocity of the ego—a balancing—a revealing of support: "who in me abides" (Greek: "meno"—μένω—"remains," "is fully remaining").

"He does the works" (Greek, "poi-ai tä hergä"—ποιεῖ τὰ ἔργα—"creates the works")—This "poi-ai"—ποιεῖ- is the world from which our word "poet" comes.

Vs. 11. "believe in me": contrast this "pistoiete moi"—πιστεύετέ μοι—with "believest thou not,"—"oo pistoi-ais—οὐ—πιστεύεις—in Verse 10.

1) 6:35—Connected with "Bread of Life"
2) 7:38—Connected with "Living Water"
3) 11:25—Connected with "Resurrection and the Life"
4) 11:26—Connected with "dying and Life"
5) 12:44—Connected with "him that sent me"
6) 12:46—Connected with "Light of the world"
7) 14:12—This is the Crown of the whole series, and is the last mention of this formula. Here connected with the "greater works."

Vs. 12. Opens with special, solemn formula, "Amen, Amen"—"Greater"—In Greek, "Maitsonä"—μείζονα.

1) Scene with Nathanael—1:51
2) Scene with the Man Born Blind—5:20
3) "Greater Works"—14:12.

"Because"—Greek, "oti"—ὅτι—Special Johannine word.

"Go to my Father": In Greek, "poroi-omai"—πορεύομαι—"travel."

In this Verse 12 we may say, He who opens himself to Christ, the Christ will do great works in him. So our ego is in his Higher Ego. It is to do that which the Christ wishes in us. We learn to let Him pray in us. And then our praying, our prayer, is successful. The prayer of petition, the "asking" prayer, belongs to the past. Meditation, which is without personal interest, in which we are interested in God's affairs, rather than seeking to have him interested in our own—this is the prayer of the present and future. We must die to our own personal affairs, in order to be resurrected to the point where God is interested in us.

Vs. 13. "in the Son": note the objectivity from "me" and "my" to "the Son."

Vs. 14. "he does" to "he will do" (Vs 13 to 14).

Vs. 15. "commandments": In Greek, "entoläs"—ἐντολὰς—"aims," "goals," "objectives."

"my": In Greek, "emäs"—ἐμὰς—Very strong "MY."

Vs. 16. The "Paraclete" (King James Version: "Comforter")—An "advocate," or "spiritual helper," one who works for another on his or her behalf. A very hard word to translate. This is one of the mysteries in the Gospel of John. It appears in this Gospel five times as follows:

The Paraclete:

1) "The Spirit of Truth"—14:16—"The Father will give."
2) "The Holy Spirit"—14:26—"The Father will send."
3) "The Paraclete "comes"—15:26—"I will send from the Father."
4) "The Paraclete"—16:7—"I will send him to you."
5) "The Spirit of Truth"—16:13—"When the Spirit of Truth comes."

Vs. 17. "world": In Greek, "kosmos"—κόσμος—"the sense world."

"receive": In Greek, "läbain"—λαβεῖν—"see."

"see and know": a contrast here.

"in you": In Greek, "en"—ἐν—"within you."

Vs. 18. "comfortless": In Greek, orphänoos"—ὀρφανούς—"orphans."

"I shall come": In Greek, "erschomai"—ἔρχομαι—"I am coming."

Vs. 19. "a little": In Greek, "mekron"—μικρὸν—special Johannine word—points to the reappearance of Christ.

"ye see" = "ye will see."

Vs. 20. "In that day": the future. "Know"—Stress on this "know" (Gnosis).

1) "I in my Father"
2) "Ye in me"
3) "I in you"

Note the development:

1) 10:38—a) "In me is the Father," b) "and I in Him."
2) 14:20—a) "I in my Father," b) "Ye in me," c) "I in you.
3) 17:21—a) "Thou, Father in me," b) "I in Thee," c) "They in us."

This is a genuine metamorphosis. In the third saying (John 17:21), he includes them—all those who believe. A special trinity:

1) The Father
2) The Christ
3) The Disciples (us)

In Ch. 10:38, the direction is towards the future—knowing connected with the future. A development to come.

Vs. 21. "Keeps": In Greek, "taron"—τηρῶν—A cultivation, a repetition, the work a gardener does; a "keeping alive" of something in the soul through systematic meditation. Not a "keeping" like a bookkeeper! It is a keeping something alive, cultivating, by meditation, repetition, rhythm.

Note the structure:

"He that has my aims and cultivates them, he it is that loves me:

1) But he that loves me
2) Shall be loved by my Father
3) And I will love him more

   And will reveal myself to him."

In this verse, the Greek word "AGAPE" "ägäpon"—ἀγαπῶν—appears:

The Father, The Christ, the Disciples = "agape" (love).

The use of "agape" ("love") in John's Gospel:

1) The Father loves the world—(sent his "unique" Son, "only revered" Son)
2) The Father loves the Son, the Christ—(seven times in John's Gospel)
3) The Father loves the Disciples—(Ch. 14:21)
4) The Christ loves the Father—(Ch. 14)
5) The Christ loves the Disciples
6) The Disciples love the Christ
7) The Disciples love each other

NB. Last two—The Disciples do not show love for the Father!

— The word "agape" grows, is used much more frequently in John's Gospel, after the Lazarus scene, and it is especially emphasized in Chapters 13 and 14 onward to the end of the Gospel.

Vs. 22. Dr. Rittlemeyer pointed out that there is some connection between this Judas and Iscariot, on the basis of ideals. It is a seeking of glory for, and before the sense world (kosmos).

"to manifest": In Greek, "emfänetsain"—ἐμφανίζειν—(from "noomai" phonetically) ("to show")—"phenomenon" is derived from this! And the best translation might be, "reveal"—in the sense of "make visible," as a phenomenon.

"reveal thyself to us, and not to the sense world": (This "to us" is strongly implied in the Greek).

Vs. 23. "Love me" (agape):—the use of agape (love) is always in a sense of 1) command, 2) a promise, or 3) a condition. It is never in the naked statement, "He loved me," in John's Gospel. Only at the end of the Gospel it stands in the question, "Do you love me?" It, however, is not a statement or indication that this is in existence on Peter's part. So often a person meditates, strives, keeps the words of Christ alive, but does not "love" him—(Vs 24, for example)

"we will come": Note the plural of "we"—Points to new waves, new impulses, new release of loving forces. In Chapter 10, this "we" is concealed. Now fine degrees of metamorphosis come out.

"abode": In Greek, "mo-en"—μὁὴν—"meno"—μένω—"remain," "tarry"—A key word for John's Gospel.

This was the Gospel for Whitsuntide in the Old Church—the Holy Spirit is included here.

Vs. 26. "Paraclete, the Holy Spirit": (see above Vs. 16)

"In my name": that which is connected with Christ, which is moving to the Christ.

"remembrance": A passing over to a kind of clairvoyance, a kind of "spiritual memory."

Vs. 27. A threefold statement:

1) "Peace I leave with you"
2) "My peace I give to you"
3) "Not as the world gives, give I to you"

— Note verbs, "leave" and "give." "My" peace—strong "my."

"Let not your heart (kardia) be shaken, nor let it fear (or "be cowardly").

1) "Peace" is a substance, spread out, remaining behind him when he leaves. A kind of leaven.
2) "My peace" My (emen—ἐμὴν)—He gives his own Higher Ego. An aspect of the Son.
3) The sphere of the Holy Spirit—a kind of inner judgment. Expressed through the contrary, the opposite, by a nega-

tion—"NOT"—Points to his "giving" as being a special kind of giving—not like other things in the world.

"fear, be afraid": "daile-äto"—δειλιάτω—(dialate)—enlargement.

Vs. 28. "I am going away," and "I am coming" is a three-time repeated formula here:

"If you loved":—note the conditional tense here.

1) "Going to the Father": 14:12
2) "Going to the Father": 16:10
3) "Going to the Father": 14:28

A special, highly solemn motif of John. "Going"—"I travel"

"Father greater than I": This is connected with the "greater works." He goes to the Father and obtains these forces. He says, "The Father is greater than I," out of a basis of equality. It is NOT a proof against His divinity, but actually for His divinity. Otherwise, it would represent a kind of over-familiarity. He is included in the Father.

Vs. 29. "It": A mysterious word here. Refers to the Mystery of Golgotha.

"you may believe": "you shall have the confidence."

Vs. 30. "ruler of this world": "too kosmoo ärschon"—τοῦ κόσμου ἄρχων.

In:

1) Ch. 12:31—he "will be cast out"—The future
2) Ch. 14:30—he "comes"—aspect of the present, of the Son
3) Ch. 16:11—he "is judged"—already past—finished

"in me": In Greek, en emoi—ἐν ἐμοὶ—"in myself." He has no hold at all—'all men have the traitor in themselves, but in me he has no hold at all'—in myself.

Vs. 31. "Rise up, etc.": A lifting up to a higher sphere.

John 15:1-27

1. I am the true vine, and my Father is the husbandman.
2. Every branch in me that beareth not fruit he taketh away, and every branch that beareth fruit, he purgeth it, that it may bring forth more fruit.
3. Now ye are clean through the word which I have spoken unto you.
4. Abide in me, and I in you. As the branch cannot bear fruit of itself, except it abide in the vine; no more can ye, except ye abide in me.
5. I am the vine, ye are the branches. He that abideth in me, and I in him, the same bringeth forth much fruit, for without me ye can do nothing.
6. If a man abide not in me, he is cast forth as a branch, and is withered; and men gather them, and cast them into the fire, and they are burned.
7. If ye abide in me, and my words abide in you, ye shall ask what ye will, and it shall be done unto you.
8. Herein is my Father glorified, that ye bear much fruit; so shall ye be my disciples.
9. As the Father hath loved me, so have I loved you, continue in my love.
10. If ye keep my commandments, ye shall abide in my love, even as I have kept my Father's commandments, and abide in his love.
11. These things have I spoken unto you, that my joy might remain in you, and that your joy might be full.
12. This is my commandment: that ye love one another, as I have loved you.

13. Greater love hath no man than this, that a man lay down his life for his friends.
14. Ye are my friends, if ye do whatsoever I command you.
15. Henceforth I call you not servants; for the servant knoweth not what his lord doeth; but I have called you friends, for all things that I have heard of my Father I have made known unto you.
16. Ye have not chosen me, but I have chosen you, and ordained you, that ye should go and bring forth fruit, and that your fruit should remain: that whatsoever ye shall ask of the Father in my name, he may give it you.
17. These things I command you, that ye love one another.
18. If the world hate you, ye know that it hated me before it hated you.
19. If ye were of the world, the world would love its own: but because ye are not of the world, but I have chosen you out of the world, therefore the world hateth you.
20. Remember the word that I said unto you, The servant is not greater than his lord. If they have persecuted me, they will also persecute you; if they have kept my saying, they will keep yours also.
21. But all these things will they do unto you for my name's sake, because they know not him that sent me.
22. If I had not come and spoken unto them, they had not had sin: but now they have no cloak for their sin.
23. He that hateth me hateth my Father also.
24. If I had not done among them the works which no other man did, they had not had sin: but now have they both seen and hated both me and my Father.
25. But this cometh to pass, that the word might be fulfilled that is written in their law: They hated me without a cause.

26. But when the Comforter is come, who I will send unto you from the Father, even the Spirit of truth, which proceedeth from the Father, he shall testify of me.

27. And ye also shall bear witness, because ye have been with me from the beginning.

Vs. 1. "I Am"—"ago aime"—Ἐγώ εἰμι—Last of the seven "I AM's."

"Husbandman": In Greek, "ga-orgos"—γεωργός—"ge"—"earth"—"orgos" = "worker" (Our name George derived from this.)

First "I Am" = Bread—seventh "I Am" = Wine.

"Bread" = "Life"—"Wine" = "Truth"—And here are the Two Trees of Paradise!

"I am the truth of that which the vine means"—which is indicated by the picture of the vine.

Vs. 2. "he purgeth" = "he cleanses": In Greek, "Käthairai"—καθαίρει—a purification, a catharsis.

"more fruit": In Greek, "plai-onä kärpon"—πλείονα καρπὸν—more, the purpose of the purification, a development, a going on. A progress out of it.

Vs. 3. Only the fact that Christ spoke had an effect of purification upon them. The aura of the Logos, working etherically in the world. Here the element of the word is restored to its original spirituality.

Vs. 4. In 6:56 we have the chapter of the bread. Here in 15:4, we have the chapter of the wine. In this Chapter 15, the word "meno"—μένω—(abide, remain, tarry) is used again and again. This motif dawns in 6:56 and increases greatly now. Note the development:

1) "Abide in me": (mainäte en emoi) (μείνατε ἐν ἐμοί) (Vs 4)

2) "He that abides in me": (ho menon en emoi) (ὁ μένων ἐν ἐμοί) (Vs 5)

3) "If you abide in me": (a-än meina en emoi) (ἐὰν μείνῃ ἐν ἐμοί) (Vs 7)

   a) In Verse 1, we are with the Father

   b) In Verse 5 ("I am the vine")—to the Disciples— The aspect of the Holy Spirit

   c) In Verse 6 ("If ye abide in me"(mena en emoi) (μένῃ ἐν ἐμοί)—the Son.

Vs. 5. "ye are able to do nothing": refers to the Chapter 14.

In Chapter 5:19, can't do anything without the Father

In Chapter 15:5, can't do anything without the Son.

Vs. 6. The negative aspect—"If anyone does not abide."

Vs. 7. This is the third time in the affirmative

Verses 4, 5, 7, = "Abide in me."

1) Verse 4: Imperative saying—"Abide in me"—the Father aspect

2) Verse 5: "Whoever"—"He"—The single individual out of the multitude—the Son aspect.

3) "If": a conditional, more the Holy Spirit aspect—The world of potentiality—plural "you."

The matter is left to their freedom. "My words"—not "my Ego"—It is by abiding in "my words" that the ability to abide in "my Ego" comes about. "Keeps my words": refers to 14:23. Through meditation on His words, we bring them to life in us. The Gospels are the bridge which leads us to the past in order to lead us to the actual meeting with Christ in the present. Through meditation upon the characteristic handwriting in the letters of a friend who has died, we can see him as he is now in the spiritual world. So through meditation on the words of Christ, we can contact him as he is now. (When reading to the dead, it is helpful to concentrate on a familiar, characteristic gesture, his or her walk, or the look of a friend—something connected particularly with him or her.)

In the Cinderella story, in order to fit the glass slipper, one sister cut off her toes (Luciferic part of the foot), the other her heel (Ahrimanic part).

There is a promise for the future in Verse 7—"be done" = "it shall happen to you."

Vs. 8. "In this is manifested my Father. . . . Ye shall become my disciples": In Greek, "emoi"—ἐμοί.

There *became* a human, but the Ego *WAS* (Chapter 1).

Vs. 9. Note the threefold structure here:

1) "As the Father loved me"
2) "I also loved you"
3) "Abide in my love"

This word "As": In Greek, "käthos"—καθὼσ = "Likewise"—which is repeated again in Verse 10—is important as a Johannine word. It adds to and extends the chain, the coverage of his words. In the threefold extension above, he extends this "ägäpa"—ἀγάπη—(love) to his disciples.

"continue"—"mainäte"—μείνατε—(from meno—μένω) "remain," "abide," "live" in my agape. "Be at home" in my agape.

"Agape" love comes out much more in Chapters 14 and 15, finally reaching a climax in Chapter 15.

Vs. 10. "If ye keep": Refers to cultivation, to meditation, to repeating and tending, to pondering.

There are three steps:

1) "Abide in me"—myself
2) "Abide in my words"—knowledge
3) "Abide in my love"—life (knowledge and life, the two Trees of Paradise). There is a graduation, a leading upward, step by step, to this "agape."

Vs. 11. "your joy may be full": This should be read: "be fulfilled," because "plarotha"—πληρωθῇ—is a verb. It is the root of the noun, "plaromä"—πλήρωμα—fullness.

"joy": Joy out of the Higher Ego—"not as the world gives." It can be an extension of His words about "My peace I give unto you."— So there is a gradual metamorphosis of the one first main statement going on: "I in you"—"I in you" = "my words", "my love", "my joy"—It is like meditating about this one idea, "I in you". So, this represents a great meditation on the subject of this mystical communion, "I in you"—and all these things (words, love, peace, joy) come out, like the many facets of a diamond, which produce many colors as the stone is turned in the sunlight. In connection with this 15:11, compare the negative aspect, in Chapter 8:37—"my words have no place in you."

"fulfilled" (plarotha) (πληρωθῇ) from "plaro-o"—πληρόω. This is a motif of John's Gospel—(Pleroma). Reference to John the Baptist, see Ch. 1:16.

"my joy": This typical Johannine motif begins in Ch. 3:29 "this my joy is therefore fulfilled." And this same motif continues through the Gospel to Easter, when (Ch. 20:20) the disciples were "glad, when they saw the Lord." The word doxa (glory) is another very typical motif of this Gospel.

Vs. 13. "lay down his life": his "psooschen"—(ψυχὴν)—his "soul" —This formula first appears in Chapter 10:15, et sequ, but note the metamorphosis now in 15:13. This verse points to a guarantee, a complete dedication of his "soul" to his friends.

No greater sacrifice can be made than that of your own soul—It is not a matter of "friends" or "enemies" in this verse. This verse points to the greatest sacrifice which anyone can make—it is a definition of "the greatest sacrifice."

"friends": In Greek, "felon"—φίλων—here is introduced a new motif. It is continued in Ch. 15:14—and appears three times:

1) for his friends" (15:13)
2) "my friends" (15:14)
3) "I called you friends" (15:15)

It is important to remember that whenever John introduces a new motif into his Gospel, he repeats it three times in order to give and build the emphasis upon it. Example: "bridegroom" (3:29), and many others. Note the development of this theme:

1) "gives for his friends" (15:13)—the friend who gives.
2) "you are my friends"(15:14)—direct
3) "I have named you friends" (15:15)—the name of the friend.

"Servants": (dooloos) (δούλους): This is an Old Testament motif. "The servant of the Lord," etc. This holds good no longer. A new level of possibility now opens. This is the level of "felos"—φίλος—(friend), and this "friend" is connected with knowledge—the sphere of the Holy Spirit. The "servant" is one who has no insight, no knowledge of the "telos"—τέλος—, the "aims" or "goals."—In other words, the "servant" stage is the stage of the old piety.—And now a new possibility opens to where there can be a higher state where the servant can see the purposes, aims, goals of the Lord on the basis of the "friend." This is like a child in relation to a parent. At first the child sees no purposes, no aims, no problems of the family and parents. He or she simply obeys. But later, he or she is let into the more intimate secrets of the family.

In Verse 14: "Ye are my friends if ye practice (poi-ate) (ποιῆτε) whatsoever I command you." The word "command" is "entel-lomai"—ἐντέλλομαι—related to "telos"—τέλος—"aim," "goal," "purpose"—and to "Tetelestai"—Τετέλεσται—the last word spoken from the cross.

"I heard": Related to 5:28 ("hear his voice"), also in Ch. 8:38 & 43 ("ye have heard of your father." and "ye cannot hear my word"). Also Ch. 11:41 & 42—("thou hast heard me," and "thou hearest me always").

Vs. 16. "that your fruit should last": (meno—μένω—remain, abide, last)—be permanent.

Seven Fulfillments of All Asking of the Disciples

    1) 14:13   5) 16:23

    2) 14:14   6) 16:24

    3) 15:7   7) 16:26

    4) 15:16

Vs. 17. This verse makes a cut, an incision, into the flow of the chapter.

Vs. 18. A look into the opposite of "agape"—into "hatred." To look into the "agape" carries with it the necessity to suffer from what is in the lower sense world the "hatred." This is the indispensable condition of knowledge of the higher, the spiritual, the divine, the agape. In this chapter of "love" (agape), John speaks in an apocalyptic way of the future. It is a "germ of the Apocalypse." It is a way of looking at the Act of Consecration:

1) The Cup—". . . the might of man's adversary Thou takest from me."

2) The Bread—". . . keep strong my soul, that it continue to live."

    The Bread points to the creation, something from the past.

    The Wine points to the future, to the Apocalypse.

"Darkness and Light": In Greek, "skote-ä"—σκοτία—and "fos"—φῶς—motif of John's Gospel—The Persian Motif in John's Gospel.

"mesa-o"—μισέω—"Hate"—Used seven times in the last part of Chapter 15 as follows: 1-2) 15:18 (two times); 3) 15:19; 4-5) 15:23 (two times); 6) 15:24; 7) 15:25.—This points to the mystery of hatred, the other side of hatred.—Who sees the one (agape) has to experience the other also.

Vs. 19. "If ye were of this world": This is a kind of background, a Johannine formula.—The suffering of Christ will be the suffering of the follower, as seen in the Apocalypse. The followers of Christ have to share his destiny, have to know him in the right way, *because without suffering we shall never come to an understanding of the Mystery of Golgotha.* Christianity does not do away with the necessity of suffering for Christians. There is nothing in the Apocalypse to indicate that we shall be relieved of suffering, but we can escape somewhat. We, like all, must die, but our dying can lead us upward instead of downward. If we see our suffering as a Communion with Christ, with spiritual effect in it, it is helpful. But, if we see it without the Christ, it is hell. Rejecting Christ is rejecting the Father. The reality of the Father God can only be found again by grasping our personal ego and connecting it with Christ. (This is all on Verses 19-25.)

Vs. 25. Note: "Their law": Now the Jews are a quite strange people to Him. "your law": (As in Ch. 8:17)—He separates himself from the Jews, but not so completely as in 15:25—"they hated me without a cause": Greek, "dora-än"—δωρεάν—"in the way of a gift": ("Gratis" = "grace).

There are two kinds of hatred:

1) Hatred arising out of causes, reasons: this we can understand.

2) Hatred arising out of karma, destiny: this we cannot understand.

A gift is an act of grace—a true gift. It is a creative action from above. And here (15:25) this hatred is like a caricature of a true gift. We often feel hatred coming to us only because the representatives of Christianity in the world are not worthy of Christianity, but they are never worthy of Christianity. But here (15:25) we see that Christ Himself, who is a worthy representative of Christianity, is hated freely! This is a hatred which comes out of the deeper layers of the soul.—Something like a "natural hated" will rise against the Christ—and He was the ideal representative of Christianity. So we need not be amazed or astonished when we find this hatred directed against us, even when it arises from within us. Indeed, we are lucky if we are not crucified, for our Master was, and we are not greater than our Lord! The verse could read: "They have hated me as one gives a present (a gift). (This is a quotation from Psalms 35:19, 69:4). And in this quotation from Ps. 35:19 here in John 15:25, we can see that John uses his quotations from the Old Testament in a much greater sense, a much deeper and wider application than the thoughts were originally used. They become much more transparent, translucent, and creative in his hands. This is the result of his seventy years of meditation on these things. Thus he did not quote in a pedantic or scholarly way, but truly creatively. The quotations from the Old Testament by John are really a chapter, a story, in themselves. Work should be done on this!

Vs. 26. "The Paraclete": In Greek, "päräklatos"—παράκλητος. Here the sevenfold mystery of hatred is connected with the Holy Spirit!—The aspect of the Comforter now comes in as a comfort for us in the face of this hatred. It is *not* enough to be a good person.—That will not relieve us of this hatred.—All will not "like us" at once because we are "good."

Vs. 27. The disciples are brought together with the Holy Spirit, a growing into the the work of the Holy Spirit. "The Holy Spirit goes forth from the Father, sent by the Son"—this is the Russian Orthodox viewpoint—more to the Past—A Luciferic aspect. The Roman Catholics, through the addition of the famous word, "filoque" (and the Son), say, "the Holy Ghost goes forth from the Father and the Son"—as in the alteration of the Nicean Creed.—This is more Ahrimanic. We try to take the way which will advance with the development of the human being.

John 16:1-33

1. These things have I spoken unto you, that you should not be offended.
2. They shall put you out of the synagogues: yea, the time cometh, that whosoever killeth you will think that he doeth God service.
3. And these things will they do unto you, because they have not known the Father, nor me.
4. But these things have I told you, that when the time shall come, ye may remember that I told you of them. And these things I said unto you at the beginning, because I was with you.
5. But now I go my way to him that sent me; and none of you asketh me, Whither goest thou?
6. But because I have said these things unto you, sorrow hath filled your heart.
7. Nevertheless I tell you the truth. It is expedient for you that I go away: for if I go not away, the Comforter will not come unto you; but if I depart, I will send him unto you.
8. And when he is come, he will reprove the world of sin, and of righteousness, and of judgment:
9. Of sin, because they believe not on me;
10. Of righteousness, because I go to my Father, and ye see me no more;
11. Of Judgment, because the prince of this world is judged.
12. I have yet many things to say unto you, but ye cannot bear them now.
13. Howbeit when he, the Spirit of truth, is come, he will guide you into all truth, for he shall not speak of himself; but

John 16:1–33

whatsoever he shall hear, that shall he speak, and he will shew you things to come.

14. He shall glorify me, for he shall receive of mine, and shall show it unto you.

15. All things that the Father hath are mine: therefore said I, that he shall take of mine, and shall shew it unto you.

16. A little while, and ye shall not see me again, and again, a little while, and ye shall see me, because I go to the Father.

17. Then said some of his disciples among themselves, What is this, that he saith unto us, A little while, and ye shall not see me, and again, a little while, and ye shall see me, and, Because I go to the Father?

18. They said therefore, What is this that he saith, A little while? We cannot tell what he saith.

19. Now Jesus knew that they were desirous to ask him and said unto them, Do ye enquire among yourselves of that I said, A little while, and ye shall not see me, and again, a little while, and ye shall see me?

20. Verily, verily, I say unto you that ye shall weep and lament, but the world shall rejoice; and ye shall be sorrowful, but your sorrow shall be turned into joy.

21. A woman when she is in travail hath sorrow, because her hour hath come, but as soon as she is delivered of the child, she remembereth no more the anguish, for joy that a man is born into the world.

22. And ye now therefore have sorrow, but I will see you again, and your heart shall rejoice, and your joy no man taketh from you.

23. And in that day ye shall ask me nothing. Verily, verily, I say unto you, whatsoever ye shall ask the Father in my name, he will give it you.

24. Hitherto have ye asked nothing in my name: ask, and ye shall receive, that your joy may be full.

25. These things have I spoken to you in proverbs, but the time cometh, when I shall no more speak unto you in proverbs, but I shall shew you plainly of the Father.

26. At that day ye shall ask in my name, and I say not unto you, that I will pray the Father for you:

27. For the Father himself loveth you, because ye have loved me, and have believed that I came out from God.

28. I came forth from the Father, and am come into the world: again I leave the world, and go to the Father.

29. His disciples said unto him, Lo, now speakest thou plainly, and speakest no proverb.

30. Now are we sure that thou knowest all things, and needest not that any man should ask thee: by this we believe that thou camest forth from God.

31. Jesus answered them, Do ye now believe?

32. Behold, the hour cometh, yea, now is come, that ye shall be scattered, every man to his own, and shall leave me alone: and yet I am never alone, because the Father is with me.

33. These things I have spoken unto you, that in me ye might have peace. In the world ye shall have tribulation: but be of good cheer, I have overcome the world.

Vs. 1. "offended": In Greek, "skändälisthate"—σκανδαλισθῆτε—"That you should not fall into a trap"—Like the Grimm Fairy Tale of the wicked mother who got her boy to put his head into a box to get apples, then brought down the lid and chopped his head off. His sphere of consciousness was cut off. This verse admonishes the disciples not to lose their consciousness in face of what He has told them is to come.

John 16:1–33

Vs. 2. "out of the synagogues": Greek, "äposoonägogoos"— ἀποσυναγώγους—"syn" = "together." "agoge" = "lead." The Apocalypse speaks of the Synagogue of Satan: "They will cast you out of the Community."

"God Service": A cultic sacrifice, a religious deed, act.

The appearance of the Christ is a crisis, a revolution. Old ties are going to decay. In Tacitus, we read that he said, "The Christians are enemies of humankind, because they believe in love." The love of the Christians appears to the Romans as hate. Ch. 16:2–8 reminds us of the events around the healing of the blind man in Chapter 9.

"The time comes" (Vs 2): In Greek, "erschetai horä"—ἔρχεται ὥρα—"the hour comes." They think they do God a service because they think the Christians threaten the divine foundations of the world.

Vs. 4. Apocalyptic aspect. A pointing to the future. This verse is a link between the Gospel and the Apocalypse. Christianity had no illusions about things going better on earth, advancing. That is an idea of eighteenth-century rationalism. For the Christians, the servant is not better than the Master, and the Master was crucified, so the servant is fortunate if he does not suffer the same fate! The famous phrase, "Christ extra nos"—and we grow into it. In Colossians, Paul points out that we fill up what Christ has left over in His Passion, pointing to the fact that there is something "left over" for the human being to do. For example, the martyrs entered into communion with Christ, the Mystery of Golgotha went on in them.

The Holy Spirit presupposes an "unholy" spirit, an evil spirit! It presupposes a higher consciousness distinguishing the spirits. We have to distinguish the *Holy* Spirit. In the Trinity, the Father and Son have no qualifications, but the Holy Spirit is qualified by the word *"Holy."*

Paraclete (Greek) = *Advocatus* (Latin) = *Advocate*. In Greek, *Para clete* includes root meaning—to call—sum it up. Paraclete—*The challenger!*

Vs. 5.—He points out that they should have asked him where he was going:

1) "I go to him"—a motif of Chapter 16:5, 16:10, 16:28

2) "I travel to the Father"—14:12, 14:28

3) "I come to thee"- 17:11, 17:13. (N.B. seven times in all)

There are three separate distinct verbs in Greek here—"go" "travel" "come."

Vs. 6. This is a reproach to them, because they are not objective enough. They do not take enough interest in the objective side of the work of Christ.

"Grief, sorrow": Greek, "Loopa"—λύπη—Corresponds exactly to the German word "Betrübnis," meaning grief, which is an expression of being "dimmed through tears."—Goethe used this word in the sense of "Trübe," where the heart is not a clear mirror.

Vs. 7. "expedient": "Good" in Greek original. It is good for them that he changes his material existence for one that is invisible. He must take on that kind of existence which will make Him available to all places on earth and in all time.

"The Paraclete": this is the fourth reference. Note the very fine interplay, the delicate metamorphosis which is going on. "I will send"—here the Father disappears behind. Here the Christ is the link between the Father and the Holy Spirit.

Vs. 8. Comforter "argues": Creates holy unrest. Thought and counter-thought does not leave us alone—makes for development—gives us unquietness of heart, moving us to God—argues about sin—no belief in Christianity—all sick.

Righteousness—right—originally meant "direction"—"right and left path."

Judgment (crisis): Greek, "kresa-os"—κρίσεως—Evolution can only proceed from crisis to crisis—we have share in this battle.

"reprove":—Latin, "Arguet" (Vulgate)—English, "argue"—Active aspect of the Comforter. Greek, "elexsai"—ἐλέγξει—"convict"— "give a consciousness to." He is to bring about a consciousness of 3 things: (1) sin; (2) righteousness; (3) judgment.

Vs. 9. Sin: The great cardinal sin of the Old Testament was in not being obedient to the Ten Commandments. An external, objective obedience to that which is outside one's self. The Rabbis in the time of Christ had to learn 300 positive and negative laws or commandments. The Gospel makes the point that Christ had never learned laws. In the great Commandment, "Ye should love one another," the laws—all 300 of them—are reduced to a single aspect. It is a grandiose reduction of the Old Testament to one commandment.

Sin—according to this Verse (16:9) then, is lack of faith in Christ. Actions which are done out of the connection of the heart with Christ are not sinful: all others are, regardless of their nature! Sin is a state of not being connected with Christ, to remain in our own natures. Luther had the right idea—not the single deeds, but the whole soil is to be considered—not to stress the good and bad actions, but to consider the soil, the root of the tree.

In Chapter 6:28, they speak of "works" (plural), but he points to "work" (singular) in 6:29. So he reduces all good works to one good, divine work: to make the connection, to open one's self to Christ. And here, in 16:9, all evil works are reduced to one sin, that of not being connected with Christ.

Vs. 10. Here righteousness is connected with the idea of the Ascension—that He changes to the invisible sphere for their benefit. In German, the word "Gericht" (righteousness, judgment) implies that upon which one can build—the correct foundations. So the right foundation for righteousness has to come from the sphere of the resurrection. This verse indicates that we have to look to the invisible for the foundation of the new world out of that which is possible "in itself"—and righteousness is the foundation of the new world, the New Jerusalem. Righteousness is a substance which has a guarantee to be eternal—Righteousness is a higher substance to be filled with a divine glory—a brightness, a shining that is righteousness.

Vs. 11. Here is another of the numbered Satanic names, "Prince of the World," in John's Gospel. Note that he "has been judged"—the perfect tense—completed—the act is done. But this has not yet been done outwardly at this point in the Gospel narrative. Here in saying this, Christ is lifted up in the sphere where the victory already approaches and is done, finished, completed. Then He has to return to the sphere in which it will be accomplished. For example, He can say, "I have overcome the world"—but after that comes Gethsemane and Golgotha! It is like the Apocalypse: first comes a great shout of triumph—"He that overcometh!" etc.—a great hymn of victory over the evil, and then after that, the Anti-Christ is set up on earth. It shows two different levels of consciousness: one, where the deed is seen as accomplished, and the other, which goes before it. It is like a kind of timelessness.

Each human being in himself or herself is the sole authority in spiritual things. I myself must take a stand for what is spiritual in the world and in me. Another may say, "All that is hallucination," but I have to take my stand. I have to make a place in my inner life for what is spiritual, and then stand behind it! The Greeks said, "The human being is the measure of all things."

Vs. 12-13. These verses are proof that the New Testament is not the final word, that something is left open. The Deed of Golgotha is to go on and on, and to become more understood in the future. Verse 13 leaves the matter open for the future, that not all is finished in the New Testament. The whole future is required to know what happened through the Mystery of Golgotha. Anthroposophy represents a vast body of knowledge which is really intended for understanding the Mystery of Golgotha in all its depth. All thinking is selfless, like the light. Light is like knowledge, an unobserved element, non-observed. Mere thinking is a spiritual force, and is a proof of spirituality. Truth is a selfless element—it does not speak of itself—like the light, making all things visible.

"He will lead": In the Greek it is, "He will guide you on the path."

Vs. 13. "Things coming": Greek, "erschomenä"—ἐρχόμενα—The apocalyptic theme: "He will announce": Greek, "änäggelai"—ἀναγελει—points to the "angelos," the "messenger," the "revealer." In Luke, the Trinity consists of: (1) the Father, (2) the Son, (3) the Angels:

One Side: (1) The Father, (2) the Son, (3) the Angels

Other Side: (1) The Father, (2) the Son, (3) Holy Spirit

Other Side: (1) The Father, (2) the Son, (3) the Saints, Church

Other Side: (1) The Father, (2) the Son, (3) the Apostles, Disciples.

The Angels, Saints, Church, Apostles, Disciples at various times in the Gospels and Epistles take the place of the third member of the Trinity.

SEVEN ASPECTS OF THE PARACLETE:

1) 14:17—The Paraclete is non-existent for the sense world, the physical world.

2) 14:26—The Paraclete as a teacher, a faculty for the human being—a working in the sphere of remembrance, of memory—the etheric.

3) 15:26—the Paraclete points to the faculty of "bearing witness": In Greek, "märtooraite"—μαρτυρεῖτε—"martyrs"—"witnesses who suffer hatred and experience love." The emotional, astral side.

4) 16:7—The Paraclete will reprove the world of sin—brings about a crisis in the world—a decision—necessity to "believe in ME" (Vs 9)—Points to the Ego—the "I AM" of Christ.

5) 16:13—The Paraclete will announce "things coming"—the full extent of the revelation, the apocalyptic side. This is the "Manas" activity.

6) 16:14—The Paraclete will "reveal," "manifest," "glorify" the Christ. This is the "Buddhi" side.

7) 16:15—The Paraclete will, through the manifestation of the things of the Son, reveal the Father God in the future.

Note: Numbers 5, 6, and 7 above are "buds" of the future possibility.

Verse 16:15 ends the Paraclete theme in John's Gospel. Only John's Gospel has the aspect of the Paraclete. It will be noted that the Paraclete at first is large (14:17), then it narrows more and more to the knowledge of the Father God. The aspect of coverage first is wide and then narrows down to include only one theme. It is like Anthroposophy, first very general, and at last narrowing to the Mystery of Golgotha, as the central theme, sum and substance.

Vs. 15. This verse must be compared with 17:10. The latter verse is a continuation of and a completion of this theme on a higher level. This theme is also to be found in the Prodigal Son Parable in Luke, "... all that I have is thine." And in this moment, the sphere of Luke touches that of John. From third person to direct address.

Vs. 16. Here a special Johannine theme word appears: In Greek, "Mekron"—Μικρὸν—"a little."—This word appears seven times here in the Greek text: 1-2) 16:16 (twice); 3-4) 16:17 (twice); 5) 16:18; 6-7) 16:19 (twice). This word "Mikron" (a little) points to the terrible events of His Passion as seen from above, from the Logos aspect. The apocalyptic aspect of His Passion. From such a height, apocalyptic events in the world seem to take only "a little while." It is a reduction of that which takes place on the physical plane to its proper, real size in relation to all other events. Thus the Passion, seen from this aspect, is only "a little while." There are THREE ASPECTS OF, OR WAYS TO VIEW, THE PASSION:

1) From the LOGOS aspect

2) From the CHRIST aspect

3) From the JESUS aspect

Vs. 19. This verse presents a picture of the whole world evolution:

John 16:1–33

1) First, humanity sees (saw) God
2) Then, lost (loses) sight of Him
3) Then, they will see Him again.

Vs. 20–21. The parable in embryo of the birth. This is a very deep and significant parable here, and especially because of this particular spot it occupies in the Gospel in its relation to all the other parts. All pain on earth should be a new birth to a higher connection with God, the birth of the higher human being. In Verse 20, his death is a rejoicing for the world because it brings about the redemption of the world. In Verse 21, not "a man," but "for joy that the human being is born into the world."

Also in Verse 21, "her hour is come," is a link, a leading over, to Chapter 17: "My hour is come."

Vs. 22. This verse is a compilation of 15:11, "that your joy may be fulfilled."

"see you": They not only see him, but He sees them. This points to the great mystery which was well known in Medieval times: "The look with which I see God is the same look with which God sees me." As we look, so are we looked at, or upon. The Altar picture looks at us in this way. It is as Paul says, "I shall know as I am known." Of the person who can love Christ, the Father can love that person more than otherwise. It is a new chance for the Spirit to help us. The flowers reveal their nature in their blossom.

"Joy": This "joy" (the word is repeated three times in Verses 20, 21, 22) is founded on inwardness, and can't be touched from outside. Because this joy is not given from outside, it can't be taken away by anything from outside. For example, in surface layers of the soul, we may be in pain, yet at the same moment, in yet deeper layers of the soul is joy. This joy which is founded in Christ, comes from the Higher Ego, and this is true of "my peace," and "my commandment," etc.

"your heart": Greek, "hoomon ha kärde-ä"—ὑμῶν ἡ καρδία—The mystery of the heart, which belongs to your innermost being. The heart is the innermost center of the ego.

"I will see you again": this is the verse which, of all of John's Gospel, first struck Dr. Rittlemeyer when he was still a Lutheran Pastor in Nüremburg. It was a great moment in his life. He loved the part of Brahm's "Requiem" which begins with these words, and frequently played it on his piano. (He was an accomplished pianist). While waiting to take a train for Berlin, his last leave-taking from his home—for he died on this journey, in Hamburg—he sat down at the piano and played this selection. (Mrs. Rittlemeyer told Dr. Frieling this).

Vs. 23. The higher worlds cannot give, unless we hold up empty vessels. (Note the last part of the Foundation Stone mantram on this.) The disciples give to their souls the proper shape into which the spiritual gifts can be given.

Fulfilled: (Related to "plaro-ä"—πλήρωα—"Fullness")

1) 3:29—"Peplarotai"—πεπλήρωται
2) 15:11—"Plarotha"—πληρωθῇ
3) 16:24 — "Peplaromena" — πεπληρωμένη — (Perfect Tense) Fulfilled in You.—"The fulfillment of the spiritual world will be in your joy."

See in the Midnight Hour Scene of the Fourth Mystery Drama, Maria's speech of joy. Also the "Iphigenia" of Goethe speaks of "the sea of joy."

Vs. 25. "proverbs": not good. Should read, "hidden words." The term "allegories" is too technical, too cold.

"Plainly": Should read, "directly." The word is the real thing, not an image. (Imagination) of something, on which we have to work.

"The Father": The last, ultimate, spiritual reality.

Vs. 26. Now a very intimate sphere is reached. This verse is not an intercession, but points to the fact that Christ is now related to the disciples. He is *in* them; he is not removed from them, but is *in* them!

John 16:1–33

Vs. 27. Not "the Father loveth," but "the Father likes,": Greek, "felai"—φιλεῖ.

Here begins one of the MOST CENTRAL EXPOSITIONS OF THE GOSPEL OF JOHN:

- How Christ comes out of eternity, goes through the world, and returns to eternity again. This is a very special and deep Meditation of Christ. It is spoken out of the deepest Intuition, in which one spirit speaks to another spirit, and the disciples really understand Him now.

- "I came out from beside God": (as from a sitting position).

Vs. 28. (I came out of the innermost being of the Father.)

1) "I came out from the Father"
2) "And have come into the world"
3) "I leave the world and go to the Father"

Vs. 29. "Lo": Greek, "Eda"—Ἴδε—(idea) = "Look!" They really understood Him now!

"Now": Greek, "noon"—νῦν—very forceful form—"in italics."

Vs. 30. Again the "Now"—Very forcefully! (Verse 30 should be compared with Verse 26).

"Anyone": There is now no need of questions coming from outside to raise knowledge from the subconscious to the conscious.

"We believe" = "On this rests our faith."

Vs. 32. "Scattered": Greek, "skorpisthate"—σκορπισθῆτε—The English word "Scorpion" related to this. The Gospel of John has to do with the sign of the Scorpion.

"To his own": Greek, "tä ede-ä"—τὰ Ἴδια—(appears three times). Through the Scorpion, each will be thrown into the prison of his or her own personal world.

"TÄ EDE-Ä"—τὰ Ἴδια—("His Own")

1) "Unto his own"—1:11
2) "To his own (personality)"—16:32
3) "Took her to his own"—19:27

This is balanced by, "I am not alone":

1) "I am not alone"—8:16
2) "Father hath not left me alone"—8:29
3) "I am not alone"—16:32

16:33—This is a continuation of 14:27—The Peace.

Greek, "airanen"—εἰρήνην—peace

"airanan" ("Peace"):

1) "Peace I leave"—14:27
2) "My peace I give"—14:27
3) "Peace in me"—16:33—This is the third aspect of the Holy Spirit.

"In me Peace": Greek, "En emoi airanen"—ἐν ἐμοί εἰρήνην—"Peace in my Ego"

"Tribulation": Greek, "Thlepsin"—θλῖψιν—The action of millstones, grinding, polishing, the pressure of the millstones of matter—what we experience in the world, the grinding down action by matter of the world upon our soul forces.

"I (Ego) have overcome the world": "my "I" has overcome the world."—The obstacle of a world "kosmon"—κόσμον—which has become separated from God. This hindrance has to be overcome—(points to the use of "overcome" in the Apocalypse). The obstacle between the spiritual world and its effect upon us has to be overcome. This is our necessity.

"Overcome": Greek, "nenekakä"—νενίκηκα—from "neka"—νίκη—meaning "victory"—So victory is included!

Apocalypse "overcomes": Greek, "nekä-o"—νικάω—And there are seven promises connected with this.

The human being is not finished. The creative act goes on, and human beings must participate in their own creation by "overcoming" the obstacles, by overcoming a certain force. That which is the specifically human element in the world can only come into being through "overcoming." We have to become good by our own effort. We have to live with and overcome sin and death, so they become our goodness. It is not enough to be passively good in the world. The human being is essentially a victor. The Apocalypse begins here (16:33) in John's Gospel. Overcome: Greek, "nenikakä"—νενίκηκα; in Apocalypse 5:5, it is "enekasen"—ἐνίκησεν. So this verse (16:33) is the germ of the whole Apocalypse.

John 17:1-26

1. These words spake Jesus, and lifted up his eyes to heaven, and said, Father, the hour is come; glorify thy Son, that thy Son may also glorify thee.
2. As thou hast given him power over all flesh, that he should give eternal life to as many as thou hast given him.
3. And this is life eternal, that they might know thee the only true God, and Jesus Christ, whom thou hast sent.
4. I have glorified thee on the earth: I have finished the work which thou gavest me to do.
5. And now, O Father, glorify me with thine own self with the glory which I had with thee before the world was.
6. I have manifested thy name unto the men which thou gavest me out of the world: thine they were, and thou gavest them me; and they have kept thy word.
7. Now they have known that all things whatsoever thou has given me are of thee.
8. For I have given unto them the words which thou gavest me; and they have received them, and have known surely that I came out from thee, and they have believed that thou didst send me.
9. I pray for them: I pray not for the world, but for them which thou hast given me; for they are thine.
10. And all mine are thine, and thine are mine; and I am glorified in them.
11. And now I am no more in the world, but these are in the world, and I come to thee. Holy Father, keep through thine own name those whom thou has given me that they may be one, as we are.

John 17:1–26

12. While I was with them in the world, I kept them in thy name, those that thou gavest me I have kept, and none of them is lost, but the son of perdition; that the scripture might be fulfilled.

13. And now come I to thee, and these things I speak in the world, that they might have my joy fulfilled in themselves.

14. I have given them thy word; and the world hath hated them, because they are not of the world, even as I am not of the world.

15. I pray not that thou shouldest take them out of the world, but that thou shouldest keep them from the evil.

16. They are not of the world, even as I am not of the world.

17. Sanctify them through thy truth; thy word is truth.

18. As thou hast sent me into the world, even so have I also sent them into the world.

19. And for their sakes I sanctify myself, that they also might be sanctified through the truth.

20. Neither pray I for these alone, but for them also which shall believe on me through their word;

21. That they all may be one; as thou Father, are in me, and I in thee, that they also may be one in us: that the world may believe that thou hast sent me.

22. And the glory which thou gavest me I have given them; that they may be one, even as we are one:

23. I in them and thou in me, that they may be made perfect in one; and that the world may know that thou hast sent me, and hast loved them, as thou hast loved me.

24. Father, I will that they also, whom thou hast given me, be with me where I am; that they may behold my glory, which thou hast given me, for thou lovest me before the foundation of the world.

25. O righteous Father, the world hath not known thee, but I have known thee, and these have known that thou hast me.

26. And I have declared unto them thy name, and will declare it, that the love wherewith thou hast loved me may be in them, and I in them.

THE "HIGH PRIESTLY PRAYER"

First Part of the High Priestly Prayer

This is the third prayer in John's Gospel. All three of the prayers begin with the word, "Father" (Pater).

1) "Father, I thank Thee" 11:41
2) "Father, save me" 12:27
3) "Father, the hour is come" 17:1

The High Priestly prayer is divided into three parts:

1) Verses 1–5—To the Father—The eternal relation of Christ to the Father. (Past)
2) Verses 6–19—To the Disciples—Aspect of the Present.
3) Verses 20–26—To the Future of humanity.

This prayer is related to the Prologue, which is in three parts:

1) Verses 1–5—The Father and the Word
2) Verses 6–13—Regarding John the Baptist
3) Verses 14–18—To the future

"The Hour has come" (the third and last reference)

1) "The hour is come" 12:23
2) "His hour was come" 13:1
3) "The hour is come" 17:1

John 17:1–26

"glorify" = "make cognizable." One depends upon the other: the Son on the Father, the Father on the Son.

Vs. 2. "As" Greek, "käthos"—καθὼς—This plays a great role as a word in John's Gospel. It points to the fact that there are mirrors in the world, gradations, reflections.

"Authority": (King James Version—"Power"). In Greek, "exoosiän"—ἐξουσίαν—related to the "Exusiae."

"Flesh": In Greek, "särkos"—σαρκός—This key word of John is mentioned here for the last time. This "authority over all flesh" refers especially to the physical body. The Exusiae formed the ego, and the ego formed the physical body ("flesh," "Sarks"). This verse anticipates Easter.

"All . . . him": In Greek, "pän . . . auto"—πᾶν . . . αὐτῷ—as in 6:38. From the neuter ("all") to the definite ("him").

"Life eternal": In Greek, "Tso-en ai-on-e-on"—ζωὴν αἰώνιον—Related to Chapter 6—the whole question of "life."

Vs. 3.—"Life eternal . . . Know": In Greek, "Tso-en ai-one-on . . . genoskosin"—ζωὴν αἰώνιον . . . γινώσκωσιν. Here life and knowledge are united again. The two trees of Paradise are reunited.

"only": Greek, "monon"—μόνον—(related to "meno"—μένω) = "unique." It corresponds to the ego. Without an ego in the human, the human being could not recognize the Ego in God. It is not the difference between Monotheism and Polytheism in a narrow sense.

"monos"—μόνος—("meno"—μένω) That which is kept for eternity. This points to the famous words of Plantinus—"The escape of the unique one to the sphere of the unique one." What is escaped is "Latha"—λήθη—"forgetfulness."

In this passage, the Christ is in the Logos consciousness, and looks down upon himself below. The prayer is based on three levels of consciousness:

1) Sphere of the Logos consciousness
2) Sphere of the Christ consciousness
3) Sphere of the Jesus consciousness

Compare in the Prologue 1:17 with 17:3—"Jesus Christ."

Vs. 4. A changing of level here. From third person to first person: "From Jesus Christ" to "I." First it is objective in "the son," then it grows to subjective "I." Here we come to the sphere of personal intercourse, in which the "I" and the "Thee" are together.

"Completed": In Greek, "etelaithsä"—ἐτελείθσα—This word includes the word "telos"—τέλος—which appears three times in John's Gospel:

1) "To finish his work" (4:34) (connection with "poi-a-o"—ποιέω)
2) "Given me to finish" (5:36)
3) "The work I finished" (17:4)

This points to the fact that human beings are not on earth as a trial or probation prepatory to heaven or hell. Through their work on earth, they add something which is not superficial, something which will act to bring the world to perfection. Their work has real meaning for the world, because it is a continuation of world creation.

"thou gavest me": this work was given as a gift, as a grace—and here the last trace of Lucifer is wiped out.

Vs. 5. This points to the pre-earthly existence of Christ—an aspect of the Christ. This appears three times in John's Gospel:

1) "Before Abraham was, I am"—8:58
2) "Before the world was"—17:5
3) "Before the foundations"—17:24

Before there was a material, sense world.

This is the End of the First Section of this Prayer

The Second Part of the High Priestly Prayer (Vs 6–19)

Vs. 6. Here we come to a new sphere—that of the Disciples.

"Gavest": In Greek, "dedokäs"—δέδωκας—"given" (dedicated)

"they have preserved Thy Logos": in Greek, "logon"—λόγον—The way for the preservation of the world goes through the human beings who love Christ.

Vs. 7. "Thou hast given": Compare: 16:15, 17:9, and 17:10. In 17:9, he gives back all to the Father—It is a kind of Offertory, an answer to a divine sacrifice.

Vs. 8. "Words": Greek, "hramätä"- ῥήματα—Not "Logos." Note that this "hramätä"—ῥήματα—has to do with the quality or action expressed in the Greek word, "hra-o"—ῥέω—meaning "flow"—and points to the etheric stream going through the words.

Vs. 9. "Known and believed": the Light of Knowledge and the Warmth of Belief.

Vs. 11. A future aspect. Like "I have overcome the world." A difference between levels here. In this verse, the special Johannine key word "*kai*" ("but," or "and") appears three times.

"I come to Thee": This is the last and most personal formula.

"Name"—the name is a summary of all that which can be known of a being.

"käthos"—καθὼς—Another special Johannine key word—"As."

"hen"—ἕν—("one")—this is another special word—seven times:

1) "I and my Father are one" (10:30)

2) "Gather together in one" (11:52)

3) "That they may be one" (17:11)

4) "That they all may be one" (17:21)

5) "They may be one in us" (17:22)

6) "They may be one as we" (17:22)

7) "They may be perfected into one" (17:23)

Here we can see how Chapter 10 anticipates Chapter 17, and it should be studied in connection with it.

There are three forms of ONE in Greek (masculine, feminine, neuter), and all are used in John's Gospel. In the masculine sense, one (unus in Latin) points to the mystery of the Ego. Above, the seven-times-used "ONE" is the neuter form, "hen"—ἕν—(Latin, unum)—and this mysterious form is a specialty of John's Gospel. It is like "that holy thing" referred to by Gabriel in Luke's Gospel. It is that which belongs to the Holy Spirit—That which is superpersonal (God).

The "as we" in 17:11 refers to "I and my Father" in 10:30.

"We": Greek, "hamais"—ἡμεῖς—this is a new word in John's Gospel. It points to the fact that John's Gospel is the Gospel of the "We." In the Prologue, the human "We"—"hamais"—ἡμεῖς—appears three times:

1) "among us" (1:14) (Christmas)

2) "we beheld" (1:14) (Easter)

3) "we received" (1:16) (Whitsuntide)

These represent three growing phases of the "we" in the Prologue of the Gospel.

In the High Priestly Prayer (Chapter 17) we have the "divine We" shown three times:

1) "they may be one as we" (17:11)

2) "they may be one in us" (17:21)

3) "they may be one as we" (17:22)

The real Ego of Christ is the root of all real community in the world.

Vs. 12. "the son of perdition": A typical Oriental saying. An expression of the background of the individual. The prophecy of the scriptures in the stars, the eternal necessities in the world—the tragic and eternal necessities.

Vs. 13. The third and last time in John's Gospel of the key expression: "I come to thee."

1) 15:11—"Your joy might be fulfilled"
2) 16:24—"Your joy may be fulfilled"
3) 17:13—"My joy fulfilled in themselves"

The last (17:13) is a flowing together of the other two.

"My": In Greek, "emen"—ἐμήν—from "emoi"—ἐμοί—The first time this word appears in the High Priestly Prayer.

"Fulfilled": Greek, "peplaromenen"—πεπληρωμένην—"Full"—but in the very "fullest" sense—"very full."

"In them": Greek, "En autois"—ἐν αὐτοῖς—"In their very selves."

Vs. 14. "Ek"—ἐκ—("Of")—Greek—The word really is to be translated "from"—and points to that which is not rooted, nourished, or subsisting in the sense world. This is a very important key word of the Gospels and Epistles of John.

Vs. 15. Note that this is a negative, and the negations are very interesting in John's Gospel. Pay special attention to them. Christianity is not Buddhistic. It is Buddhistic and not Christian to wish or seek to escape from the sense world. It means something that we are in the sense world. Human beings have to be exposed to the evil in order to reach their goals. They have to take risks. "Them" refers to all who wish to follow Christ.

Vs. 17. "Sanctify": This is the meaning of sacrifice. It is an offering made through sacrifice.

Vs. 18. "sent them into the world"—this is repeated in Chapters 20 and 21. There he "breathed upon them," etc.

"As"—Käthos—καθώς—a proportion.

The Third Part of the High Priestly Prayer (Vs 20–26)

Vs. 20. This verse opens the third part of the prayer with a view to the fulfillment of the Holy Spirit in the future.

Vs. 21. This verse points to Chapter 14.

Vs. 22. The last formula of the whole theme.—This formula first appears in Chapter 10. It is like the development in Goethe's *Metamorphosis of Plants*, very delicate and gentle, but clear.

Vs. 23. "Perfected": In Greek, "Tetelai-omenoi"—τετελειωμένοι—from "telos"—τέλος—, "aim" or "goal."

— The personal sphere is reached in this verse. In this verse (23), "the world may know," whereas in Verse 21, "the world may believe." In Verse 23 the highest of all Johannine words appears: "AGAPE."

Vs. 24. From "hoos"—οὕς—("whom" or "what")—that which is more neutral, neuter, to "käkainoi"—κἀκεῖνοι—("they")—the personal form: to the single individual.

— Third time: "they be with me where I am"—see the notes for Chapter 14:3.

— The formula "they can come" (positive) is used three times.

— The formula "they cannot come" (negative) is used three times.

— This verse 24 contains the third aspect of the pre-existence of Christ.

"My Glory" is like "My Joy"—it is the glory which Thou hast given me. It represents a kind of Christianization of Lucifer by identifying His [Christ's] "MY" with what "Thou hast given me." It is a connecting of giving with love, and this overcomes Lucifer. The connecting of "power over all flesh," overcomes Ahriman.

"Foundation of the World": Greek, "kätäbolas kosmoo"—καταβολῆς κόσμου. "To Throw Down": "throwing off," in the sense that the animals are said to "throw off" their young—as a young being is "thrown off." It is a throwing out of the Spirit into the sphere where the creation can be realized, recognized, can become a reality.

Vs. 25. "know": In Greek, "egnosän"—ἔγνωσαν—the highest form of "knowing" (Gnosis, Gnostic) in the Greek language is referred to here. They did not know the Father, but they did know the Christ, the "Me"—the "I AM."

Vs. 26. This verse is an exact reflection of Ch. 12:28. The following from this verse is the highest formulation, the highest metamorphosis of all Christianity:

"That the Love wherewith Thou hast loved me, may be in them, and I in them."

— This is a gentle metamorphosis which runs through the whole chapter, embracing "Thou in me," and "I in the Father."

Special Note:

17:11—"Holy Father"—is connected with "preserve me from evil."

17:25—"Righteous Father"—connected with the deepest necessities of the karma-knowledge. A pointing to the highest sphere of knowledge where the mysteries of the world find their solution, and the workings and necessities of karma become clear to one.

John 18:1-40

1. When Jesus had spoken these words, he went forth with his disciples over the brook Cedron, where was a garden, into the which he entered, and his disciples.
2. And Judas also, which betrayed him, knew the place, for Jesus ofttimes resorted thither with his disciples.
3. Judas then, having received a band of men and officers from the chief priests and Pharisees, cometh thither with lanterns and torches and weapons.
4. Jesus therefore, knowing all things that should come upon him, went forth, and said unto them, Whom seek ye?
5. They answered him, Jesus of Nazareth. Jesus said unto them, I am he. And Judas also, which betrayed him, stood with them.
6. As soon then as he had said unto them, I am he, they went backward, and fell to the ground.
7. Then asked he them again, Whom seek ye? And they said, Jesus of Nazareth.
8. Jesus answered, I have told you that I am he; if therefore ye seek me, let these go their way.
9. That the saying might be fulfilled, which he spake, Of them which thou gavest me have I lost none.
10. Then Simon Peter having a sword drew it, and smote the high priest's servant, and cut off his right ear. The servant's name was Malchus.
11. Then said Jesus unto Peter, Put up thy sword into the sheath; the cup which my Father hath given me, shall I not drink it?
12. Then the band and the captain and officers of the Jews took Jesus, and bound him,

13. And led him away to Annas first; for he was father-in-law to Caiaphas, which was the high priest that same year.

14. Now Caiaphas was he, which gave counsel to the Jews, that it was expedient that one man should die for the people.

15. And Simon Peter followed Jesus, and so did another disciple, and that disciple was known unto the high priest, and went in with Jesus into the palace of the high priest.

16. But Peter stood at the door without. Then went out that other disciple, which was known unto the high priest, and spake unto her that kept the door, and brought in Peter.

17. Then saith the damsel that kept the door unto Peter, Art not thou also one of this man's disciples? He saith, I am not.

18. And the servants and officers stood there, who had made a fire of coals, for it was cold, and they warmed themselves, and Peter stood with them, and warmed himself.

19. The high priest then asked Jesus of his disciples, and of his doctrine.

20. Jesus answered him, I spake openly to the world; I ever taught in the synagogue, and in the temple, whither the Jews always resort; and in secret have I said nothing.

21. Why askest thou me? Ask them which heard me, what I have said unto them; behold, they know what I have said.

22. And when he had thus spoken, one of the officers which stood by struck Jesus with the palm of his hand, saying, Answerest thou the high priest so?

23. Jesus answered him, If I have spoken evil, bear witness of the evil: but if well, why smitest thou me?

24. Now Annas had sent him bound unto Caiaphas the high priest.

25. And Simon Peter stood and warmed himself. They said therefore unto him, Art not thou also one of his disciples? He denied it, and said, I am not.

26. One of the servants of the high priest, being his kinsman whose ear Peter cut off, saith, Did I not see thee in the garden with him?

27. Peter then denied again, and immediately the cock crew.

28. Then led they Jesus from Caiaphas unto the hall of judgment, and it was early; and they themselves went not into the judgment hall, lest they should be defiled; but that they might eat the Passover.

29. Pilate then went out unto them, and said, What accusation bring ye against this man?

30. They answered and said unto him, If he were not a malefactor, we would not have delivered him up to thee.

31. Then said Pilate unto them, Take ye him, and judge him according to your law. The Jews therefore said unto him, It is not lawful for us to put any man to death:

32. That the saying of Jesus might be fulfilled, which he spake, signifying what death he should die.

33. Then Pilate entered into the judgment hall again, and called Jesus, and said unto him, Art thou the King of the Jews?

34. Jesus answered him, Sayest thou this thing of thyself, or did others tell it thee of me?

35. Pilate answered, Am I a Jew? Thine own nation, and the chief priests have delivered thee unto me; what hast thou done?

36. Jesus answered, My kingdom is not of this world: if my kingdom were of this world, then would my servants fight, that I should not be delivered to the Jews, but now is my kingdom not from hence.

37. Pilate therefore said unto him, Art thou a king then? Jesus answered, Thou sayest that I am a king. To this end was I born, and for this cause came I into the world, that I should

bear witness unto the truth. Every one that is of the truth heareth my voice.

38. Pilate saith unto him, What is truth? And when he said this, he went out again unto the Jews, and saith unto them, I find in him no fault at all.

39. But ye have a custom, that I should release unto you one at the Passover: will ye therefore that I release unto you the King of the Jews?

40. Then cried they all again, saying, Not this man, but Barabbas. Now Barabbas was a robber.

Vs. 1. "Kedron"—κεδρών—is the brook in the valley between the Mount of Olives and the mountain on which the Temple was built.

Vs. 4. The first speech of Christ

Vs. 5. The first speech of the "Ago aime"—Εγώ είμι—(I Am).

Vs. 6. The second speech of the "Ago aime)—Εγώ είμι—(I Am) (Quoted)

Vs. 8. The third speech of the "Ago aime)—Εγώ είμι—(I Am)—More directly.

Vs. 6. "Fell to the Ground": In Greek, "schämai"—χαμαί—From which "chemistry," "alchemy," etc., are derived. It is an Egyptian word, not a Greek word!

Vs. 11. "Doing the will of God" is like the "food."

"Suffering the will of God" is like the "drink" (the Cup). (See Chapter 4 of John's Gospel. Also Rittlemeyer's "Studies in the Gospel of John."

Vs. 12. "Captain": Greek, "schele-ärschos"—χιλίαρχος—Commander of a thousand soldiers—A very high ranking officer—the head of the Roman garrison in Jerusalem.

Vs. 13. Annas—a man of 80 years, a dreadful Saduccee figure—Ahrimanic man like the Doge Dandallo of Venice. Interested only in revenues and the commissions and income from the Temple—in business, not in religion at all!

"That year": As quoted before, Ch. 11:49.

Vs. 14. "expedient that one"—Ch. 11:50 (Quoted first after the Lazarus scene).

Vs. 15. "Another disciple": John—This shows that he had connections in the Temple at Jerusalem.

Christ had Three Trials:

1) The Trial before Annas
2) The Trial before Caiaphas
3) The Trial before Pilate and the People

(This is a kind of opposite to the three Christmas services.)

— The Trials before Annas and Caiaphas were not really trials with judgements following, because it was Jewish law that no judgement of death could be given at night, in the night. (The indication of morning comes in Verse 28, "it was early." (Beginning of the "Peter interpolation" scene.)

Vs. 17. Peter's first Denial: "Ook aime"—Οὐκ εἰμί—after the three times "Ago aime"—Εγώ εἰμί—of Christ.

Vs. 19. The Beginning of the hearings before Caiphas.

Vs. 20. The sixth speech of Jesus.

Vs. 23. The seventh speech of Jesus.

Vs. **25.** A return to the "Peter scene"—the second "Ook aime"—Οὐκ εἰμί.

Vs. 27. The third "ook eime" only indicated—The other Gospels give more details of Peter's reaction.

In Verses 20 and 21, "Ego" ("I") spoken by Christ three times before the second and third "Ook aime"—Οὐκ εἰμί—of Peter.

From Verse 27, the Christ speaks only seven times more before the resurrection:

To Pilate he speaks four times.

On the cross he speaks three times—a total of seven.

In the Gospels of Matthew and Mark, the Caiaphas scene (Vs 20-23, John's Gospel, Ch. 18) and Luke only speak of the morning assembly.

"Warming" in Verse 18 is taken up and continued onward in Verse 25.

Beginning with verse 28 come seven scenes, passing from outside (exoteric) to inside (esoteric), very interestingly arranged from a dramatic compositional standpoint.

Scene 1

Vs. 29. An Outside Scene—more exoteric nature. It begins with a very routine Roman legalistic question. Typical of the Roman judiciary. Pilate was in Jerusalem at this time because of possible revolutions when 10 million people gathered in Jerusalem for the Passover season. It created a very difficult and tense atmosphere. Pilate did not live in this "strange" Jewish religious center, but at Caesarea on the sea. When the Romans sought to set up Caligula's statue in the Temple in Jerusalem, 40,000 Jews went out to Caesarea to offer themselves as a sacrifice before the Romans' swords rather than let the Temple be profaned by the erection of a human statue. Even the Roman Aquilae ("eagles") carried at the head of each Legion, were not permitted to be brought or carried into Jerusalem. Such was the religious fanaticism of the Jews at this time. Therefore, at this Passover time, Pilate, his chief army officer, and Pilate's wife were in Jerusalem. Matthew's Gospel gives details concerning Pilate's wife and her dream.

Vs. 30. Their reply shows how "touchy' and "on edge" the Jews were at this moment.

Vs. 30–31. Tiberius, the Roman Emperor, had removed the right of "legis gladii" (capital punishment) from the Jews just at this time. If the Jews had had the right of capital punishment, they would have stoned Jesus to death, because that was their custom. The crucifixion was the Roman method. Thus the Christ had prophesied long before that He would die by a "lifting-up." In Greek, "hoopso-o"—ὑψόω—and had repeated this three times in John's Gospel. Therefore, this kind of death was essential.

Scene 2

Vs. 33. Note the frequency of the word "in" here. This is one of the most esoteric of the seven scenes.

Vs. 34. This is the first of the four Jesus-speeches to Pilate.

Vs. 36. This is the second of the four Jesus-speeches to Pilate.

— The "MY" (capitals)—"MY Kingdom"—the Kingdom of the Higher Ego. In this Verse 36, the words, "My Kingdom," occur three times. The Greek text says, "My kingdom is not *from* this world."—It does not have its roots or origin or existence in this sense world.

Vs. 37. The third of the Jesus-speeches to Pilate. This is one of the *most essential elements of Christianity*—that one frees the other person, in order that the other person may recognize the truth. "You say it"—"You must say it"—"Soo Legais"—Σὺ Λέγεις—Jesus does not ask for confirmation. It is Pilate's ("your") part to acknowledge Christianity.

"I" (Ego)—All of the Passion is done out of the utmost clarity of consciousness.

"Heareth my voice":

1) The voice of the Bridegroom—Cana Wedding

2) Sheperd's voice—Chapter 10

3) "Heareth my voice"—Ch. 18:37.

Verse 37 has a Threefold Structure:

1) "Thou sayest I am a King"—The Father
2) "For this cause ... unto the truth"—The Son—Christ
3) "Everyone ... my voice"—The Holy Spirit.

Scene 3

Vs. 38. "He went out"—exoteric

Vs. 40. "a robber" or "a murderer"—A special "short line"—a Johaninne insertion—typical of John. It is like the line after the scene in Ch. 13, vs 30. In some early versions of John's Gospel, Barabbas has a first name "Jesus," i.e., "Jesus-Barabbas."

In Chapter 19 the scene here goes straight on—no break in the continuity—note the Greek text.

John 19:1-42

1. Then Pilate therefore took Jesus, and scourged him.
2. And the soldiers platted a crown of thorns, and put it on his head, and they put on him a purple robe,
3. And said, Hail, King of the Jews! and they smote him with their hands.
4. Pilate therefore went forth again, and saith unto them, Behold, I bring him forth to you, that ye may know that I find no fault in him.
5. Then came Jesus forth, wearing the crown of thorns, and the purple robe. And Pilate saith unto them, Behold the Man!
6. When the chief priests therefore and officers saw him, they cried out, saying, Crucify him, crucify him. Pilate saith unto them, Take ye him, and crucify him, for I find no fault in him.
7. The Jews answered him, We have a law, and by our law he ought to die, because he made himself the Son of God.
8. When Pilate therefore heard that saying, he was the more afraid,
9. And went again into the judgment hall, and saith unto Jesus, Whence art thou? But Jesus gave him no answer.
10. Then saith Pilate unto him, Speakest thou not unto me? Knowest thou not that I have power to crucify thee, and have power to release thee?
11. Jesus answered, Thou couldst have no power at all against me, except it were given thee from above: therefore he that delivered me unto thee hath the greater sin.
12. And from thenceforth Pilate sought to release him, but the Jews cried out, saying, If thou let this man go, thou are not

Caesar's friend; whosoever make himself a King speaketh against Caesar.

13. When Pilate therefore heard that saying, he brought Jesus forth, and sat down in the judgment seat in a place that is called the Pavement, but in the Hebrew, Gabbatha.

14. And it was the preparation of the Passover, and about the sixth hour, and he saith unto the Jews, Behold your King!

15. But they cried out, Away with him, away with him, crucify him. Pilate saith unto them, Shall I crucify your King? The chief priests answered, We have no King but Caesar.

16. Then delivered he him therefore unto them to be crucified. And they took Jesus and led him away.

17. And he bearing his cross went forth into a place called the place of a skull, which is called in the Hebrew Golgotha:

18. Where they crucified him, and two others with him, on either side one, and Jesus in the midst.

19. And Pilate wrote a title, and put it on the cross. And the writing was, JESUS OF NAZARETH THE KING OF THE JEWS.

20. This title then read many of the Jews: for the place where Jesus was crucified was nigh to the city: and it was written in Hebrew, and Greek, and Latin.

21. Then said the chief priests of the Jews to Pilate, Write not, the King of the Jews, but that he said, I am King of the Jews.

22. Pilate answered, What I have written I have written.

23. Then the soldiers, when they had crucified Jesus, took his garments, and made four parts, to every soldier a part; and also his coat. Now the coat was without seam, woven from the top throughout.

24. They said therefore among themselves, Let us not rend it, but cast lots for it, whose it shall be: that the scripture might

be fulfilled, which saith, They parted my raiment among them, and for my vesture they did cast lots. These things therefore the soldiers did.

25. Now there stood by the cross of Jesus his mother, and his mother's sister, Mary the wife of Cleophas, and Mary Magdalene.

26. When Jesus therefore saw his mother, and the disciple standing by, whom he loved, he saith unto his mother, Woman, behold thy son!

27. Then saith he unto the disciple, Behold thy mother! And from that hour the disciple took her unto his own home.

28. After this, Jesus, knowing that all things were now accomplished, that the scripture might be fulfilled, saith, I thirst.

29. Now there was set a vessel full of vinegar, and they filled a sponge with vinegar, and put it upon hyssop, and put it to his mouth.

30. When Jesus therefore had received the vinegar, he said, It is finished: and he bowed his head, and gave up the ghost.

31. The Jews, therefore, because it was the preparation, that the bodies should not remain upon the cross on the Sabbath day (for that Sabbath day was an high day), besought Pilate that their legs might be broken, and that they might be taken away.

32. Then came the soldiers, and brake the legs of the first, and of the other which was crucified with him.

33. But when they came to Jesus, and saw that he was dead already, they brake not his legs,

34. But one of the soldiers with a spear pierced his side, and forthwith came there out blood and water.

35. And he that saw it bare record, and his record is true: and he knoweth that he saith true, that ye might believe.

36. For these things were done, that the scripture should be fulfilled, A bone of him shall not be broken.

37. And again another scripture saith, They shall look on him whom they pierced.

38. And after this Joseph of Arimathea, being a disciple of Jesus, but secretly for fear of the Jews, besought Pilate that he might take away the body of Jesus, and Pilate gave him leave. He came therefore, and took the body of Jesus.

39. And there came also Nicodemus, which at first came to Jesus by night, and brought a mixture of myrrh and aloes, about an hundred pound in weight.

40. Then took they the body of Jesus, and wound it up in linen clothes with the spices, as the manner of the Jews is to bury.

41. Now in the place where he was crucified there was a garden; and in the garden a new sepulchre, wherein was never man yet laid.

42. There laid they Jesus therefore because of the Jews' preparation day; for the sepulchre was nigh at hand.

Scene 4

The First Mystical scene—"The Flagellation."

Vs. 1. There is a great Johannine reserve in this scene. He omits all the terrible details about the Flagellation—how the victim was stretched out on a convex slab or post, so all the blows would raise huge welts and cuts immediately, the bleeding, etc. And many died from heart failure under this. "Scourged him" is all it says. And yet this reserve is very "telling" also. And all is contained in Verse 1.

Vs. 2. The Second Mystical scene—"The Crowning with Thorns." The Greek word for "thorn" is "äkänthon"—ἀκανθῶν—from which "akanthus" is derived.

1) The Robe—Feeling
2) The Crown—Thinking
3) The Reed (scepter)—Willing

The threefold human being!

Scene 5

Vs. 4. This is a markedly "exoteric" scene. Note the frequency in the Greek text of the prefix "Ex," "Ex," "Ex." "EX" in Greek: "ex"—= ἐξ.

"I find no fault in him"—said three times:

1) 18:36
2) 19:4
3) 19:6

Vs. 5. "Ecce homo!" "Edoo ho änthropos"—Ἰδού ὁ ἄνθρωπος! "Behold MAN!."

"Behold the archetype of the human being!"

- Here the mysteries are made public, are shown to all the world. "ecce homo"—contains prefix "ex."

Vs. 6. "Crucify, crucify": This is said twice by the Saducees, and once by Pilate;—three times in all in this verse.

Note that the Pharisees are not mentioned. Bad as they were, they were not as bad as the Sadducees, the Temple Rulers, who had sold themselves to Rome for the sake of money concessions and privilege. The Sadducees were complete cynics where religion was concerned.

Vs. 8. "More afraid": This indicates that Pilate had been afraid before. This is perhaps an echo of what is explained in full in Matthew as the dream of Pilate's wife—but here only in the background. He was not previously sure of the justice of all this, or of his position on it in relation to his duty to Rome.

NOTE ON MATTHEW'S GOSPEL: Matthew's Gospel has all the dreams. There are five dreams in Matthew, because that Gospel is particularly connected with the spirituality of the past, the spiritual life of the Old Testament, the Jewish, the pre-Christian world, the old spirituality in which dreams played a great role.

Scene 6

The sixth Pilate scene, and the third esoteric scene. Now we are "inside" again.

Vs. 9. "Of what religion art thou?"—A typical Johannine expression.

Vs. 10. "Power": In Greek, "exoose-än"—ἐξουσίαν—Typical of Roman authority. The word "Power" is spoken three times—two times by Pilate and one time by Jesus.

Vs. 11. This is the fourth word of Jesus, and the last to Pilate:

"From above": Typical Johannine motif.

1) "From heaven"—3:27
2) "From the Father"—6:65
3) "From above"—19:11

"He": the Jews, and perhaps also Judas, but this pronoun refers especially to the Jews as a whole.

Vs. 12. Here the voices of the Jews come as a kind of "offstage voice"—an offstage speech chorus—through thick, stony walls from the street into this inner room where Pilate is with Jesus. The Jews say what perhaps they would not have dared to say to Pilate openly or directly.

"Caesar's friend": the "friend" motif of John.

Vs. 13. Note "heard"—that is, Pilate heard the voices from afar, penetrating into the inner room.

Scene 7

This is an "exoteric" scene: note "forth."

Three scenes are esoteric.

Four scenes are exoteric.

Vs. 13. "Gäbäthä"—Γαββαθᾶ—is a name, but it does not mean "pavement."

Vs. 14. The Passover motif again.

"The sixth hour" was about 12 noon.

Matthew, Mark, Luke indicate Christ hung on the cross from 9:00 AM to 3:00 PM. John indicates he hung there only three hours, from 12 noon to 3:00 PM, thus making Pilate's surprise that Jesus had died in so short a time more comprehensible. The nails were used as a favor to Christ, to permit a quicker death because of more bleeding. In Mark, Pilate is astonished that Jesus died so soon. Often victims crucified lived for twenty-four to forty-eight hours on the cross—in terrible agony. It was an unbelievably slow and horribly painful, agonizing death. One should just hang from one's hands from a branch of a tree, or from a projection overhead, just 10 minutes and see how it feels. Then multiply this by three hours or more!

Rudolf Steiner said that, at the time of the Transfiguration, if Jesus had been a Buddha, he would have died. All the struggles of Christ from the Transfiguration onward, were to stay in the body—to stay alive. This accounts for Gethsamane—for the struggle there. It was not a struggle against what was coming, but a struggle to stay alive to meet it. He had to stay in the physical body if He was going to experience physical death. This is the answer to the nineteenth century rationalists who had the terrible thought that Jesus really did not die on the cross but was only overcome in those three hours and lost consciousness, and then in the cool tomb, and with the spices and ointments, he merely revived. A terrible conclusion.

Notes on the Apocalypse of John
(in response to a question posed
by Paul Allen to Dr. Frieling):

— The sections of the Apocalypse correspond to the sections of the Act of Consecration of Man. Each is sharply divided by "thundering, lightning, and voices"

— The Last, the "Vials"—The same angel that shows the Babylon, that which has to be destroyed, also shows the Heavenly City which grows more and more distinct.

— The Vision of the God-Crowned Woman stands in the very midst of the Apocalypse, and there the name Michael is mentioned once, but this is a key to understanding of the Michael nature of the whole Apocalypse. (fighting, etc)

— Dr. Frieling said he considers the works which Dr. Bock did on the "Notes of Introduction" and the tranlation of the Epistles to be his most mature and important literary work.

— The Gospel—The seven Letters to the Churches

— The Offertory—The Seven Seals

— Transubstantiation—The Seven Trumpets

— Communion—The Seven Vials

Notes on the Epistles

"Hebrews" not written by St. Paul.

The Epistles have the character of seven places or churches, the same as do the seven Letters to the Churches in the Apocalypse. The seven Epistles follow:

1) Romans—Connected with the Jews and the old Jewish law and the overcoming of this by the New Law of Christ—the Moon (Soul).

2) Corinthians—Related to the Greek merchant spirit, the movability, the fluctuating impulse—Mercury.

3) Galatians—In Greek, "Gälätäs"—Γαλατάς—meaning "Celts"—the Druidic esoteric knowledge—Venus.

4) Ephesians—Related to the Mysteries—Sun

5) Phillipians—the overcoming of troubles—the influence of Mars overcome by the peaceful powers, as when Buddha works on Mars.

6) Colossians—Wisdom of the Mysteries emphasized. Ephesians and Colossians belong together. Related to Jupiter.

7) Thessalonians—Thessälonikais—Θεσσαλόνικεις—in Greece. Deals with "last things"—the return of Christ, the Last Judgment, Apocalypse, the dead souls, the mystery of iniquity, the Anti-Christ—Saturn.

An interesting figure is formed when we note that—

a) three letters are written to places in Asia

b) three letters are written to places in Greece

c) one Letter is written to a place in Italy.

The Epistle of Jude is very precious because of the reference to Michael as fighting with the Devil over the corpse of Moses. Jude was the brother of Jesus. Jude and II Peter belong together.

In Acts, a great turning point is reached in Chapter 16 when they touched Europe. Luke and Mark travelled with Paul on his journeys.

John 19:1–42 (continued)

Vs. 14. "Preparation": In Greek, "päräskoi-a"—παρασκευὴ—The old word or name for Friday. Thus the motif of Good Friday is hidden here.

"King":—this reflects the last day when the Jews really were together as a people—on Palm Sunday.

Vs. 15. "Crucify": this is the third time this formula is in the mouth of the Jews.

John 19:1–42

"No King but Caesar": Here the Jewish people commit suicide! They throw away their legal status as a nation. They acknowledge they have no aim, no spiritual representative, no King. Caesar is merely an Ahrimanic caricature of the ego. Judas Iscariot, according to Dr. Steiner, was the reincarnation of Judas Maccabeus.

Today, in Roman Catholicism, we have the combination of Jewish and Roman elements. The Jewish laws and Commandments combined with Roman juristic power and soldier, militaristic elements. It is these two forces which delivered Christ to die on Golgotha, and still do so!

Vs. 17. Golgotha in Hebrew is "Gulgoleth." Golgotha in Latin is "Calvaria." The phrase "place of a skull" in Greek is "kräne-oo topon"—κρανίου τόπον—(English word, "cranium"). The place of a skull, Golgotha, points to the principle of the intellect, the human consciousness on the earth, intellectuality, cut off from heaven. In the Gospel of John we have an extremely notable combination of the ego versus the clearness of the physical environment of the earthly world. The topographical notices of John are very accurate and interesting. In Verse 20 is such a topographical notice: "For near the city was the place."

Vs. 20. The "three languages" is mentioned only by St. John. These represent the three languages of the Greco-Roman Cultural Epoch in which the Mystery of Golgotha took place.

(Chapters 3 through 7 of Daniel were originally written in Aramaic.)

Vs. 22. Pilate's revenge against the Jews. A really typical, dry, hard cynical Roman remark! If they want to execute their King as a common criminal, then that is up to them! But this gave him the chance for an ironical revenge. Pilate is strong, but too late. He uses really monumental words here, in a truly Roman formulation.

Spengler, in his terrible way, said the Pilate's question, "What is truth?" is the only positive element in the whole New Testament.

Vs. 23. In reference to the "parting of the garments," see the Kassel cycle on St. John's Gospel by Dr. Steiner, *The Gospel of St. John and Its Relation to the Other Gospels.*

"Four"a is the number of Space, the direction in Space. The "Cloak" is like the atmosphere around the earth.

"Top to bottom": this can read, "From above," and it has a double meaning—one in the sense of "from the top to bottom," and the other, in the sense it is used in the Nicodemus scene, "from above"—i.e., "from heaven." Each of the four parts of the clothes falls to the earthly powers, which make a play, a game, of power over them.

Note on Division of Chapter 19:

Verse 17 ends the Pilate scene.

1) Verses 17-18—The Way to Golgotha and Crucifixion

3) Verses 19-22—The Title on the Cross

3) Verses 23-24—The Soldiers and the Garments

4) Verses 25-27—The Mother and John

5) Verses 28-30—The Death on the Cross

6) Verses 31-37—The Body, Spear, Blood, Water, Bones

7) Verses 38-42—The Burial

In all these seven scenes, as given in John, there is a most admirable reticence. He gives only the barest facts, but these are fully enough!

Vs. 25. The three Marys are representative of the threefold soul members:

1) Mary, the Mother = The Consciousness Soul

2) Mary Cleophas = The Intellectual Soul

3) Mary Magdalene = The Sentient Soul

(If one studies the Grünewald representation of the Crucifixion, these three soul members stand out clearly represented).

Vs. 26. "Woman": the Greek word, "Goonai"—Γύναι—was used at the Cana Wedding. This word is not a reproach in the Greek language, but refers to the principle of womanhood as such. In this verse (26) we can see how the female principle and the male principle are united in a harmonious way so they can work together. They are brought together for this purpose.

Vs. 27. "ais tä ede-ä"—εἰς τά ἴδια—"To his own"

1) John 1:11 (Prologue)—"Came to his own"

2) John 16:32 (skorpisthate—σκορπισθῆτε)—"Scattered each to his own"

3) John 19:27 (Crucifixion)—"Took her to his own"

Mary was the carrier of the Sophia through her pain and suffering. In this moment, the Sophia (Mary) is united with the anthropos (John)! In other words, the human being (anthropos) takes wisdom (Sophia) into his own ego. (Anthroposophy!)

The Apocrypha: All of the Apocrypha were written in Greek. "The Wisdom of Solomon" is the most interesting of all the Books of the Apocrypha. It deals very much with the Sophia. Also with problems of pre-existence, almost Reincarnation. Maccabees contains material concerning services for the dead. It was rejected by Luther and the other Protestants for this reason.

Vs. 28. This starts the fifth scene—The Act of Dying. "Knowing"— He is superior through his consciousness.

Vs. 29. "Hoossopo"—ὑσσώπῳ—: A cleansing agent used by the Jews to assist them in avoiding touching decay. It was required by Jewish law. Vinegar: related to the wine. Like the earthly part of the wine. An awakening influence.

Vs. 30. "Tetelestai"—Τετέλεσται- Used three times. Two times in Verse 28, and once in Verse 30. This is the keyword for his death. In this verse we have the clear picture that His head had been upright before, and now He "bowed his head"—and this becomes a CONSCIOUS ACT OF DYING.

In Bach's "Matthew Passion," the key is in the minor. In Bach's "Johannes Passion," the key is in the major, with the opening choral being, "The Glory of God be manifested upon earth." And the Passion in John is really in the major mood. The action is clear, and the whole is the work of a fully conscious Ego. First Christ knows the Passion consciously, then he DOES it. It is like a ritual book, and he FINISHES it consciously. To consciously conclude a thing is really the result of an act of the ego, otherwise things merely stop. Conscious Beginning and Conscious Conclusions of something are ACTS OF THE EGO.

1) CONSCIOUS BEGINNING = ÄRSCHEN—αρχήν—

2) CONSCIOUS CONCLUSION = TELOS—τέλος—

"FULFILL"—Points to Genesis—to Creation

"FULFILL"—Points to Apocalypse—To Michael and the Conclusion of things.

An animal can't "take leave" at death—it is taken away in death. To conclude with consciousness is the great act of the ego.

Vs. 31. Begins the Sixth Scene.

Preperations: Greek, "päräskoi-a"—παρασκευὴ—The old word for Friday. The Sabbath was Saturday, and the preparation extended to Friday evening at 6 pm, when the Sabbath began.

"Their legs broken": This was done with heavy iron rods. The thigh bones were broken with heavy blows. Thus putrifaction was speeded, and also if the victim was not yet dead, this prevented his running away. They were crippled and remained prisoners.

Vs. 32. They did not break the bones of Christ; i.e., they did not interfere with his skeleton.

Vs. 34. Blood and Water: There is something of a mystery here, because when a person dies, at that moment the blood immediately ceases to flow. Therefore, there is something of a special alchemy in the body of Christ. There is a connection between water and wine—water and blood.

Vs. 35. "He who has seen" = John

"He knows" = God or Christ (not quite clear)

"Witness": In Greek, "märtoore-ä"—μαρτυρία—martyr—A very special word in the Gospel of John and in the Apocalypse.

"Ye" "hoomais"—ὑμεῖς—This address to the reader is quite unique in John. No other Gospel speaks directly to the reader in this way.

Bones—see the Kassel cycle on St. John's Gospel by Rudolf Steiner.

Vs. 36. "Not a bone shall be broken": Refers to Exodus 12:46—A requirement of the perfect condition of the Passover Lamb—it had to be perfect. So, we have "Behold the Lamb of God . . ." in the beginning of the Gospel of St John, and now again here at the end—a frame. This is not mentioned in the other Gospels. This theme is continued in the Apocalypse.

The word "Lamb" in the John Gospel is "ämnos"—ἀμνός

The word "Lamb" in the Apocalypse is "ärne-oo"—ἀρνίου—and "ärne-on"—ἀρνίον.

Vs. 37. "Whom they pierced": Refers to Zachariah 12:10. This is a remnant of the Babalonian-Tamas cult, where the sacrifice is rendered holy by piercing it with a spear. The same cult is found among the Teutonic peoples, where Wotan sacrifices are consecrated with a spear. Among the Vikings, King Vika hung upon a tree and was pierced by a spear in order that the winds might blow.

John 19:37 is linked with Matthew 24:30 and Revelation 1:7.

Vs. 38. This begins the seventh scene—and the last—the funeral of Christ—the Burial, on Friday evening.

Joseph of Arimathea.

He appears in all four Gospels, with different aspects stressed in him, with the character of each Gospel.

1. Mark: he "took courage"—"heart" (Lion).
2. Matthew: he was "a rich man"—Jewish aspect.

3   Luke: he was a member of the Sanhedrin, "a good and just man" who did not agree with the treatment of Christ. The quality of his soul is stressed.

4   John: he was a disciple of Jesus, but in secret, for fear of the Jews.

Vs. 39. Nicodemus—Only John connects Nicodemus and Joseph of Arimathea. And only John shows Nicodemus bringing the spices—and a large quantity of spices too.

"Nooktos"—νυκτὸς—"At night"

1) First appearance, Nikodemus—Positive Degree—3:2

2) Second appearance, Nikodemus—Comparative Degree—7:50

3) Third appearance, Nikodemus—Superlative Degree—19:39

Vs. 40. "Spices": in Greek, "äromäton"—αρωμάτων—This refers to the Myrrh of the Wise Men (Magi) of Matthew, thus connecting Nicodemus with the Hebrew spirit of Matthew's Gospel.

"a custom among the Jews": in contrast to the Egyptian methods of burial preparations.

John meditated the contents of this Gospel for seventy years. Before this, he wrote the Apocalypse, in which his Greek is very poor. However, in this Gospel, his Greek has greatly improved to the point where one can say that, while the Gospel is not in the most fluent Greek, nevertheless, it is not incorrect Greek by any means.

Chapter 21 was probably added by others, doubtless the editors of the Gospel manuscript. It was written to explain and conclude things which were left "open" in his Gospel. Perhaps in the circle of those who finished this after John's death, were Andrew and Phillip, in whom John was definitely much interested, as we can see from his Gospel.

Vs. 41. A topographical remark of John. None of the other Gospels say anything about a garden. In this, and in his many other details, we can see that John had an exact knowledge of the topography of Jerusalem. John's topographical references are an interesting study in themselves. There was a very good and interesting book titled, "The Topography of the Gospel of St John." It was a fine theological book.

Note in Vs 41, the three uses of "en"—ἐν:

1) "en"—ἐν—"in the place"
2) "en"—ἐν—"in the garden"
3) "en"—ἐν—"in which no one . . ." (refers to the tomb)

"new tomb": Specifically clean. Stress on the fact that no other corpse had ever been placed there. No disintegration or decomposition had ever taken place there. It was free from this.

Vs. 42. "Preparation"—"Päräskoi-an"—παρασκευὴν—(Friday).

There was an old law among the Jews that the priests, when dressed and robed for service, could not look on a corpse. If they did so, it meant they could perform no rituals before going through several days of purification. Such an instance is found in the play by Fanny Werfel, *Paul Among the Jews*, in which the son of the High Priest dies, and the father cannot even look upon the boy's corpse before going to the temple.

"Near": About eighty steps from the cross was the garden. The cross and garden form an ellipse, point to point.

This ends the Burial of Jesus, and the seventh scene in this part of the chapter.

John 20:1-31

1. The first day of the week cometh Mary Magdalene early, when it was yet dark, unto the sepulchre, and seeth the stone taken away from the sepulchre.

2. Then she runneth, and cometh to Simon Peter, and to the other disciple, whom Jesus loved, and saith unto them, They have taken away the Lord out of the sepulchre, and we know not where they have laid him.

3. Peter therefore went forth, and that other disciple, and came to the sepulchre.

4. So they ran both together, and the other disciple did outrun Peter, and came first to the sepulchre.

5. And he stooping down, and looking in, saw the linen clothes lying; yet went he not in.

6. Then cometh Simon Peter following him, and went into the sepulchre, and seeth the linen clothes lie,

7. And the napkin, that was about his head, not lying with the linen clothes, but wrapped together in a place by itself.

8. Then went in also that other disciple, which came first to the sepulchre, and he saw, and believed.

9. For as yet they knew not the scripture, that he must rise again from the dead.

10. Then the disciples went away again unto their own home.

11. But Mary stood without at the sepulchre weeping, and as she wept, she stooped down, and looked into the sepulchre,

12. And seeth two angels in white sitting, the one at the head, and the other at the feet, where the body of Jesus had lain.

13. And they said unto her, Woman why weepest thou? She saith unto them, Because they have taken away my Lord, and I know not where they have laid him.

14. And when she had thus said, she turned herself back, and saw Jesus standing, and knew not that it was Jesus.

15. Jesus saith unto her, Woman, why weepest thou? Whom seekest thou? She, supposing him to be the gardener, saith unto him, Sir, if thou have borne him hence, tell me where thou hast laid him, and I will take him away.

16. Jesus saith unto her, Mary. She turned herself, and saith unto him, Rabboni, which is to say, Master.

17. Jesus saith unto her, Touch me not, for I am not yet ascended to my Father, but go to my brethren, and say unto them, I ascend unto my Father, and your Father; and to my God, and your God.

18. Mary Magdalene came and told the disciples that she had seen the Lord, and that he had spoken these things unto her.

19. Then the same day at evening, being the first day of the week, when the doors were shut where the disciples were assembled for fear of the Jews, came Jesus and stood in their midst, and saith unto them, Peace be unto you.

20. And when he had so said, he shewed unto them his hands and his side, Then were the disciples glad, when they saw the Lord.

21. Then said Jesus unto them again, Peace be unto you, as my Father hath sent me, even so send I you.

22. And when he had said this, he breathed on them, and saith unto them, Receive ye the Holy Ghost.

23. Whose soever sins ye remit, they are remitted unto them; and whose soever ye retain, they are retained.

24. But Thomas, one of the twelve, called Didymus, was not with them when Jesus came.

25. The other disciples therefore said unto him, We have seen the Lord. But he said unto them, Except I shall see in his hands the print of the nails, and put my finger into the print of the nails, and thrust my hand into his side, I will not believe.

26. And after eight days again his disciples were within, and Thomas with them; then came Jesus, the doors being shut, and stood in the midst, and said, Peace be unto you.

27. Then saith he to Thomas, Reach hither thy finger, and behold my hands; and reach hither thy hand, and thrust it into my side; and be not faithless, but believing.

28. And Thomas answered and said unto him, My Lord and my God.

29. Jesus saith unto him, Thomas, because thou hast seen me, thou hast believed: blessed are they that have not seen, and yet have believed.

30. And many other signs truly did Jesus in the presence of his disciples, which are not written in this book:

31. But these are written, that ye might believe that Jesus is the Christ, the Son of God; and that believing ye might have life through his name.

Vss. 1 & 2. Note the present tense form of the verbs here, for "life." Note the verb for "seeing."

Vs. 2. John speaks only of Mary Magdalene at the tomb. But here she says "We." Here John presupposes knowledge of the other three Gospels, and their story of the other woman who also went to the tomb.

John 20:1–31

"She runs": This is something special in John's Gospel account. In Verse 4, Peter and John also "run" to the tomb.

"Whom Jesus loved": In the Greek text, "whom Jesus liked"—"efelai"—ἐφίλει.

Vs. 3. "Peter and the other disciple": This is a pre-picture of the Peter and John activities of the Acts.

Vs. 5. It is interesting that John only looks into the tomb at first, but does not enter, while Peter (Vs. 6) enters into the tomb. Peter has much more of the impulse to incarnate into earthly things than John does.

Vs. 7. "the Napkin": Points to the Lazarus-John experiences, the tomb at Bethesda. Note that it is John who sees it.

Vs. 8 & 9. Special remarks of John. They are inserted and are the results of his meditation. After all these events are complete and in the later years he "believed"—otherwise Verse 9 does not make sense.

"Scripture": Does not refer to any specific verse of the Old Testament, but to that which has been written from eternity, to that which is a divine necessity, that which has to be.

Vs. 11 & 12. Verbs—Note change of tense, which brings life into the whole thing: "stood," "wept," "stooped," then "beholds"—present tense! Note the importance of "seeing"—here as shown in the development of the verbs.

"Verbs for Seeing":

1) Blepo—βλέπω—"to glance"—"to look"—German word "blick" derived from this.

2) Tha-orai—θεωρεῖ—"to look with meaning"—English word "theory" derived from this.

3) aidon—εἶδον—from "aido"—εἴδω—"to see," in the sense of "idea."

THE ANGELS OF THE RESURRECTION

1) Matthew—The Angel of the Earthquake—Angel of the Lord—The Angels intervening in earthly events—This is the EXUSIAI aspect.

2) Mark—"The Young Man"—the aspect of youthful forces—This is the ARCHAI aspect.

3) Luke—"Two men" sitting *in* the grave—The "two men" at the Ascension. This is the ARCHANGEL aspect.

4) John—The ANGEL aspect.

The sequence here descends from Heaven to Earth: From Exusiai to Angel aspect. Dr. Steiner said that one angel stands at the head and one at the foot of every corpse.

Vs. 13. "Goonai"—Γύναι—This is the same word that is used in connection with the Wedding at Cana; it points to the first "sign" in the Gospel. It refers to the feminine principle, and is by no means a reproach. She is not aware of the angels, because she is so absorbed in Christ. The psychology of John is exact and coherent.

"My Lord": The "My" stresses the intimate aspect.

Vs. 14. "Him": Greek, "auton"—αὐτόν—Used three times, showing how preoccupied she is with the thought of Christ.

A) "Carry off him"

B) "where you laid him"

C) "Take him away"

In the Easter scene, Christ speaks three times:

1) "Woman, why weepest thou?"—Verse (15)

2) "Mary"—(Verse 16) (her name)

3) "Touch me not," etc. (he charges her) (Verse 17)

Vs. 16. "Turns": What is behind us is always a mystery. There is an occult sphere behind us. Turning represents a kind of conversion, or change of heart and thought and will. The eyes cross in their seeing. And this crossing has to do with the "ego." In the Apocalypse, there is the phrase "I heard behind me," and "I turned to see," indicating a passing to an occult state of seeing. Here Mary turns with the speaking of her name. This is a decisive turning point in her life and experience.

The recognition of the Christ's voice by Mary also makes us recall the sayings: 1) at Cana about "the voice of the bridegroom," and 2) in Chapter 10 about the sheep hearing the voice of the shepherd.

"Räbbooni"—Ραββουνί: The phrase, "that is to say, teacher (or Master)," was added later. "Rabboni" does not mean master or teacher. It is a much greater word, which is only used for God. The "i" on the end of the word "Rabboni" means "of me" or "my." The word should be translated "My God."

Vs. 17. "Änäbebakä"—ἀναβέβηκα (from ἀναβαίνω): "I ascend"— A key word for the Gospel of John. As we know, the Gospel of John starts after the Baptism in the Jordan, and stops before the Ascension, yet both events in essence are contained in this Gospel. Therefore, here in this Verse 17, is the BEGINNING OF THE PROCESS OF THE ASCENSION. Both the Resurrection and the Ascension are processes which continue. The process of the Resurrection is shown in Verse 17. Having been raised from the dead, Christ now goes into the Father sphere. Then when Christ meets Thomas a week later, he asks Thomas to touch Him, showing that a process of development has continued meanwhile. Christ must first complete the process. The Son forces can then work in the sphere of personal connections (Thomas, Emmaus, etc.)

1) The Son forces working in the sphere of personal connections.

2) The Father forces working in the sphere of the body.

These two forces work together.

The Resurrection body goes through a process, and the last moment, the completing moment of this process is the Ascension.

Thus the Gospel of John begins after the Baptism and ends before the Ascension, but the aroma of both is poured out over the Gospel.

"ädelphoos moo"—ἀδελφούς μου: "My Brothers": There are three steps:

1) Servants
2) Friends
3) Brothers (Brethren).

With this calling of them "brothers," a new stream, a new possibility of heritage is opened. We have to maintain a bodily relationship to Christ. This appears only after the Resurrection. And thus we are all related to the Resurrection body of Christ, which is for all of us. This word also appears in Matthew, at the end of Chapter 25, near to the Resurrection story. There it is more concealed. "These are my brothers" "ädelphoos moo"—ἀδελφούς μου. Note that the "änäbebakä"—ἀναβέβηκα—(from "änäbaino"—ἀναβαίνω) here is in the present tense: "I ascend" or "I am ascending"—a process is clearly indicated going on.

"My Father and your Father," "My God and Your God"—There is separation here.

Goethe said that in unity and oneness there is confusion and no meaning. In separation there is room for Devotion. This statement of Christ makes a distinction—knowing who He (Christ) is, and who I am. There is a gap between. And of course, ultimately this gap has to be bridged, but it is not bridged yet. We have to be aware, we have to have a real feeling for the levels and distances in the spiritual world, and this verse helps us to such an awareness.

Clergymen have often spoken about how the words "Our Father" must have sounded when the Christ prayed them. In other words, how Christ must have prayed the Lord's Prayer. They convey the meaning that Christ praying "Our Father" was praying to God as from one standpoint for all—as though we and Christ are all on the same level as far as God is concerned, so far as an understanding of and an approach to God are concerned.—And that is all an error. The Christ gave the Lord's Prayer. He gave it, the "Our Father," but TO THE DISCIPLES! It was for them. There is absolutely no indication that He prayed this prayer for Himself. And all of this can bring about a feeling of Communion as well as a feeling of distance. So Christ in this passage indicates a distance which has to be overcome in a living way—otherwise there is nothing for the human being but confusion, and a confounding of oneself with God, a putting of oneself on a level with God.

In the old theological teaching, the human being was conceived as being at a "stabilized distance" from God. And this distance then had to be covered by the human being in reaching God. In the mystical sense, the distance exists between the human being and God, but this is a flowing distance, i.e., when one moves towards God, God moves too. So the progression becomes infinite! Christ never says "OUR" Father—He uses other pronouns.

Chapter 15 of I Corinthians is THE OLDEST RECORD OF EASTER. The Gospels are of later writing. The differences are interesting. For example in John we have Peter and John running to the tomb. In Luke, we have only Peter running to the grave, looking into it, and returning home in wonderment.

In 1 Corinthian Chapter 15 account of the Resurrection, Paul speaks only of men as having witnessed the events, because as a typical Jew of his time, for Paul, women were not reliable or of importance.

SEVEN STEPS TO THE ASCENSION

The actual beginning takes place on EARTH—in the figure of the empty tomb.

1. Sunday Morning: Mary Magdalene comes to the tomb. The soul aspect, astral, the sphere of personal feelings ("My Master," "My Lord," etc.) The MOON—aspect of Resurrection.

2. Sunday Afternoon: The walk to Emmaus—the two disciples walking on the way. In connection with the "explaining the Scriptures," the word "Hermnaiston"—appears—comes from "hermnoi-o"—ἑρμνεύω = to interpret or to translate—the picture of the winged shoes of Hermes-Mercury. The MERCURY aspect of Resurrection.

3. The Easter Sunday Evening meeting with the disciples. The higher love. Breathing the Holy Spirit. The overcoming of the Luciferic in the breathing in them. The power of healing, the healing of sins. This is the VENUS—aspect of the Resurrection.

4. The Sunday after Easter one week later. The octave. The Thomas acknowledgment—all doubts of Thomas melt away. This is perhaps the greatest of all acknowledgments: "God and the God of my ego"—"Koore-os"—Κύριος—and "Tha-os moo"—Θεός μου—old cultic words—this is the link to the Apocalypse. A great acknowledgment for Christ, later used by the Emperor Dometian for himself. A formula of the cult of the old Sun gods, used in old mantric hymns. In his *Theosophy* Dr. Steiner says that, when we come to the Sun sphere, "all doubts melt away." This is the SUN aspect of the resurrection.

5. The scenes in Matthew 28 and John 21: The mountain and the lake in Galilee. A growing into the cosmic sphere. An enlarging. The sending of the disciples. The initiation of the great conquest of the earth, of world conquest, a beginning of a new energy.—The unification of blood through the blood of Christ. Encouragement—adding to the strength of the heart. This is the MARS aspect of the resurrection.

6. The draft of fishes—the spiritual fullness. The organization of churches—the indication of the leading personalities—the Institution—The Lambs—the ordering, the proper arranging of things. This is the JUPITER wisdom aspect of the Resurrection.

7. Ascension—The Mount of Olives—Jesus—the forest. The SATURN aspect of the resurrection.

With this seventh Saturn step, we come to the ultimate limits of the planetary spheres and pass over into the mystery of the Father sphere.

Thus Ascension is a process which is still going on. We see that the process goes to the ultimate limits of the planetary regions—the Saturn sphere—and all is completed. The physical body is built up by the fixed start, etc.

In Chapter 20, Verse 17 we have the beginning of the Ascension process, so John's Gospel here includes the aroma of Ascension, although the actual Ascension event is not given in detail. But the process definitely begins here.

In the Russian Orthodox Church, on Easter and each Sunday to the eve of Ascension, the gospel at evensong is John 20:19-25, which is read in many languages.

In Ch. 20, Vs 22, we have the first touches of the Whitsuntide experience. The first hint of the dawn.

Note that the first (20:17) is a morning story. A passing through the garden and standing before the rock tomb. The Ascension picture—the Father forces. Note that the second (20:22) is an evening story. A closed room. The doors are closed. The doors of the senses are closed. The twelve are sitting. A going out of the body for a working of the Holy Spirit—a meditative time. "In the midst" (20:19)—a quality, a central being in the true center—they felt Christ to be the true center.

"Peace to you": this wonderful and very important formula is spoken three times: Chapter 20: Verses 19, 21, 26.

"Grace and Peace": In his writings, St. Paul combines the two wonderful qualities:

1) "schäres"—χάρις—"Grace"—the GREEK aspect.
2) "Airana"—Εἰρήνη—"Peace"—the HEBREW aspect, found in the words "Shalom," "Salem,"—"Peace."

The first Gospel begins with "schäres"—χάρις—(Grace)—Matthew.

The fourth Gospel begins with "Airana"—Εἰρήνη—Shalom (Peace)—John.

"Peace to you": "Airana humen"—Εἰρήνη ὑμῖν—is a formula repeated three times:

1) 20: 19—The Father aspect
2) 20:21—The Son aspect (personal)
3) 20:22—The Holy Spirit aspect

Vs. 20. "Rejoiced"—This is the last appearance of this important word in the Gospel of John.

Vs. 21. "käthos"—καθὼς—"As"—A special Johannine word. Verse 21 is in three parts:

1) "Peace to you"
2) "As the Father has sent me forth"
3) "I also send you"

In the "Closed Room Scene" (Ch. 20) The Christ speaks three times:

1) "Peace to You" (Vs 19)—The Father aspect
2) "Peace to You. As the Father has sent me forth, I also send you" (Vs 21)—The Son, the personal, "I", the Christ aspect.
3) "Receive the Holy Spirit" (Vs 22)—The aspect of knowledge for remission of sins, knowing—the Holy Spirit aspect

Vs. 22. "Breathed into" (them)—This breathing is like a reminder of Genesis—the breathing into Adam. Here the creation of the human being is renewed by the New Adam!

This verse is in a threefold form:

1) "Receive the Holy Spirit"—Holy Ghost aspect
2) "Of whomsoever you may forgive the sins, they are forgiven to them"—the Son aspect
3) "Of whomsoever you may retain, they are retained"—the Father aspect

— The Karmic necessities. He brings the sphere of ordering of karma to the human being.—It is now entrusted to human beings themselves to order things on earth. What you don't do in any one incarnation, is kept for another incarnation. It is much more than arbitrariness or surface understanding of this verse in the usual theological sense.

— The "you" here refers to all who are connected with and have the mission of the Risen Christ.

— This scene takes place on Sunday morning.

Vs. 24. Thomas is he who has said, "Let us die with him."—He is deeply connected with Lazarus and the experience of death and resurrection. He has a deep mystical attraction to the sphere of death, goes deeper into the death experience of Golgotha than the others. This is a new time of revelation of the Christ, especially for Thomas.

In the first wave of Christianity, the element of feeling predominated—more feminine—the Mary faith. In our own time Christianity is based more on the element of knowledge—more masculine—the Thomas type.

"Thomas, called Didymus" "The Twins"—the sign of Gemini—connected with knowledge. Here we have duality (Twins)—the "two souls" in one breast—as in Faust. Thomas is interested in the wounds. He is interested in what Christ experiences in the human body which has been brought to the higher spheres. This has an eternal meaning. Chapter 5 of the Apocalypse is the continuation of Golgotha in the higher worlds. Here we see that the Mystery of Golgotha has an importance forever. It is established once for all.

Here the experience of Golgotha—the marks of Golgotha—have been brought into the higher worlds.

The God is suffering from us. All human sufferings are suffered in God much more.

Vs. 26. "Within": In Greek, "eso"—ἔσω—In the esoteric sphere, the inner experience.

"comes": In Greek, "erschetai"—ἔρχεται—Note the present tense—vivid, alive quality.

"In the midst": Not a materialistic thing like a mere description of a physical position. The disciples are like the signs of the Zodiac and Christ stands in the center like a world center. The "I"—the "Ich"—stands here like the Heart of the World.

Three appearances of Christ

1) To Mary in the Garden—he speaks three times
2) To Disciples in the Evening—he speaks three times
3) To Thomas in the Room—he speaks three times

In his speeches to Thomas, Christ says:

1) "Peace to you" (V. 26)—The Father sphere
2) "Bring thy finger," etc. (V. 27)—The Son sphere—personal
3) "Because thou hast seen," etc. (V. 29)—knowing, etc.,—Holy Spirit.

The Sphere of the Risen Christ:

1) "Saw"—As in Matt. 28—They only saw him—Imagination
2) "Heard"—More developed in later Gospels—Inspiration
3) "Touch"—"eat"—Fully developed in John—Intuition.

The hands have to do with Gemini, the Twins. Hands and Feet, a duality—"Believing" versus "Not Believing": In Greek, "pistos"—πιστός—versus "äpistos"—ἄπιστος—whether one has the connection with the pectoral region, the region of the heart, or not.

Thomas has to add to the evidence. He begins with the understanding, then adds the warmth of heart. He is truly a modern human being. In the olden times, they started with the warmth of the heart, then added the understanding. This "apistos" is characteristic of the modern human being.

Vs. 28. "My Lord and My God"—This is the greatest confession in the whole Gospel. One now sees Christ in relation to one's own ego. Christ is the Kurios and the God of our own ego. This is a balancing of the beginning and the end of the Gospel:

1) In the Prologue
2) In Chapter 20—Out of the mouth of a human being

Vs. 29. Here is a picture of how to grow from the brain downwards! The seeing and believing. The benediction upon those who do not have the understanding, but have the feeling of the heart. Thomas here is the forerunner of quite another type of human being than we find in the Gospels.

Verse 29—the third saying is more in the direction of the Holy Spirit.

Vss. 30 & 31. The actual conclusion of the Gospel of John.

"In his name"—this is like the Prologue

"You"—Into the form of direct address to the reader. The personal relationship to the reader—we feel personally addressed by John.

"Name"—His name is "Ago aime"—Ἐγώ εἰμι—"I am the I AM"—In these verses we have faith (Pistis) and Knowledge (Gnosis) connected. A name is the manifestation of what we know of another.

John 21:1-25

1. After these things Jesus shewed himself again to the Disciples at the sea of Tiberias; and on this wise shewed he himself.

2. There were together Simon Peter, and Thomas called Didymus, and Nathanael of Cana in Galilee, and the sons of Zebedee, and two other of his disciples.

3. Simon Peter saith unto them, I go a fishing. They say unto him, We also go with thee. They went forth, and entered into a ship immediately; and that night they caught nothing.

4. But when the morning was now come, Jesus stood on the shore, but the disciples did not know that it was Jesus.

5. Then Jesus said unto them, Children, have ye any meat? They answered him, No.

6. And he said unto them, Cast the net on the right side of the ship, and ye shall find. They cast therefore, and now they were not able to draw it for the multitude of fishes.

7. Therefore that disciple whom Jesus loved saith unto Peter, It is the Lord. Now when Simon Peter heard that it was the Lord, he girt his fisher's coat unto him (for he was naked), and did cast himself into the sea.

8. And the other disciples came in a little ship (for they were not far from land, but as it were two hundred cubits), dragging the net with fishes.

9. As soon as they were come to land, they saw a fire of coals there, and fish laid thereon, and bread.

10. Jesus saith unto them, Bring of the fish which ye have now caught.

11. Simon Peter went up, and drew the net to land full of great fishes, an hundred and fifty and three: and for all there were so many, yet was not the net broken.

12. Jesus saith unto them, Come and dine. And none of the disciples durst ask him, Who art thou? knowing that it was the Lord.

13. Jesus then cometh, and taketh bread, and giveth them, and fish likewise.

14. This is now the third time that Jesus shewed himself to his disciples, after that he was risen from the dead.

15. So when they had dined, Jesus saith to Simon Peter, Simon, Son of Jonas, lovest thou me more than these? He saith unto him, Yea Lord; thou knowest that I love thee. He saith unto him, Feed my Lambs.

16. He saith to him again the second time, Simon, Son of Jonas, lovest thou me? He saith unto him, Yea Lord; thou knowest that I love thee. He saith unto him, Feed my Sheep.

17. He saith to him the third time, Simon, Son of Jonas, lovest thou me? Peter was grieved because he said unto him the third time, Lovest thou me? And he said unto him, Lord, thou knowest all things, thou knowest that I love thee. Jesus said unto him, Feed my Sheep.

18. Verily, Verily, I say unto thee, When thou wast young, thou girdest thyself, and walkedst whither thou wouldest, but when thou shalt be old, thou shalt stretch forth thy hands, and another shall gird thee, and carry thee whither thou wouldest not.

19. This spake he, signifying by what death he should glorify God. And when he had spoken this, he saith unto him, Follow me.

20. Then Peter turning about, seeth the disciple whom Jesus loved following, which also leaned on his breast at supper, and said, Lord, which is he that betrayeth thee?

21. Peter seeing him saith to Jesus, Lord, and what shall this man do?

22. Jesus saith unto him, If I will that he tarry till I come, what is that to thee? Follow thou me.

23. Then went this saying abroad among the brethren, that the disciple should not die; yet Jesus said not unto him, He Shall not die, but, If I will that he tarry till I come, what is that to thee?

24. This is the disciple which testifieth of these things, and wrote these things, and we know that his testimony is true.

25. And there are also many other things which Jesus did, the which, if they should be written every one, I suppose that even the world itself could not contain the books that should be written. Amen.

The style of Chapter 21 is different from the rest of the Gospel. In this chapter, Christ speaks twelve times.

Vs. 2. Here seven disciples are named:

In Chapter 6, the twelve appear at first.

In Chapter 1, five are named.

In Chapters 5 and 7, three have names, and four have no names.

Nathanael: Note that Nathanael was the last one mentioned in Chapter 1, and then immediately, the scene passes directly to the Cana Wedding. Here in Chapter 21, we learn for the first time that he lived in Cana, that he had very much to do with Cana. He was an initiate belonging to the sphere of Cana, and is named in this verse for the last time. The "two sons of Zebedee" are John and James. The "Two others" are a mystery—we don't know who they are.

Vs. 3. Peter shown as the active human being.

Vs. 4. The scene at dawn

Vs. 5. "Paide-ä"—Παιδία—"little children"—like "tekniä"—τεκνία—in Ch. 13:33. This is a typical Johannine reference and expression. It is not a sentimental statement or reference. It is an address to what, though only a germ in them, will grow to fullness and maturity—it addresses the spiritual seed in each of them.

In Luke, Chapter 5, Christ tells them to go the middle of the lake. The shore is left far behind. Water is more connected with the cosmos. On the water, Christ is not the same as on the earth. There Christ unfolds his cosmic powers. The net breaks.

In John, Chapter 21, the scene takes place near the shore. The net did not break. It appears as a balance to the story in Luke. It is not the same story at all. In Luke, Chapter 5, Christ is more outside, more in the cosmic character. They have caught nothing in the night. The human being's sleep and dreaming yields no fruit at all. We are poor in our sleep life. The morning hours should have golden treasures for us of inspiration. And Christ opens this treasure for us again. In Luke Chapter 5, the whole scene is like a daydream. Peter experiences Christ supernaturally, beginning in this moment. He feels that Christ is not a human being, but he cannot bring this into his everyday consciousness, so the net is broken.

In John 21:4—The Christ stands on land, on the earth. Since Golgotha, Christ is connected with the earth. His connection with the earth is established. Now the net does not break. The Christ sends them strong powers from the earth.

1) The Right Side—more earthly, more active, masculine

2) The Left Side—Heart, etheric, feminine, heavenly, receiving

If a human being becomes active, then through the help of Christ, his or her night experience will become fruitful.

Vs. 3. "exelthon"—ἐξῆλθον—"Went Out"—Connected with our word "exhale"—a going out into a night experience as in sleep and dream.

Vs. 4. "knew not"—like a dream experience—the same type of experience is seen in the Magdalene scene and at Emmaus.

Vs. 5. He addresses the child in them. They have nothing with which to feed the germ of the future in the human being. Do you have any food for the child in your soul?

Vs. 7. "IT IS THE LORD"—"HO KOORE-OS ESTIN"—Ὁ κύριός ἐστιν

This sacred formula appears three times in Chapter 21:

1) In Vs. 7—John to Peter
2) In Vs. 7—Peter hears
3) In Vs. 12—They know

It means, "He is the beginning" (koore-os)—κύριός—The I Am of the Christ experienced from the outside. He says, "I AM"—they recognize the Ego of Christ. It is the recognition by the disciples of the "Ago aime"—Ἐγώ εἰμι. Dr. Rittlemeyer speaks of the atmosphere of the dream in this scene. Then a flash of reality suddenly springs up with the pronouncing of this sacred formula.

Vs. 8. They are near the shore: the Christ is connected with the earth.

Vs. 9. "They see"—the present tense suddenly appears. A vivid sense of reality.

This Chapter 21 is interesting because here Christ speaks twelve times. In the other chapters he speaks either three times or seven times.

Vs. 11. The Fishes represent the door to the lower sphere of the dark signs of the Zodiac. The net was not rent, otherwise the wealth of the night experience would be lost to the human being.

In Feeding the 5,000, 5 loaves are used—(Mark)

In Feeding the 4,000, seven loaves are used—(Mark)

These refer to the seven light signs and five dark signs of the Zodiac.

Vs. 12. This is like a dream, the knowing and not knowing—becoming clearer, then fading out, etc.

Vs. 13. "Comes"—He makes a new effort to manifest himself to their consciousness. It is like the scene in Matthew 14, where the steps are progressive. "Walking," "Speaking," "Coming."

The Three Steps of the Eucharist:

1) Comes
2) Takes
3) Gives
    a) In Chapter 6, the Bread is in the foreground.
    b) In Chapter 21, the Fish are in the foreground.

   Between stands the Mystery of Golgotha.

Vs. 14. "third time"—This represents the Third Degree, the third step or the third quality of the appearance of the Risen Christ.

The first appearance in Chapter 21 was in Galilee—in the cosmic character.

The second appearance was in Jerusalem—in the house, the earthly, the night.

The third appearance has to do with the cosmos, the morning—The beginning of a New World and not the end of an old one!

Vs. 15-17. The three charges here are the balance of the three denials! This is a purgatorial experience for Peter. Note carefully the Greek text for comparative words in the three questions and answers. Each has three parts:

1) The question of Christ

2) The answer of Peter

3) The charge of Christ. How Christ words His question and how Paul words his answer is always mistranslated from the Greek—.

Vss. 15 & 16. In each of these verses Jesus asks: "*lovest* thou me . . . ?" He uses the word "ägäpäs," which comes from "ägäpa"—αγαπε—meaning "love." And Peter answers: "Yea, Lord, you know that I *care for* you." Peter uses the term, "felo"—φιλῶ—meaning "to like," or "to care."

Vs. 17. Then Jesus asks in the third question: "do you *care* for me?' Jesus uses the term "felais," which comes from "felo"—φιλῶ—to care, or to like. And it then says that Peter is grieved, because this time, Jesus asks: "Do you *care* for me?" Jesus no longer asks, "Do you *love* me?" but "Do you *care* for me?" Perhaps as if to ask, Do you *even care* for me?

Vs. 19. Signifying—The Greek word, "Semainon"—σημαίνων—"sign."

Vs. 20. "Sees"—the vivid quality.

"At supper . . . betraying"—the picture of Judas called up here. Peter, John, Judas—a special group. Think of da Vinci's *Last Supper*.

Vs. 22. "Abide"—The Johannine "meno"—μένω.

This is the last word of the Christ in John's Gospel. In John, the continuing consciousness is lighted, which remains. This is the bridge from the time of the Apostles until Christ's return. This is the task of the Johannine stream, the esoteric Christianity running underground through the outward, the exoteric world of Petrine Christianity.

This verse is the word of Christ's return. The whole of the Apocalypse stands here like a germ."Until I come"—like Chapter 14 of John's Gospel.

Vs. 23. An editorial reminder:

"Abide until I come"—this important formula is stressed by this repetition—It is underlined. The sacred task of John is pointed to—the eternal light which must be kept burning until the direct relationship to Christ can once more be established, can begin anew.

Vs. 24. Compare Chapter 10:41 (". . . all things that John spake concerning this man were true") with 21:24—(". . . we know his testimony is true"). In the first instance, John the Baptist is being spoken of. In the second instance, John the Evangelist is spoken of. Here the two John's are placed side by side.

Note the jump from the "we" in Verse 24 to the "I" in Verse 25.

Chapter 21 was probably written by members of the Johannine circle at Ephesus after the death of John.

Notes on the Compostion of Mark's Gospel
Based on Conversations with Dr. Freiling
New York, April 17, 1951

The Gospel opens with John the Baptist.

Part 1

Capricorn: John Baptist. Turning, changing mind. Opposite sign, Cancer (1:1–3).

Aquarius: Baptizing in Jordan (1:4–8).

Pisces: Baptism of Christ—Always the Christ sign. The Virgin stands as opposite sign (1:9–22).

Aries: Expulsion of Evil spirits so a person can stand on his or her own feet. So one can restore one's ego.—Expulsion of foreign spirituality. The bringing back to the normal state of mind. The vertical, upright posture, lifted head (1: 23–39).

Taurus: The Taurus sections are always large. The healing of sick people is always Taurus. The Taurus connected with the throat—the healing word, speech with magic power. The sphere of the healing word of Christ. The Logos sphere is the Taurus sphere. Healing motif. The Pharisees appear. They represent the word which has died, which has become a dead tradition, in distinction to Christ's Word which lives and heals—the living Word. The opposite sign of Taurus is Scorpio—the enemy and intrigue—the sting—in the background here. Eating is a sign of Taurus. Taurus is that which leads into the earth and earthly incarnation. Healing on the Sabbath, a part of the the struggle between the Living Word and dead tradition (from 1:40 to 3:12).

Gemini: Creating of the twelvehood. Gemini is always related to the mountain, the holy mountains. Gemini represents the highest point of the heavens that the sun reaches. In the Zarathustra teaching of Persia, the mountain plays a great role—light and darkness. The sun makes the circle of the Apostles. Christ creates the circle (3:13–19).

Crab: From the mountain to the narrow room of the house. Inwardness. Narrowing influence of matter. The bodily sphere. Madness and misunderstanding. Aspect of materialism. The family—son of the mother—narrowness of family ties. Imprisoning (3:19–34).

Leo: The lion is not represented as such, because it pervades the whole Gospel as the sign of St. Mark. It is more in the background. The hero motif, courage of heart, belongs to Leo. This is touched upon in the "strong man" theme in 3:27.

Virgo: The logos as a seed—picture of the mother. The Virgin. All the imaginations concerning the seed from 3:34 through 4:34.

Libra: Balance. Inner balance as opposed to the restoration of inner calm. Opposite sign of Libra is Aries—compare above. The Libra section is 4:35–41.

Scorpio: One of the dark signs. The netherworld, the underworld. The opposite sign is Taurus. The opposite to the first possessed man is the Taurus healing of the leper in 1:40, et se. The healing power of Christ's word works here in Ch. 5 too. The sexual sphere which doesn't function (5:21) belongs to Scorpio. His original word is present—the Aramaic word, and Aramaic words are special—only in Mark's Gospel—for example, 5:41. The magic word—reminder of Taurus—The sting of death—odors—scattering—all Scorpio. People not believing, not able to work, adversary, hindrance of healing forces—all belong to Scorpio (5:1 through 6:6).

Saggitarius: This is the special sign of the Church. Here Jupiter is in his own house. Saggitarius is the sign of metaphysics and the Church. It is thinking far off from goal. The streaming of the blessing of the Milky Way. Saggitarius is the sign of the Mystery of Golgotha. Sign of death where, or in which, new life is released. In the background is the opposite sign of Gemini, when Christ sends the disciples two-by-two—(Twins) (6:7–13).

(End of the first Zodiacal Round in Mark's Gospel)

Part 2

Capricorn: The King Herod versus John the Baptist theme. Black magic. The turning point—the demons. The opposite aspect of the Twelve Holy Nights, for the Twelve Holy Nights can have more than one aspect—more than the Christmas aspect. Stubbornness, not to turn with what comes. To remain with the old forces and become hostile to new and to seek to kill the new (6:14-28).

Waterman: Baptism and Funeral. The funeral is the octave of the Baptism, since there are seven Sacraments. Here in Mark is the funeral of John the Baptist—the connection with Baptism and Burial (6:29).

Pisces: Feeding the 5,000. Special Christological sign, together with the Virgin. Pisces and Virgo form the horizontal. Saggitarius and the Twins form the verticle. Together they form the cross. Virgin belongs to the bread, to wheat, to the seed imagination. "Thou art my beloved son"—this belongs to the Baptism in the Jordan and Pisces. Pisces and Virgo are opposite signs. Pisces is the constellation of the Last Supper. (6:30-46)

Aries: Stilling the storm. Opposite to the healing of human beings. The opposite of Libra, balance. More of the Ego in Aries—standing upright—lifted head. "Be courageous" is Aries. "I Am"—(6:47-52).

Taurus: Opposite to Scorpio where Christ couldn't heal. Old laws and words dried up into traditions—the washing hands controversy. Living and dead words—Food and Eating—typically Taurus. In 7:22 is the catalog of twelve things out of the human being—objectionable qualities. Matthew gives seven bad qualities in his list. In 7:11 an Aramaic word appears. In 7:34 is another Aramaic word. Typical Taurus. Also "band of his tongue" (7:35) typically Taurus (6:35-7:37).

(Gemini, Cancer, and Leo are omitted in the Gospel at this point.)

Virgo: Feeding the 4,000. The Christological axis of the Virgin and the Fishes. Here only a little fish and much bread—characteristic of the "bread" quality of the Virgin. Virgo is a Day or Light sign.

In the Feeding of the 5,000, which took place in the Fishes—(see above)—in the Night or Dark sign of the Pisces, two fish are specified. (8:1-9)

Libra: Going over the sea. The cosmic balancing element here (8:10).

Scorpio: Disputation with the Pharisees regarding the sign. Misunderstanding of the disciples. The warning about the leaven of Pharisees and of Herod. The Herodians believed Herod to be the Messiah. It was not only a political movement. The mind which darkens the spiritual eyes (8:17-19). Healing of the blind man, in connection with not understanding in 8:21. The eyes opened in a counterpicture of not understanding—the action of Scorpio is to make blind (8:11-26).

Saggitarius: The confession of Peter. Church. The Golgotha constellation. Connected with the death of Christ. The announcement of the Passion (8:27-31).

(End of Second Zodiacal Round)

Part 3

Capricorn: Satan—Stubbornness. (v. 33) A picture of the winter, but without Christmas. Peter is related to some of the old, pre-Christian powers of Carpricorn. Changing mind—repentance (v. 34). Capricorn and Waterman (Aquarius) belong to John the Baptist.—the role in the Transfiguration where John the Baptist appears as Elias (8:32-9:3).

Aquarius: Mingles with Capricorn, especially in connection with the Transfiguration (9:4-6).

Pisces: "Thou art my beloved Son" (9:7-13).

Aries: The vertical, rising from the horizontal position, the upright head. Note healing of the boy, beginning with 9:14—and, "raised him up and he arose" (9:27)—emphasis on the vertical. The boy was restored in his own ego qualities. Note the many very vivid small physical details—this is very typical of Mark. The action. The opposite sign of Aries is Libra and the picture of the pigs (9:14-17).

Taurus: The Word. 9:31—The second announcement of death. Before, in Saggitarius, near to Scorpio, was the first announcement of Christ's death. (8:31). The opposite sign of Taurus is Scorpio, which is spoken of by Dostoyevski in *The Possessed*, where he speaks of "Legions," the collective spirit. Scorpio is related to Judas, suicide, self-harm, the sexual sphere, dimming of consciousness after death, not understanding, the sting, the lower world, betrayal.

The speaking of Christ is always Taurus, the doctrine. In Chapter 10, in the controversy with the Pharisees we have Scorpio in the background. Divorce, controversy, Scorpio—Then the "little children" follow immediately after the discussion of divorce in Chapter 10:13. Blessing is a function of the healing word belonging to Taurus. The rich man. 10:32—the third announcement of His Passion. Scorpio in the background (9:28 to 10:31).

Gemini: The going to the holy mountain. It is clear in Ch. 10:35—two sons, two pillars—right and left side—A looking back to the Transfiguration—in Vs. 37. To Moses and Elias. Not simply ambition here. (10:32-45).

Cancer: Entrance into the materialistic sphere of Jericho. Jericho is from "Jeriach" meaning "Moon" in Hebrew. Jericho means "City of the Moon." Entering into matter—typical of the Cancer type. The Fig tree, Cleansing of the Temple—All Cancer (From 10:46 to 14:2).

Leo: Not included as such.

Virgo: The Woman in Bethany. To Virgo belongs the Last Supper, all the Feedings, Baptisms, Transfiguration—now the Last Supper which is the axis of Virgo and Pisce. (From 14:3-27).

Libra: Gethsemane—Fighting and struggling for balance in the Ego. Struggle with the Ego to maintain self in the body. In 14:36 is another Aramaic word (14:27-42).

Scorpio: The Judas theme and the whole Passion. Pilate. Peter's denial—this last is typical Scorpio (From 14:43 to 15:21).

Saggitarius: The Golgotha constellation. The death of Christ (From 15:22 to 15:33).

Part 4

The Opening of the Fourth Round of the Zodiac

Capricorn: The Elias-John motif—John the Baptist motif is always Capricorn (From 15:34 to 15:41).

Aquarius: Burial. The Octave of the Baptism in the Jordan (From 15:42 to 15:47).

Pisces: the Resurrection (From 16:1-8).

(The last part of Mark is a doubtful addition following Verse 8.)

In Mark's Gospel there are four Parables only:

a) In Chapter 4—Three Parables about Seed, Grain, Wheat

b) In Chapter 12—One Parable about Vineyard and Wine

The two sets of parables concern BREAD and WINE.

Notes on the General Character of the Apocalypse
Conversation with Dr. Freiling, April 24, 1951

"The Letters to the Churches" refer to the Gospel in the Act of Consecration of Man.

Chapters 4 and 5 form an introduction to the opening of the Seals. The first of the Seven Seals is opened in Chapter 6.

Chapter 4 is like unveiling of the chalice—the entrance into a more Imaginative sphere—the sphere of images, Imagination—as in the Act of Consecration.

The formula of transition between one part of the Apocalypse and another is "lightnings, thundering, voices," etc. This divides, as the sections of the Act of Consecration are divided.

From Seals to Trumpets—Ch. 8:5, 6.—The entrance into a more Inspirational sphere—from Imagination to Inspiration.

The formula of transition appears in:

1) 4:5—Churches to Seals (Gospel to Offertory)
2) 8:5—Seals to Trumpets (Offertory to Transubstantiation)
3) 11:19—Trumpets to Vials (Transubstantiation to Communion)

Note the metamorphosis and slight changes in this formula, how it grows from point to point.

8:1—"Silence"—This is an Inspirational silence. It is like the silent incensing of the Altar before the Transubstantiation. It is the introduction to the Inspirational Sphere—From Imagination to Inspiration (Trumpets).

Four of the Angels with Trumpets are similar in character, judging by the effect of their work, while three of them are dissimilar.

The transition from the sixth to the seventh Trumpet occurs between 9:13 and 11:15. Therefore, all of the "Angel with the book," "the Angels loosed," "the measuring of the Temple," etc.—all belong to the sphere of the sixth Trumpet.

Chapter 12 belongs to the seventh Trumpet.

In 12:7 occurs the "Michael reference"—and this is the only reference to Michael in the Apocalypse. But it is in the very midst of the Apocalypse, and shows it is Michael who stands behind the Apocalypse.

The Trumpets represent the sphere of Inspiration, the Transubstantiation in the Act of Consecration.

The Vials are represented as beginning in Ch. 16:1, and continuing through 16:17. At 16:18 the fomula of division is repeated, but with a slight change, metamorphosis.

Chapter 17 belongs to the sphere of the Vials. In fact, the remainder of the Apocalypse is in the sphere of the seventh Vial.

The Vials represent the counterpicture to the Communion. All that which is in the way of the direct communion with the Divine World, has to be thrown out. It is not worthy to pass to the sphere of the Communion. In any consideration of Communion there has to be considered "Excommunion"—the unworthy have to be thrown out.

The Communion versus Excommunion

New Jerusalem versus Babylon—Chapter 17 et sequence.

In Chapter 19 is the Vision of the Last Judgment.

In Chapter 20 is the Vision of the Dead.

In Chapter 21 is the Vision of the New Jerusalem.

There are four steps: 1) Communion; 2) Intuition; 3) Reality; and 4) New World.

All that is not worthy to enter into the sphere of the Communion is thrown out. Communion is a sphere of being, and is involved with Excommunion. The human beings are free, have free will to enter in or not. If they do not, then they must suffer and will be thrown out—but they have free will to choose. Those who do not accept Christ, and instead go their own way—then materialism comes out.

The Seven Seals are more in the sphere of the human being. The intelligence is spiritualized.—6:2-8.

6:13—the Falling of the Stars from Heaven.—This is a cosmic event. The Scorpions appear.

6:12—The Sixth Seal—Directed more to the earth, to nature. The picture of the world changes through intellectualism.—Here in Chapter 6, the events are seen from the standpoint of the human being. The Moon—the lower side of the moon which poisons the astrality, etc.-6:13—"The Stars fall to earth"—the ideals of humanity are lost. The human being is no longer directed from outside.— Heaven is no longer the book of wisdom and revelation through the stars. One must find one's wisdom and revelation within—in one's free ego.

6:14 "Mountains and Islands": The people of old had great reverence for the "Holy mountain" and the "sacred islands"—Patmos is an example—as places of initiation. All the places on the earth where spiritual inspiration could come are unspiritualized. All the old ways of revelation are gone. All is gone from nature, and nature itself is unspiritualized.

6:15 "dens and rocks"—the picture of a flight into materialism. Materialism is a flight into matter, in order to avoid having a meeting with the threshold of the spiritual world. People use alcohol, drugs, etc., to dim down consciousness, thus to avoid the meeting.

In Chapter 8, there is a going more and more into the sphere of nature—the figures of hail, fire, blood.

8:7—One-third of the earth: This perhaps refers to one-third of our natures:

1) In our thoughts we are alone. The divine element has withdrawn entirely from that part of us, and comes only as we invite it.

2) In all our feelings there is some divinity—even in base feelings there is something that is divine. Ahriman has not entirely taken them over—they are not entirely Ahrimanized, as our thinking processes are.

8:7 "all green grass was burnt up": Here we are reminded of the "green grass" at the Feeding of the 5,000. The picture of the growing, the life forces, the etheric forces in the world, destroyed by the human intellect. This is a "scorched earth," as we know it in modern warfare.

8:8 "cast into the sea," etc. : Here the spirituality of the element of the water is attacked—through the human intellect, the "brain beast."

8:9 "creatures died . . . ships destroyed": the creatures are the living, etheric part of the sea, which is also attacked.

The ships remind us of Plato and of Tristan and Isolde. They point to the etheric sphere—to beauty—this verse indicated the loss of spiritual beauty. A ship represents the faculty to go into the spiritual sphere, the love of and going out into the spiritual sphere of the arts and beauty. This points to the fairy tales and their use of the ship motif.

Today we do not really "know" the spheres of air and water. We have only transferred the conditions of the solid ground into our airplanes and ocean liners. We may, and do, sail through the air and over the water, but we don't know either.

8:10, 11—"There fell a great star from heaven. . . ."—A cosmic catastrophe. "River and wells . . ."—The old inspiration ceases to work out of these.

8:12—"Sun, moon, stars"—These lose one-third part of their light. In our time, living in a great city, we can see this has already happened.

Trumpets: Mean an awakening call. All external loss of spirituality in nature, has to be replaced within the human being! One has to build up one's spiritual Intuitional sphere. The Trumpets are a call to do this.

In Chapter 9, the word "five" appears three times: In 9:1, 5, 10. The word "Scorpion" appears three times: In 9:3, 5, 10.

9:1—The Abyss. That which is "bottomless": The Egyptians had the concept that the world is built over an abyss. What is below the world has to remain below, has to remain covered. It is always a presupposition that the abyss is always covered. Now in Chapter 9, what is covered comes out, emerges. A picture of the bottomless sphere, depths of the human soul. Culture is that which comes from below, in a sense, but remains under control. Otherwise, it is not culture. And in our time culture is unfettered, out of control.

In his first book, Dr. Sigmund Freud, the psychiatrist, said, as a motto for his life: "If I cannot bend the gods to my purpose, I will summon the demons of the lower world to work my will."

Chapter 9 presents a picture of moral collapse, step-by-step, slowly and inexorably. The consequences of a materialistic way of life, and materialism in general, are shown here. It is a highly impressive imagination. The Fallen Angel opens the abyss. The smoke is the counter-picture to the incense in Ch. 8:4. Locusts out of the smoke (9:3)—An oriental picture of the locusts, largely lost in meaning to us in the Western world. The locusts respresent the destroying force which destroys every green thing in the world—all which is living (etheric) in the world. There are beings with the lust to kill. All of this is a picture of what happens in the human being.

9:14—"bound in the river Euphrates"—This is a collectivism coming from the East—the collective consciousness, the heaps of humanity, the "anthill masses" of human beings. In Roman times this meant the country of Parthia, the limit of the extent of the Roman Empire—in our time, China, perhaps.

Chapter 13 is the setting up of the kingdom of the AntiChrist.

1) The Dragon in the Air—(12:3-4, 13)—The astrality of the airy element taken over by the AntiChrist.

2) The Beast out of the Sea—(13:1 et seq.) The etheric, the watery element—the human being shaped back to animal form.

3) The Beast out of the Earth—(13:11)—The most terrible of the three. Has many heads—indication of extreme cleverness. A climax of intellectual magical powers. The caricature of creative power, power of creation, in the word "poi-a-o"- ποιέω—"works"—appears seven times ("poi-ai"—ποιει— "poi-a"—ποιῇ—"poi-asai"—ποιῆσαι—"poi-asa"—ποιήσῃ):

Ch. 13: Verse 12 (2x); Verse 13 (2x); Verse 14 (2x); Verse 15 (1x).

Chapter 14: This is the counter-picture; the world of growing good in contrast, in opposition to the world of growing evil, as seen in Chapter 13.

The Harpers: A new sphere of Art, of Feeling life.

The Psalms: All of a growing, metamorphosing, increasing picture. Life activity.

The Name written in the Forehead: (Ch. 3:12)

A:

1) The Name of God (Father)

2) The Name of the City (Holy Spirit)

3) The Name of Christ ((Son)

First there is a fullness, then a contraction, then a complete contraction—from 1) to 3).

B: Two Names: The Father and Christ (14:1)

C: One Name: The Father (22:4)

"Which is, and was, and is to be"—Three times this Formula:

1:4; 2) 1:8; 3) 4:8

In the third repetition is the vision of the Father Ground in the Heaven.